全国高等院校专业英语规划教材

# 商务英语口语（第3版）

房玉靖　梁　晶　主编
姚　颖　邓莉洁　副主编

清华大学出版社
北京

## 内容简介

本书以商务材料为主，内容涵盖商务工作所涉及的日常交际、涉外活动和涉外业务等常见场景，以功能用途划分。全书共设 16 个单元，内容主要涉及办公、商务旅行、商务接待、商务会谈、商务会议、展览展会、求职面试、公司与产品、商标与专利、询价、报盘、讨价还价、支付、包装与运输、保险、市场营销、销售谈判、合约签订、投诉索赔等方面。

本书可满足高职高专院校商务英语、国际贸易、国际商务等相关专业的学生、从事国际商务工作的外经贸从业人员、外事人员以及广大英语爱好者的需要。

**图书在版编目 (CIP) 数据**

商务英语口语 / 房玉靖，梁晶主编 . —3 版 . —北京：
清华大学出版社，2017（2024.7重印）
（全国高等院校专业英语规划教材）
ISBN 978-7-302-46959-9

Ⅰ . ①商… Ⅱ . ①房… ②梁… Ⅲ . ①商务—英语—口语—高等职业教育—教材 Ⅳ . ① H319.9

中国版本图书馆 CIP 数据核字 (2017) 第 074130 号

责任编辑：陈立静
装帧设计：杨玉兰
责任校对：张文青
责任印制：沈 露

出版发行：清华大学出版社
　　　网　址：https://www.tup.com.cn，https://www.wqxuetang.com
　　　地　址：北京清华大学学研大厦 A 座　　邮　编：100084
　　　社总机：010-83470000　　邮　购：010-62786544
　　　投稿与读者服务：010-62776969, c-service@tup.tsinghua.edu.cn
　　　质量反馈：010-62772015, zhiliang@tup.tsinghua.edu.cn
　　　课件下载：https://www.tup.com.cn, 010-62791865
印 装 者：小森印刷（北京）有限公司
经　销：全国新华书店
开　本：185mm×260mm　　印　张：15.25　　字　数：448 千字
版　次：2010 年 3 月第 1 版　2017 年 9 月第 3 版
印　次：2024 年 7 月第 11 次印刷
定　价：45.00 元

产品编号：073132–01

# 第3版 前言

　　《商务英语口语》的第2版自2016年1月出版后，我们收到了更多的读者好评，在此感谢广大用户对本书的支持与厚爱。

　　我们根据时事的变化，对本书材料进行了进一步更新，使得信息量更大、实用性更强。升级后的第3版注重激发学生积极参与口语活动的兴趣，提高学生跨文化交际能力；突出教师与学生以及学生之间互动协作的重要性，启发学生的想象力与创造力，从而能够得体地使用工作交际用语。

　　为满足广大读者的需求，我们特意邀请发音纯正的美籍人士朗读本书的对话部分，由美国专业的影视公司进行录制，读者可欣赏到音质清晰、原汁原味的美语朗读。

　　本教材由房玉靖、梁晶担任主编，姚颖、邓莉洁担任副主编。望广大读者对本教材继续给予指正，不胜感谢。

编　者

# 前言 第2版

　　《商务英语口语》自2010年3月出版后，受到用户的广泛好评，也有不少专家和读者提出了宝贵建议。为了更好地发挥和完善教材的作用，我们对全书内容进行了修订和补充。

　　修订后的《商务英语口语》的素材仍以商务材料为主，内容上涵盖了商务工作所涉及的日常交际、涉外活动及涉外业务等常见场景，以功能用途划分。全书共设16个单元，内容主要涉及办公、商务旅行、商务接待、商务会谈、商务会议、展览展会、求职面试、公司与产品、商标与专利、询价、报盘、讨价还价、支付、包装与运输、保险、市场营销、销售谈判、合约签订、投诉索赔等方面。每个单元围绕一个主题展开，根据相应目标设置，力求系统地将背景知识、功能型对话及练习、知识点讲解、扩展练习、相关信息、思维拓展、模拟场景对话等内容联系起来。

　　本书再版时，对原版版块式结构进行了有效整合与更新。首先，增加了热身练习，类型多样、难度适中的任务使学生能够在接触本单元语言知识前对专业内容有基本了解。其次，为更加突出材料的实用性，对原有对话进行了部分改编和更新，并加入了场景介绍，使学习者更易理解对话中的角色关系和各自诉求。此外，对原有的拓展练习部分进行了整合，使得结构更紧凑。其中Role-play部分的驱动型任务，角色的任务指令更加明确，使学生对于任务要求更加明了。

　　本教材由房玉靖、梁晶担任主编，姚颖、邓莉洁担任副主编。

　　由于编者水平所限，书中难免有不足之处，敬请读者指正。

编　者

# 第1版 前言

在经济全球化进程不断加快的今天，我国改革开放进入了快速和纵深发展期，国际商务活动和经济技术的交流也日益频繁。高职高专院校商务英语专业的学生不仅需要具备熟练的英语技能，还必须具有良好的沟通技巧和娴熟的实践能力，才能适应当代商务领域各项工作的需要。"商务英语口语"课程是根据高职高专商务英语专业学生需要开设的一门职业基础必修课程，同时也是一门语言技能训练课。教育部颁布的《高职高专教育英语课程教学基本要求》中，强调打好语言基础，要求语言基本训练和语言应用能力并重。

本书是一本以交际功能和中心话题为纲要编写的口语教材，它注重将学生置于多元文化背景之中，提供真实的语言环境和标准的语言范例，强调知识性、信息性、实用性和功能性，引导学生积极主动地进行口语练习，扩展学生用英语进行交流的综合能力。本书的特点在于遵循知识与实践相结合的原则，强化对学生英语听说应用能力的训练，旨在培养具备较强英语基础技能和一定的商务贸易、商务谈判和企业管理的综合技能，能适应现代各类经贸活动要求的高级应用型专门人才。

本书以商务材料为主，内容涵盖商务工作所涉及的日常交际、涉外活动和涉外业务等常见场景，以功能用途划分。全书共设16个单元，内容主要涉及办公、商务旅行、商务接待、商务会谈、商务会议、展览展会、求职面试、公司与产品、商标与专利、询价、报盘、讨价还价、支付、包装与运输、保险、市场营销、销售谈判、合约签订、投诉索赔等方面，可满足高职高专院校商务英语、国际贸易、国际商务等相关专业的学生、从事国际商务工作的外经贸从业人员、外事人员以及广大英语爱好者的需要。

本书的版块式结构安排，系统地将背景知识、功能型对话及练习、知识点讲解、扩展练习、相关信息、思维拓展等内容联系起来。每个单元围绕一个主题展开，其中又包含 3～4 个学习目标，根据每个目标设置相关内容的对话范例、注释、句型及针对性训练，另外还设置了整个单元的语言重点。其中，Unit 1～8 语言重点部分主要是分模块的功能句型；Unit 9～16 由于涉及的内容专业性较强，所以包括贸易术语或专业术语加功能句型两部分，便于学生灵活掌握和运用。

本书由房玉靖担任主编，参加编写的有房玉靖、刘玉玲、梁晶、姚颖。本书的编写得到清华大学出版社的大力支持，在此表示衷心的感谢。

编　者

目录 CONTENTS

# Unit 1

# Office Work

## Learning Objectives

**In this unit, you will learn how to:**

- Talk on the phone
- Make & change appointments/arrangements
- Talk with associates

## Background Information

General office skills may include answering phones, faxing, basic computer skills, as well as customer service skills. Effective communication concerning these skills at workplace is extremely important to smooth and efficient business operation. There are mainly two types of communication: verbal communication (such as meetings, phone calls, speech, one to one feedbacks, etc.), and non-verbal communication (such as written or printed emails, etc.). Communication at workplace should be clear, concise and specific. In addition, there should be effective use of body language at workplace. Good communication skills will help to establish a better working relationship where as poor workplace communication skills will have negative effects on business relationships and may result in decreased productivity.

## Starting Up

Read the following tips and decide which are DOS ( √ ) and which

**are DON'TS ( × ). Compare your answers with a partner's and explain your choices.**

| When you answer the phone in the office ⋯ |
|---|
| ☐ pick it up after the first ring |
| ☐ pick it up after three or more rings |
| ☐ immediately ask who is calling and what they want |
| ☐ say your own name |
| ☐ say your company name and/or department |
| ☐ just say "Hello?" |
| ☐ have a pencil and paper ready so that you can take notes |
| ☐ try to sound friendly and helpful |
| ☐ speak quickly so that the call is soon over |
| ☐ speak clearly and slowly |
| ☐ smile |
| ☐ use the speaker phone |

 Oral Workshop

## A. Talking on the Phone

### Dialogue 1 – Asking to speak to someone

*Diana is making a call to Mr. Brown of Deep Blue Office Supply.*

**Operator**：Good morning, Deep Blue Office Supply.

**Diana**：This is Diana Wong from MAP Advertising. I'd like to speak to Mr. Brown, please.

**Operator**： Is that Michael Brown or Tony Brown?

**Diana**：I'm not sure. I want to talk to someone about the maintenance of laser printers.

**Operator**：Then you need to speak to Tony Brown. He's with After Sales Department. I'll put you through.

**Diana**：Thank you.

**Mr. Brown**：Hello, Tony Brown.

**Diana**：Hello, Mr. Brown. This is Diana Wong from MAP Advertising. I called last week about the laser printer.

**Mr. Brown**：Sorry, can you spell your name, please?

**Diana**：It's W-O-N-G. Diana Wong, from MAP Advertising.

**Mr. Brown**：Oh, yes. I remember.

**Diana**：We bought 5 laser printers from you two weeks ago, but one of them doesn't seem to work properly, and we also have some questions on maintenance. So I'm calling to see whether it's possible for you to send someone to help.

**Mr. Brown**：All right. Would tomorrow suit you?

**Diana**：That'll be great. I'm in the office all day.

**Mr. Brown**：So I'll send over an engineer around 10:00 in the morning.

**Diana**：Thank you very much, Mr. Brown.

| | | | |
|---|---|---|---|
| maintenance | 维修，保养 | put through | 接通电话 |
| laser printer | 激光打印机 | | |

## Dialogue 2 – Leaving and taking messages

*Peter Jackson of FBJ Marketing wants to speak to Paul Richards of BIG Supermarket. At the first attempt, he dials the wrong number. At the second attempt, Sara Lee, Paul's secretary answers the phone.*

**Andy**：Hello, Marketing Department. Can I help you?

**Peter**：Hello. May I speak to Paul Richards, please?

**Andy**：I'm sorry. You've got the wrong number. But he does work here. I'll try and put you through. In future his direct number is 5558770.

**Peter**：Didn't I dial that?

**Andy**：No, you rang 5558790.

**Peter**：Oh, sorry to have troubled you.

**Andy**：No problem. Hang on a moment and I'll put you through to Paul's extension.

**Peter**：Thanks.

**Sara**：Good morning, Paul Richards' office, Sara Lee speaking.

**Peter**：Oh, hi. This is Peter Jackson from FBJ Marketing. Could I speak to Paul, please?

**Sara**：I'm afraid Paul is on a training course.

**Peter**：Do you know when he'll be back?

**Sara**：I'm afraid he won't be back until tomorrow, but if it's urgent I can get a message to him this afternoon.

**Peter**：I'd really appreciate that. Could you tell him I called because I need to check the budget for supermarket promotion this coming weekend?

**Sara:** OK. You'd like to check the budget for supermarket promotion this weekend.

**Peter:** That's right.

**Sara:** I'm afraid I didn't catch your name.

**Peter:** It's Peter Jackson from FBJ Marketing.

**Sara:** Thank you, Mr. Jackson. I'll make sure he gets the message this afternoon.

**Peter:** Thank you very much.

**Sara:** You're welcome. Goodbye.

**Peter:** Bye.

| extension | 电话分机 | appreciate | 感谢 |
|-----------|---------|------------|------|
| budget | 预算 | promotion | 促销 |
| catch | 听清楚 | | |

## Practice

1. You are asked to call a client who you have never either talked with or met before. Speak to him/her and introduce yourself, explain the purpose of your call.

2. You are with After-Sales Department. Someone calls and asks to speak to Cathy, a sales representative in Sales Department. You either offer the caller the right extension number or help put him/her through to Cathy.

3. You ring up Mr. Blare and invite him to attend a cocktail party in honor of your newly-appointed CEO next Friday, 6:30 p.m. at Crystal Hotel. As Mr. Blare is in a meeting, you leave a message to his secretary and ask Mr. Blare to call back to confirm with you.

4. You leave a message to Mr. Cook, the sales manager of ABC Company, asking him to airmail you some samples by the end of the week.

5. Suppose you have booked a two-week holiday in Singapore. You receive a call about a change of departure date from Sunrise Holidays —a travel agency. As you are about to attend a meeting in two minutes, you arrange to call back.

| sales representative | 销售代表 | cocktail party | 鸡尾酒会 |
|----------------------|---------|----------------|---------|
| in honor of | 为了向某人表示敬意 | | |
| newly-appointed | 新任命的 | | |

# B. Handling Appointments/Arrangements

## Dialogue 1 – Making arrangements

*Robert Bush of HBC Trading is calling Tina Stone to discuss the arrangements for his trip to New York next week.*

**Tina：** Hello, Tina Stone speaking.

**Robert：** Hello, this is Robert Bush from HBC Trading.

**Tina：** Hi, Robert, nice to hear from you. How's everything?

**Robert：** Great. You know, I'm planning to come to New York next week.

**Tina：** Really!

**Robert：** Yes. I'll have a meeting with a client in Boston on Tuesday next week. I was hoping we could arrange to meet up either before or after.

**Tina：** So you have to be in Boston on Tuesday? That's the 7th.

**Robert：** That's right. Now, I could stop over in New York on the way in — that would be Monday. Would that be possible?

**Tina：** Ah, I'm afraid I won't be in the office on Monday.

**Robert：** Uh-huh, well, the other possibility would be to arrange it after Boston on my way home.

**Tina：** When do you plan to leave Boston?

**Robert：** Could be either Tuesday or Wednesday morning, but I would like to catch a flight back to London on Wednesday evening.

**Tina：** OK. Well, it would be best for us if you could fly in on Wednesday morning. I'll be able to pick you up at the airport, and then we could show you the new trade center.

**Robert：** That sounds good. But do you think you could fax me an itinerary for the day that's Wednesday the 8th?

**Tina：** No problem.

**Robert：** Thank you. Then I'll see you next Wednesday. Goodbye.

---

stop over　（中途）短暂停留　　　　　　pick up　（开车）接人

itinerary　行程，旅行日程

---

## Dialogue 2 – Changing an appointment

*Justin Wong is calling Mr. Smith's office to change his appointment. Mr. Smith's assistant Mary answers the call.*

**Mary：** Good morning, Mr. Smith's office. Can I help you?

**Justin**: Good morning. This is Justin Wong from J & J Footwear. I have an appointment with Mr. Smith at 2:30 p.m. tomorrow afternoon, but I'm sorry I can't keep our appointment because I'll be sent to attend an urgent meeting at the HQ.

**Mary**: Would you like to cancel it?

**Justin**: No. I wonder if it's convenient to put it off.

**Mary**: Could you hold on for a minute, Mr. Wong? I'll just look in the diary. So, when's convenient for you?

**Justin**: Later this week if possible. I gather he's away the following week.

**Mary**: Yes, that's right. He's on a business trip overseas.

**Justin**: I need to see him before he goes away. So would Friday afternoon, the same time be okay?

**Mary**: Friday afternoon … let me see … Sorry, but Mr. Smith won't be free until 3:00 p.m. Would 3:30 p.m. be all right?

**Justin**: Yes, that's fine with me. Thank you very much.

**Mary**: So, Mr. Wong, your appointment with Mr. Smith is rescheduled at 3:30 Friday afternoon.

| | | | |
|---|---|---|---|
| keep an appointment | 守约 | HQ = headquarter(s) | 总部 |
| put off | 推迟 | gather | 猜想 |
| reschedule | 将……改期；重新安排 | | |

## Practice

1. You and your partner work in the same company but in two different departments. You would like to have a short meeting regarding work sometime next week. Call him/her to arrange a time for you two to meet either in your office or your partner's.

2. Your company is planning on a launching ceremony for a new product. Talk with your team members and work out the arrangements.

3. You have arranged to meet a colleague from one of your subsidiaries. Explain that you cannot keep the appointment, give a reason, and then suggest an alternative time.

4. You call a colleague to tell her the meeting has been put off until tomorrow, but she is not in. Leave a message to her secretary.

| | | | |
|---|---|---|---|
| launch | （产品）上市 | subsidiary | 子公司 |

# C. Talks at Work

## Dialogue 1 – Receiving a guest

*Allan Johnson from ABC Trading comes to visit Mr. Eastwood by appointment. Tracy, the receptionist, receives the visitor at Reception, and contacts Mr. Eastwood's secretary Daisy.*

**Allan**：Good morning.

**Tracy**：Good morning. Can I help you?

**Allan**：Yes. I have an appointment with Mr. Eastwood at 10:00 a.m.

**Tracy**：Mr. Eastwood from Marketing Department?

**Allan**：Yes.

**Tracy**：May I have your name please?

**Allan**：I'm Allan Johnson from ABC Trading.

**Tracy**：Thank you. Please take a seat while I'm contacting Mr. Eastwood's office for you.

**Daisy**：Mr. Eastwood's office.

**Tracy**：Hello, Daisy. This is reception. Mr. Johnson is here for his 10 o'clock appointment with Mr. Eastwood.

**Daisy**：Oh, yes, Tracy. Mr. Eastwood is expecting him.

**Tracy**：I'll send him up then.

**Daisy**：Thanks.

**Tracy**：Mr. Johnson, would you please go to Room 216 on the second floor? It's the first on your right. Mr. Eastwood is expecting you.

**Allan**：Room 216, second floor.

**Tracy**：Yes. The stairs are on the left.

**Allan**：Thanks a lot.

---

expect                          等待

---

## Dialogue 2 – Requesting and offering help

*Adam and Jason are colleagues. Adam asks Jason for help.*

**Adam**：Hi, Jason, are you very busy right now?

**Jason**：Not really, no.

**Adam**：Do you think you could help me with my computer? There seems to be a problem with my network.

**Jason**：Oh, it's not just with your computer. I think the entire network is down for upgrades. It should be back up in an hour.

**Adam**：Oh, no, that'd be too late. I need the budget documents from the company network share.

**Jason**：Don't worry. I have a copy of that on my computer. Do you want it now?

**Adam**：You do? Can I get a copy?

**Jason**：Sure. But I have to put it on a USB flash disk for you since the network is down.

**Adam**：That would be great!

**Jason**：Do you have one?

**Adam**：Er … no, I forgot to take it off my computer after I finished last night at home.

**Jason**：Never mind. Use mine.

**Adam**：Sorry to trouble you.

**Jason**：Oh, that's no big case. OK, it's saving now. Here you go.

**Adam**：Thanks a lot. You really saved me a great deal of trouble.

**Jason**：No problem. I'm glad I could help.

| | | | |
|---|---|---|---|
| upgrade | 升级 | network share | 网络共享 |
| flash disk | 闪存盘 | | |

## Dialogue 3 – Giving instructions

*Sandy is newly employed and does not know how to use the software. Her supervisor Jason Lewis is telling her what to do.*

**Jason**：Hi, Sandy, how are you settling in?

**Sandy**：Just fine, thanks, Mr. Lewis. I really appreciate you taking the time to help me out with this software.

**Jason**：Sure. Now, let's get started. Could you tell me if you've worked with this program before? That will help me figure out how to proceed.

**Sandy**：I've done a little work with it, but not much. To be exact, I have read some books on it, but never run it myself.

**Jason**：Well, I think it's a good idea to have the manual at hand.

**Sandy**：Yes, you're right. So, what do I do now?

**Jason**：Just click on the button in corner. Be sure to enter the password you created. You can write it down somewhere just in case you forget. But very importantly, you need to keep it in a very safe place.

**Sandy:** I got it. What do I do next?

**Jason:** Well, what you need is to select the network you want to work with, and you're all set.

**Sandy:** Great. And do I just click on print icon to print out reports?

**Jason:** You'd better go to File-Print from the menu, just to make sure you select the right printer as we have three printers connected to different computers.

**Sandy:** I see. Thanks a lot. May I trouble you if I have further questions?

**Jason:** Sure. I'd love to help.

| | | | |
|---|---|---|---|
| proceed | 进行 | manual | 手册 |
| icon | 图标 | | |

## Practice

1. You have an appointment with someone. You arrive 30 minutes earlier than the scheduled time. Talk to the receptionist and ask if it is possible to bring forward the appointment.

2. You are new to the company. Ask one of your colleagues to proofread the English report you've just finished before handing in.

3. You are expecting an EMS parcel at the entrance of your company. As you are stuck in the negotiation, ask a colleague to pick up the package for you.

4. You explain to the new staff the regulations at your company, which may include working hours, dress code, sick leave, etc.

 Language Focus

| Talking on the Phone | |
|---|---|
| • Hello, this is … calling from …. <br> • Could I speak to .., please? <br> • I'd like to speak to …, please. <br> • Could you put me through to …? <br> • Can you give him/her this message, please? <br> • Can I leave a message for …? <br> • I must have dialed the wrong number. | • Could I ask who's calling, please? <br> • Who shall I say is calling? <br> • I'm afraid he/she is not available at the moment. Would you like to leave a message? <br> • I'll make sure he gets the message. <br> • Can you call back later? <br> • Could you hold the line a moment, please? <br> • I'm afraid you have the wrong number. <br> • Thank you for calling. |

## Making Appointments/Arrangements

| | |
|---|---|
| • I'd like to make an appointment with … | • Tuesday suits me very well. |
| • I'd like to arrange … | • Tuesday is fine for me. |
| • Does … suit you? | • I'm sorry but I can't make it then. |
| • Shall we make it …? | • I'm afraid I'm busy then. |
| • Did you have a time in mind? | • I prefer a meeting in the afternoon. |
| • When is the best/convenient time for you? | |

## Changing Appointments/arrangements

• Could we postpone/put off … to …?

• I'm sorry I can't keep our appointment because …

• I wonder if it's convenient to change our appointment from … to …?

• I'm afraid we have to cancel …because …

## Requesting Favors

• Can you spare a few minutes?

• Could you do me a favor?

• I'v got a favor to ask you. Could you …?

• Would you mind if I …?

## Offering to Help

| | |
|---|---|
| • Can I give you a hand? | • Yes, please. Thanks a lot. |
| • Would you like a hand with …? | • I'd appreciate that. |
| • Is there anything I can do for you? | • I can't thank you enough. |
| • Would you like me to …? | • That's very nice/thoughtful of you. |
| • Would you like me to help you with that? | • No, thanks. I think I can manage that. |
| • I'd be happy to …, if you'd like. | • That's very kind of you, but I prefer to do it myself. |
| • If there is anything I can do to help, please let me know. | • I think I'd prefer to do that myself because … |
| | • Yes, I will. |

 Extended Activities

## Role-play

### Task 1

**Student A：** You are the assistant to Ms. Baker, the General Manager. You have already

arranged a meeting for Ms. Baker to see John Miller, a consultant from S & M Management Consultancy. However, Ms. Baker has to be away on business to deal with some emergency and won't be able to keep the appointment. Phone Mr. Miller's office and cancel the appointment.

**Student B**: You work for S & M Management Consultancy. One of your colleagues, John Miller, is out of the office at the moment. Answer the phone for him and take a message if necessary.

## Task 2

**Student A**: You are the general manager of Global Trading, an international company. You are to invite a world-renowned expert on project management to give some lectures to your employees. Make a phone call and extend your invitation.

**Student B**: You are a well-known expert on project management. You're invited to give some lectures at Global Trading, an international company. You need to decide whether to accept or decline the invitation. If you choose to accept, settle the details; otherwise, give a reason for not being able to deliver the lectures.

## Task 3

**Student A**: You are Mr. Johnson's assistant. Answer the phone calls for your boss as he is not in the office.

**Student B**: You are Tony White, Managing Director of ABC Corporation. You would like to invite Mr. Johnson, President of BHP Trading Company, to attend a business banquet next Friday, 6:30 p.m. at Hilton Hotel. Ask Mr. Johnson to ring your office at 6377-5988.

**Student C**: You are Sara, head of Sales at The Pearls. You would like to know whether Mr. Johnson, President of BHP Trading Company, has signed the Sales Confirmation. If so, fax to 5235-6730 first, and then courier it to you.

**Student D**: You are Jack Jones, Development Manager at The Pearls. You are returning Mr. Johnson's call. Since you are out of town, Mr. Johnson can reach your mobile at 13389774128.

**Student E**: You are Bruce Lee, Director of Sales and Marketing at The Pearls. You would like to invite Mr. Johnson, President of BHP Trading Company, to visit your showroom. The latter part of next week would be best for you. You can be reached at 6230-8966, ext. 1543.

| | | | |
|---|---|---|---|
| banquet | 宴会 | courier | 快递（文件） |
| showroom | 商品陈列室 | | |

**Task 4**

**Group work：** Work in groups of 3~5. One of you acts as the manager of After-sales Department, one as a new employee, and the others the staff of the department. The manager shows the new employee around the office and introduces him/her to the other colleagues.

# Discussion

## Topic 1

What do you think is difficult about making a first-time call to a stranger?

What are the important points to consider when you have to take a message?

## Topic 2

What makes a good team? Work with your group members or partners and make a list of necessary characteristics of a good team. Explain why you think these are of great importance.

## Topic 3

You work as a receptionist. Someone wants to see the general manager with no prior appointment. How do you deal with the matter tactfully?

| | |
|---|---|
| tactfully | 婉转地 |

## Related Information

### Keys to Successful Workplace Communication

The following keys will help you unlock the door to successful communication not only at work, but also in all your relationships.

- Personal contact is important. People relate to one another better when they can meet in person and read each other's body language, so they can feel the energy the connection creates. If personal contact is not possible, the next best way to connect is by talking on the telephone.

- Develop a network. No one achieves success alone. Make an effort to become friends with people in different departments within your company, meet new people in your community, and look for experiences or interests you have in common.

- Always be courteous in your communications with others. Courtesy lets people know that you care. The words "Thank You" show that you appreciate a person's efforts. Try saying, "Would you please..." instead of just "Please...".

- Be consistent and clear in your workplace communications. Consistency builds trust. Asking "Did I explain this clearly?" will assure that people can understand what you say.

- Compromise decreases the tension associated with conflict. Ask "What is best for the company?" so that co-workers will not take the conflict personally.

- You cannot hold a person's interest if you have nothing interesting to say. Here are some of the ways you can learn to be an interesting communicator. Read your hometown paper daily. Read industry literatures so that you can know what is going on in your industry. Rehearse telling a few short personal stories about your interesting experiences.

- Listen to what others are saying and show interests in the conversation. Listening demonstrates respect and admiration. Make your conversation like a game of tennis and keep the ball going back and forth.

| courteous | 有礼貌的 | compromise | 妥协 |
| tension | 矛盾；紧张气氛 | | |

 Supplements for Reflections

## Phone Etiquette

Courtesy is as important in speaking over the phone as in talking to people face to face.

**Calling on the Phone**

A person should always be certain of the number he is dialing to avoid disturbing someone unnecessarily. If you do reach a wrong number, it is important to say "I'm sorry, I dialed the wrong number." before hanging up.

When you talk on the telephone, remember to maintain your voice quality and express yourself clearly and concisely. The person at the other end of the phone cannot see your facial expressions or gestures and the impression he receives depends on what is heard.

concisely　简洁地

## Answering the Phone

The most proper way to answer a telephone is "Hello." When the telephone is answered by someone other than the head of the office and someone says, "May I speak to Mr. X, please?" he or she should say, "Just a moment, please." If Mr. X is unable to come to the phone, the correct reply is "Mr. X can not come to the phone now. May I have your name, and he will call you back as soon as possible?"

If you must put the telephone down during the conversation, do it gently, and when you hang up, do it gently. DO NOT slam the receiver down!!! The person at the other end may still have the phone close to his ear, and then a sudden sharp bang can be hurtful as well as rude.

## Transferring a Call

Transferring calls on the phone at work is part and parcel of any business but it's amazing how damaging bad practice in this regard can be when it comes to how outsiders perceive a company. Therefore, it's important to practice good professional etiquette when it comes to call transfers.

Listen to the caller. One of the most important aspects of phone work is to listen to what the caller is saying and that means not interrupting. Sometimes you may instinctively know within a matter of a few seconds that you're going to need to transfer the call to somebody else, but don't be tempted to interrupt — hear the caller out.

Check that the person you're going to transfer to is available. The caller might have been waiting in a queuing system for quite some time before being transferred; therefore, if you need to transfer the call, make sure that the person you're going to put through to is available.

It is good etiquette to ask the caller first if it's OK to put them on hold to check if the person's available. If they agree, make sure you come back to the caller at least every minute telling them that you're trying to connect them and whether they would mind continuing to hold. If the caller decides not to hold any longer, give them the name and the number of the person they should ask for when they call back.

| perceive | 注意到 | etiquette | 礼仪 |
| instinctively | 本能地；凭直觉地 | | |

## Common Telephone Courtesy Hints

Make sure of the correct number so as not to risk disturbing strangers.

Make sure that your conversations with busy people are as brief as possible.

Time your calls so as not to interfere with the work schedule of those you call.

Make business calls well before the close of the office hours.

When the number you are calling is not answered quickly, wait long enough for someone to put aside what he or she is doing. It is very annoying to have been disturbed just to pick up the telephone and find the caller has hung up.

When transferring calls, phrases such as "I'm putting you through to…" or "I'm going to connect you to…" are far better than saying "I'm going to transfer you to…" as the latter often causes anxiety amongst callers who sometimes feel as though they could be accidentally cut off at this point.

| put aside | 忽视；忘记 |

## Questions

- What are inappropriate times to make business calls?
- What are some commonly-found bad phone habits? What else do you find in mobile phone calls?
- Suppose a caller has been put through to several persons who have not been able to assist and the caller does not wish to be transferred anymore. In situations like these, what do you do?

# Unit 2

# Business Travel

 Learning Objectives

In this unit, you will learn how to:

- Check in at an airport
- Go through immigration and customs
- Claim baggage
- Make hotel bookings
- Check in/out at a hotel

 Background Information

Traveling abroad on business can locate and cultivate new customers and improve relationships and communications with current foreign representatives and associates. In modern international business, progressing up the career ladder often brings an obligation to travel more frequently. It usually includes issues dealing with flights, hotels and car rentals. Frequent business travel— by whatever mode of transport  can be extremely stressful, and may take its toll both mentally and physically. A well-planned itinerary enables a traveler to make the best use of time abroad.

 Starting Up

Are you familiar with the following terms and expressions that are associated with business travel? Work with your partners and

**group them into different categories. Can you add more words?**

| departure | rate | housekeeping | delayed | wakeup call |
| lobby | gate | reservation | carousel | scheduled time |
| towel | terminal | late charge | trolley | boarding pass |
| transfer | suite | front desk | lounge | money exchange |
| vacancy | tip | check in/out | deposit | final call |
| economy | cabin | guest house | bellboy | baggage claim |
| concierge | security | shuttle bus | gym | toiletries |
| escalator | life vest | declaration | aisle | duty-free shops |

| Airport/Flight | Hotel/Accommodation | Both |
|---|---|---|
|  |  |  |
|  |  |  |
|  |  |  |
|  |  |  |
|  |  |  |
|  |  |  |
|  |  |  |
|  |  |  |

 Oral Workshop

## A. Preparing for a Trip

### Dialogue 1 – Booking tickets

*Michael Woods calls to book a flight ticket.*

**Clerk**：Hello. This is United Airlines.

**Michael**：I'd like to book a ticket to Los Angeles for next Monday.

**Clerk**：Which flight would you like to book? When are you planning to leave?

**Michael**：I prefer a morning flight.

**Clerk**: OK. Just a second, I'll check the schedule. We've got UA003 for Los Angeles leaving at 9:25. Is that all right?

**Michael**: Yes, that's perfect. I'd like an economy ticket with an open return.

**Clerk**: May I have your name, please?

**Michael**: Michael Woods.

**Clerk**: So, one economy class seat with an open return to Los Angeles for next Monday, Oct. 17th. Is that right?

**Michael**: That's right.

**Clerk**: Now you have been booked.

**Michael**: Thanks a lot. What time do you start to check in?

**Clerk**: Two hours before departure time. And you need to check in at least one hour before the departure time.

**Michael**: Thank you. Bye.

| | | | |
|---|---|---|---|
| open return | 回程时间不固定的往返票 | | |
| business class | 商务舱 | economy class | 经济舱 |
| first class | 头等舱 | departure time | 起飞时间 |

## Dialogue 2 – Changing reservations

*Kevin Kidd calls to change his air ticket reservation.*

**Clerk**: United Airlines. May I help you?

**Kevin**: Hello, I've bought the ticket from Hong Kong to Los Angeles on July 23rd. Can I change it to July 25th?

**Clerk**: What's your name and flight number?

**Kevin**: My name is Kevin Kidd, and the flight number is UA003 for Los Angeles.

**Clerk**: Let me check. There is one available in the morning, taking off at 10:15. Would that be all right?

**Kevin**: Yes, that's perfect. I'll take it. How can I collect my new ticket?

**Clerk**: You just show your old ticket at the check-in counter.

**Kevin**: Do I have to confirm my seat?

**Clerk**: Yes, you'd better confirm it 72 hours prior to the departure time.

**Kevin**: Thank you very much. Bye!

| take off | 起飞 | | collect | 领取 |
|----------|------|--|---------|------|
| check-in counter | 值机柜台 | | | |

## Practice

1.  You plan to pay a visit to one of your most important clients in Britain. Ask your secretary to confirm your arrangements and make preparations for you.

2.  Your boss is going to attend a conference in New York next week. As his secretary, you are responsible for planning his trip. Now call the ticket office of an airline to book a return ticket for a set date.

3.  You are on a business trip and you need to stay an extra day due to an emergency. Phone the airline office to arrange a different flight.

# B. At the Airport

### Dialogue 1 – Checking in

*The traveler is checking in at the check-in counter.*

**Clerk**：Good morning, Madam.

**Traveler**：Good morning. I'd like to check in, please.

**Clerk**：May I see your ticket and passport?

**Traveler**：Here you are.

**Clerk**：Thank you. Do you have a seating preference?

**Traveler**：I'd like to have a seat by the window, and in the front, please.

**Clerk**：Oh, I'm sorry, Madam. There isn't any window seat left. But there are some aisle seats in the front.

**Traveler**：Well, then, an aisle seat would be fine, thank you.

**Clerk**：Do you have any luggage to check in at this time?

**Traveler**：Just these two, please. Right here.

**Clerk**：Any lighter or wine in your baggage?

**Traveler**：No.

**Clerk**：Any carry-on baggage?

**Traveler**：Yes, this bag.

**Clerk**：All right. Here is your boarding card. The flight will begin boarding around 3:45, at Gate 12. And the gate will be closed 20 minutes prior to departure time. Have a pleasant flight!

**Traveler**：Thanks a lot!

---

| | | | |
|---|---|---|---|
| window seat | 靠窗座位 | aisle seat | 靠通道座位 |
| check in | 托运 | carry-on baggage | 手提行李 |
| boarding card | 登机牌 | gate | 登机口 |

## Dialogue 2 – Going through immigration

*The traveler is attending a trade fair in New York. On his arrival at the airport, he goes through the U.S. immigration.*

**Officer**：May I see your passport, please?

**Traveler**：Here you are.

**Officer**：What's the purpose of your visit, business or pleasure?

**Traveler**：Business. I'm attending a trade fair in New York.

**Officer**：How long will you be staying in the United States?

**Traveler**：About 10 days.

**Officer**：Where will you be staying?

**Traveler**：I'll be staying at Hilton Hotel.

**Officer**：Can I see your return ticket, please?

**Traveler**：Yes, here it is.

**Officer**：Do you have anything to declare?

**Traveler**：No, I don't think so.

**Officer**：Well, are you carrying any food with you?

**Traveler**：No.

**Officer**：Do you have any cigarettes or liquor?

**Traveler**：No.

**Officer**：All right. Then you go through the Green Channel. And enjoy your visit to the United States.

**Traveler**：Thank you.

---

| | |
|---|---|
| declare | 申报 |

## Dialogue 3 – Going through the Customs

*The traveler goes through the Customs at the airport.*

**Officer**：May I see your Customs Declaration Card, please?

**Traveler**：Here you are. I've already filled it out.

**Officer**：OK, sir. This is just a routine check. Would you mind opening the bag for me?

**Traveler**：All right. These are all just my personal belongings.

**Officer**：Hmm. You have five watches here. What are they for?

**Traveler**：Well, my company makes watches. They are for our display at the fair.

**Officer**：And what is this?

**Traveler**：Oh, that's some perfume I bought at London Heathrow. Is it dutiable?

**Officer**：Is it for personal use or is it a gift?

**Traveler**：It's for myself.

**Officer**：Now, everything is OK. You are through. Here is your passport. Have a nice stay.

**Traveler**：Thank you. Bye-bye!

| | | | |
|---|---|---|---|
| Customs Declaration Card | 海关申报卡 | routine check | 例行检查 |
| dutiable | 应征税的 | | |

### Dialogue 4 – Reporting missing baggage

*The traveler cannot find his baggage and reports at the airline's service desk.*

**Officer**：Can I help you, sir?

**Traveler**：Yes, I can't find my baggage.

**Officer**：Which flight were you on?

**Traveler**：CA1705, from Melbourne.

**Officer**：Right. How many pieces of baggage are missing?

**Traveler**：Two.

**Officer**：Are they both suitcases?

**Traveler**：No, one big suitcase, one small carton.

**Officer**：Can you describe them?

**Traveler**：Well, the big suitcase is dark brown and it's made of leather.

**Officer**：How big is it?

**Traveler**：About a meter long by about 70 centimeters. It's got two handles, one of them is at the side.

**Officer**：What about the carton?

**Traveler**：The carton isn't big, about 50 by 50 by 30. But with books inside, it's a bit heavy. And it's strapped.

**Officer**：Anything looks special?

**Traveler**：No, I don't think so. But they both have my name tags. Yes, there's really something.

**Officer**：What is it?

**Traveler**：It's a small national flag of Australia on the carton.

**Officer**：OK. Don't worry, sir. I'm sure we'll find them. Now can I take you name and address?

**Traveler**：My name's Tony Howard, and I will be staying at Sheraton Hotel.

**Officer**：Right. Can you give me a telephone number where I can contact you?

**Traveler**：Yes. The hotel number is 6793-5532.

**Officer**：Right. That's everything.

**Traveler**：How soon will I find them back?

**Officer**：Sorry, I can't tell. I'll first contact Melbourne airport and then Inchon Airport where the flight stopped over to check whether your baggage were mistakenly unloaded. If not, we have to wait until the next flight from Melbourne arrives. Anyway, I'll call you later today and let you know what's happening. When we find your baggage, we'll send them to you immediately.

**Traveler**：OK. Thank you very much.

| | | | |
|---|---|---|---|
| strap | 用带子固定 | stop over | 中途停留 |
| unload | 卸货 | | |

## Practice

1. You are flying to Berlin, Germany from Beijing International Airport. You are now at the check-in counter to check in.

2. You are traveling to JFK Airport, New York. Your partner works as a customs officer. Answer your partner's questions.

3. You are a businessman from the U.S. During your stay in China for a trade fair, you bought some Chinese paintings and two vases. Now you are going through customs at JFK airport in your country.

4. Suppose you are at the Lost Baggage Office at an airport. You can not find your suitcase. Describe your suitcase to the airport officer.

# C. Staying at a Hotel

## Dialogue 1 – Booking accommodation

*Tony Shaw calls to make a hotel reservation.*

**Receptionist**：Room Reservations. What can I do for you?

**Tony Shaw**：Good morning. I'd like to book a room for five nights, from November 4th to November 8th.

**Receptionist**：Yes. What kind of room would you like?

**Tony Shaw**：A single room with a bath, please.

**Receptionist**：Yes, we do have a single room available for those dates.

**Tony Shaw**：What is the rate, please?

**Receptionist**：The current rate is $90 per night.

**Tony Shaw**：I'll take it. By the way, I'd like a quiet room away from the street if that is possible.

**Receptionist**：No problem. Now, could you please tell me your name, sir?

**Tony Shaw**：Yes, it is Shaw, Tony Shaw.

**Receptionist**：How do you spell it, please?

**Tony Shaw**：It's S-H-A-W.

**Receptionist**：S-H-A-W. And what is your address, please?

**Tony Shaw**：It is 30 First Avenue, Eastwood, New South Wales 2122, Australia.

**Receptionist**：Excuse me, sir, but could you speak a little more slowly, please?

**Tony Shaw**：Sure. It's 30 First Avenue, Eastwood, New South Wales 2122, Australia.

**Receptionist**：All right, it's all settled. And our check-in time is after 1:00 p.m. We look forward to seeing you next Tuesday.

**Tony Shaw**：Thank you very much. Bye.

---

| | |
|---|---|
| rate　费用 | settle　安排；料理 |

---

## Dialogue 2 – Checking in

*Tony Shaw checks in at the hotel.*

**Receptionist**：Good afternoon, sir. Can I help you?

**Tony Shaw**：Good afternoon. I have a reservation for a single room with a bath here.

**Receptionist**：May I have your name, please?

**Tony Shaw**：Shaw, Tony Shaw.

**Receptionist**: Just a moment, sir. Yes, we do have a reservation for you, Mr. Shaw. Would you please fill out this form while I prepare your key card for you?

**Tony Shaw**: Yes, of course.

*(a couple of minutes later)*

Here you are. I think I've filled in everything.

**Receptionist**: Thank you. Here is your key, Mr. Shaw. Your room number is 1518. It is on the 15th floor and the daily rate is $90. Here is your key card. Please make sure that you have it with you all the time.

**Tony Shaw**: OK. I'll take good care of it.

**Receptionist**: Now if you are ready, Mr. Shaw, I'll call the bellboy and he'll take you to your room.

**Tony Shaw**: Yes, I'm ready. Thank you. One more thing, where is your restaurant?

**Receptionist**: The restaurant is on the second floor. We also have a cafeteria on the top floor. If you would like something to drink, you can either call room service or come down here. The bar is right behind the lobby.

**Tony Shaw**: That's great. Thanks a lot.

**Receptionist**: You're welcome. And enjoy your stay.

---

| | |
|---|---|
| fill out　　填写 ( 表格 ) | bellboy　　行李生 |

---

## Dialogue 3 – Requesting room service

*John Smith calls the hotel operator to request some room service.*

**Operator**: Room Service. What can I do for you?

**John**: I have some shirts that need to be laundered, and I'd like my suit pressed.

**Operator**: Your room number, please?

**John**: Room 1123.

**Operator**: All right, sir. There is a laundry form and a bag in your room. Please fill out the form, and then place it and the bag with your clothes, in the closet. The maid will come and pick them up.

**John**: Hold on, I can't see the laundry form. Where is it?

**Operator**: It's in the drawer of the table beside your bed.

**John**: Ah, yes, I've got it. How long will it take to get my things back?

**Operator**: The laundry will be returned to your room tomorrow before noon.

**John**: All right. I've got it all ready here.

**Operator**：We'll pick it up right away, sir.

---

| launder | 洗熨 | press | 熨平 |
| maid | 女服务员 | | |

## Dialogue 4 – Checking out

*Tony Shaw checks out.*

**Receptionist**：Good morning, sir. Can I help you?

**Tony Shaw**：Good morning. I'd like to check out.

**Receptionist**：Your name and room number, please.

**Tony Shaw**：Tony Shaw, Room 1518.

**Receptionist**：Yes, Mr. Shaw. Have you used any hotel service?

**Tony Shaw**：No, I haven't.

**Receptionist**：All right. This is your bill, Mr. Shaw. Five nights at $90 each, plus phone bills and room service, that makes a total of $495.

**Tony Shaw**：Can I pay by credit card?

**Receptionist**：Certainly.

**Tony Shaw**：Here you are.

**Receptionist**：Please sign your name here.

**Tony Shaw**：And can you please help me call a taxi?

**Receptionist**：No problem. Have a nice day. Bye-bye.

## Practice

1. You will receive some clients from Britain. Call Grand Hotel and make a reservation for two single rooms and a double room for about four days.

2. You are going to attend a conference with two colleagues in Chicago. Phone Imperial Hotel to book three single rooms with shower for two nights. Find out about the price and ask about restaurants and other facilities.

3. You are a guest to check into Holiday Inn. During the check-in, you need to fill out the Registration Form, and then ask the receptionist to find out information about hotel services (such as morning call service, laundry service, international call, etc.).

4. You are leaving the hotel. First ring the reception desk and ask them to have your bill ready. Then go to the lobby and check out.

 Language Focus

| Traveling by Air |
|---|
| • Do I have to confirm my plane reservation? |
| • I'd like to change my reservation. |
| • I'd like to reconfirm my flight. |
| • I'd like to fly economy/first /business class to … |
| • What is the baggage allowance? |

| At the Airport | |
|---|---|
| • What time do you start to check in? | • Do you have a seating preference? |
| • How much should I pay for the excess weight? | • How much money do you have with you? You don't have to pay duty on personal belongings. |
| • Where is the boarding gate for this flight? | • You will have to declare on this item and pay import duties. |

excess weight　　超重部分

| Dealing with Accommodation | |
|---|---|
| • I'd like to make a reservation for … | • What kind of rooms would you like? |
| • Do you have … available? | • How would you like to pay? |
| • I wonder if you have any vacancies for …? | • How long do you expect to stay? |
| • Is there a reduction/ discount for company bookings? | • I hope you will enjoy your stay wit us. |
| • I'd like a wake-up call/ morning call, please. | • Here's your bill. Would you like to check and see if it's correct? |
| • I'd like to check out. | |

 Extended Activities

## Role-play

### Task 1

**Student A**：You are an assistant to your manager, who asked you to book a flight to New York for him next week. Call the travel agency to book a ticket. Your boss prefers Northwest Airlines and doesn't like traveling in the evening.

**Student B:** You work at a travel agency and are responsible for ticket booking. Help your customer with his/her booking.

### Task 2

**Student A:** You have a reservation for three single rooms with bath for three nights. Due to a change of schedule, you have to revise your booking. Call the hotel to change the dates, room types and number of rooms.

**Student B:** You work at the Friendship Hotel. You are mainly responsible for taking hotel reservations on the phone.

### Task 3

**Situation:** Mr. White is trying to make a reservation for a single room from July 12 to 20 for his boss. He calls a hotel but is told all the rooms are booked. He then calls another hotel, but there are only double rooms available. He has to try a third one and make a reservation.

### Task 4

**Situation:** Sally has booked two tickets for Mr. Collins and Mr. Grant respectively for the same flight. Due to an urgent case, Mr. Collins has to put off his flight early next week. Mr. Grant will need an upgraded seat from economy class to business class, as he is going to travel with one of his clients who will fly business class.

## Discussion

### Topic 1

Try to brainstorm as many different types of transportation as possible. Which one(s) do you prefer if you are going to travel? Why?

### Topic 2

Look at the list of various airline services as below. Work in groups and choose three most important services for business travelers.

- double baggage allowance
- priority status at check-in
- exclusive business lounges
- advanced seat selection
- wider, fully reclining seats

- in-seat phone/fax facilities
- in-flight catering/free drinks
- on-board duty-free sales
- air-miles awards for frequent fliers

 Related Information

## How to Manage Business Travel?

The more organized and prepared you are for a business travel, the better you'll be able to cope with its rigors, and the more effective and productive you'll be. It will also mean you have less to catch up on when you return to the office.

Thorough planning is essential. If traveling to an unfamiliar destination, make sure you know precisely where you are going and how you are going to get there, including a means of transport at each interconnecting stage of the trip.

If you are a frequent traveler, keep a permanent list of things to take and do that can be re-used. Be sure to have all the relevant information and your itinerary easily to hand, and most importantly, allow plenty of time for delays. The more changes you make, the more changeover time is necessary.

If you only do five things, they will be:

- Arrange your trip properly;
- Plan your final day at work well;
- Set priorities for tasks before setting off;
- Take good care of yourself;
- Keep your trip as stress-free and relaxing as possible.

> changeover　更换

 Supplements for Reflections

## How to Prepare for Business Travel —— for Dummies

The most import consideration of business travel is to know why you are traveling and what you are expected to accomplish as a result. Once you have these answers, begin to plan your business trip using the following template.

### How to Plan Your Business Meetings

When you know you will be travelling, do the following：

- Have a clearly defined plan for you to follow.
- Set up appointments with your contacts.
- Plan your meetings so that there is plenty of time between appointments. This leaves you plenty of time to move around an unfamiliar city to your next meeting if necessary.
- In case electronic devices possibly distort your files during travel for any reason, email yourself every document that you will need in your destination city.
- If you will have some spare time, consider a day trip or extend your trip to include a weekend getaway.

| electronic device | 电子设备 | getaway | 离开；短假 |
| --- | --- | --- | --- |

### How to Handle Your Travel-related Business Expenses

- Review your company's policies on business travel expenses and reimbursement.
- Keep all of your receipts. Make notes on the back of each to outline the nature of the expense. This includes any tips that you give.

| reimbursement | 补偿 |
| --- | --- |

### Book Your Airline Tickets

Consider the following questions when you book your airline tickets online:

- Are there corporate discounts?
- Are there alternate days/times with cheaper airfares?
- Does the ticket have any restrictions?
- When do you need to pay for the ticket?
- Can you reserve your flight now and confirm your flight later?
- If you cancel the ticket, can it be reused?
- Will you be charged a fee for changing the ticket?
- What other airlines serve this destination?

### Book Your Lodging

Book your hotel near where you will be holding your meetings. Consider the following questions when you book your lodging online:

- Are there any hidden charges or fees?
- How much does parking cost?
- How much does the phone/internet/fax cost (local and long distance charges)?
- How much does room service cost?
- What is the hotel policy on room cancelation, early arrival or early departure?
- Does the hotel have a free airport shuttle?
- Are there any corporate discounts?

## How to Prepare for International Business Travel

If your business travel is international, consider the following：

- a passport
- a visa
- vaccinations and jet lag

| | | | |
|---|---|---|---|
| vaccination | 接种疫苗 | jet lag | 时差 |

### Study the Language, Customs and Business Culture

If you will be interacting with another culture, research that culture. You do not want to offend your business contacts.

You should also learn about the business culture and business etiquette (customs and dress code in the work place) at your destination.

| | |
|---|---|
| dress code | 着装标准 |

### Have the Right Currency on a Business Trip

If you're taking a business trip overseas, be sure to stop in at your bank ahead of time and get enough currency from your destination country to pay for small expenses before you get a chance to go to a hotel's or bank's exchange window. Also, ask your bank or host whether your ATM card is going to work for getting your destination currency at the hotel where you'll be staying or at a nearby bank.

### Personal Safety Considerations

If your business travel is international, review your destination for safety.

## Packing for a Business Meeting

Pack accordingly after reviewing your destination for the following:

- climate
- time of year
- transportation
- type of meetings (formal/informal)
- hotels/restaurants
- the length of time away from home

Bring the following stuff with you:

- a business outfit that is casual and that can be worn on the town
- clothing and accessories that can be mixed and matched
- clothing that can go from day to evening and can still work in more than one setting
- stylish, comfortable shoes

## Traveling to the Airport

Confirm the status of your flight before you depart and before you return home.

## Transportation Options

Arriving at/departing from your destination, consider the following transportation options:

- hotel shuttle
- taxi
- public transportation — use this option only if you have enough time, little luggage and are familiar with your destination

## Arriving at Your Hotel Room

- Phone home and your office to let them know that you have arrived safely. Provide them with your phone number.
- Confirm your upcoming meeting times.
- Set up your work materials near the phone and internet connection. Make it easy to find everything.
- Plug in your laptop and phone charger.

## Prepare for Your First Meeting

- Pack your briefcase with everything you will require.
- Prepare your clothing and shoes.

- Set the alarm clock and ask for a wakeup call.
- Arrange your transportation to the meeting(s).

## Rise Early on the Morning of the Meeting

- Review the details of your meeting(s).
- Enjoy a leisurely breakfast.
- Leave enough time to travel to your first meeting.

## At the End of Each Day

- Review the events of the meeting.
- Contact your office for messages; brief your supervisor.

## Checking out of Your Hotel

- Pack your bags.
- Check your room carefully to make sure you did not leave anything behind.
- Use the express check-out from your hotel.

## Upon Your Return

- Unpack your bags.
- Debrief your supervisor.
- Follow through with any commitments that you made in your business meetings.
- Complete the expense report required for business travel. Organize your receipts by category (food, transportation, lodging, airfare, etc.) when you complete your expense form.

## Questions

- What information about the destination should be considered?
- In what way do cultural factors influence your preparations?
- Decide on a place you are traveling to and make a to-do list.

# Client Reception

## Learning Objectives

**In this unit, you will learn how to:**

- Receive visitors
- Entertain visitors
- See off visitors

## Background Information

Don't let poor manners separate you from success! Hosting a client is an art. In today's business world, being an expert in your field is not always enough. The ability to get along with others, to display good manners, and to make others feel comfortable has become increasingly important. So the way we treat clients can determine whether they will choose our company over our competitors. Learn the fine art of gracious dining in a business setting. The emphasis is on demonstrating good manners and making your client feel pampered.

Good conduct and consideration with clients is not an altruistic pursuit. It's a critical issue facing all businesses today. Companies who fail to recognize this fact will put at risk not only their reputation but also their very survival. Strong companies make etiquette and ethics — good conduct and conscience in business — a core value and a strategic imperative.

 Starting Up

A receptionist plays a variety of roles that center on representing the company to clients, customers and guests. Add to the list below the main job duties of a receptionist and the skills needed to successfully perform these duties.

| Receptionist Duties | Receptionist Skills |
| --- | --- |
| ☆ Greeting visitors | ☆ Communication skills |

 Oral Workshop

## A. Welcoming Clients

### Dialogue 1 – Meeting at the airport

*Frank works at Global Import & Export Company. He comes to the airport to meet Mr. Smith, an American client of the company.*

**Frank:** Excuse me, are you Mr. Smith from the United States?

**Mr. Smith:** Yes. And you are...

**Frank:** I'm Frank from Global Import & Export Company. I'm here to pick you up.

**Mr. Smith:** Nice to meet you, Frank. Thanks for meeting me at the airport.

**Frank:** You are welcome. Very pleased to meet you. I would have been here earlier if I hadn't been held up in a traffic jam.

**Mr. Smith:** I'm glad you could make it.

**Frank**：We've been looking forward to your arrival. How was you flight?

**Mr. Smith**：Just Wonderful! Good food and good service.

**Frank**：Is this your first visit to Beijing?

**Mr. Smith**：Yes. I hope it won't be my last one.

**Frank**：Direct contact is good for both sides.

**Mr. Smith**：Yes. That's why I am here.

**Frank**：OK. I think you'd like to freshen up a bit. Maybe have a rest to overcome jet lag. Our car is out in the parking lot to take you to your hotel.

**Mr. Smith**：Thank you so much. That's very considerate of you.

---

freshen up    梳洗一番              considerate    考虑周到的

---

## Dialogue 2 – Receiving a client in the company

*Mr. Smith comes to visit Mr. Black, the General Manager(GM) of Edmond Company.*
*Victoria greets and receives him at the reception.*

**Victoria**：Good morning. May I help you?

**Mr. Smith**：Yes. I'm Tony Smith. I have an appointment with Mr. Black at 9:30.

**Victoria**：He's in the office. Let me call him, and he'll be right out to see you.

**Mr. Smith**：Thanks.

**Victoria**：I'm sorry, but Mr. Wilson is taking a long distance call. Do you mind waiting for a few minutes?

**Mr. Smith**：No, not at all.

**Victoria**：Would you like some tea?

**Mr. Smith**：Yes, please.

**Victoria**：How do you like your tea? Strong or mild?

**Mr. Smith**：Not too strong, I'm afraid.

(a couple of minutes later)

**Mr. Black**：Mr. Smith, it's a great pleasure to see you.

**Mr. Smith**：Glad to meet you, Mr. Black. I've been looking forward to our meeting.

**Mr. Black**：I'm sorry to have kept you waiting, but I was on a long distance call.

**Mr. Smith**：No problem.

**Mr. Black**：Thank you very much for coming all the way to meet me here in person.

## Practice

1.  You come from Veego Company. You are waiting at the airport to welcome an

American businessman who comes to China to visit your company.

2. You are the secretary to the general manager of Veego Company. Greet and welcome the American businessman when he comes to your company for the first visit.

# B. Entertaining Clients

## Dialogue 1 – At a welcome party

*Mr. Smith meets Mr. Brown and Mr. Black of Global Import & Export Company at a welcome party.*

**Mr. Black**: Mr. Smith, I'd like to introduce you to Mr. Brown, our president.

**Mr. Smith**: Nice to meet you, Mr. Brown.

**Mr. Brown**: How do you do, Mr. Smith? It is indeed a great pleasure to meet with you. I understand that you had a pleasant flight and have settled into your room.

**Mr. Smith**: Yes, everything is just fine.

**Mr. Brown**: We look forward to meeting with you over the next few days.

**Mr. Black**: We have ordered one of our favorite wines called "Pleasure" for you.

**Mr. Smith**: That's very kind of you.

**Mr. Brown**: For our special guests, we've arranged the menu in advance. We hope our selection of dishes this evening will be to your liking.

**Mr. Black**: Since this is the first time we have the honor of entertaining you at dinner, we thought that you might like to try some local traditional dishes, which are famous here.

**Mr. Smith**: That sounds wonderful.

**Mr. Black**: Please help yourself.

**Mr. Brown**: Your offices are located in Chicago. Do you also live there?

**Mr. Smith**: Chicago is a large and busy city, at least in the States. I live outside Chicago and drive to work everyday.

**Mr. Black**: Is that convenient?

**Mr. Smith**: Yes, it is.

**Mr. Brown**: Now, I'd like to propose a toast to our special guest, Mr. Smith. Once again I express our great appreciation for honoring our company with your visit. I hope that our discussions over the next few days will be fruitful and to our mutual benefits.

**Mr. Black**: I also hope that our business negotiations will mark the beginning of a long and friendly relationship between us!

**Mr. Smith:** Thank you, Mr. Brown and Mr. Black. I am very pleased to be here. Your welcome and reception are greatly appreciated. May I propose a toast to our hosts and our cooperation?

**Mr. Black:** To our long friendship…Cheers!

**Mr. Brown:** To our friendly cooperation…Cheers!

| | | | |
|---|---|---|---|
| to one's liking | 合……口味 | mutual | 共同的 |

### Dialogue 2 – Taking a client shopping

*Frank offers to take Mr. Smith shopping.*

**Frank:** Mr. Smith, we would like to take you on a quick tour of the downtown area for a little sightseeing.

**Mr. Smith:** That would be great, but what I really like to do now is some shopping.

**Frank:** Oh, of course, no problem. What did you have in mind, Mr. Smith?

**Mr. Smith:** I'd like to find some souvenirs for my friends, and my wife would like to buy some jade as well.

**Frank:** Alright. Let me see … there's an Ancient Culture Street nearby where you will find all kinds of handicrafts and souvenirs.

**Mr. Smith:** Could I find jade there, too?

**Frank:** Don't worry. There's a jade market about a 5-minute taxi ride from here.

**Mr. Smith:** That'd be great!

*(three hours later)*

**Mr. Smith:** Thank you very much for the shopping tour, Frank.

**Frank:** My pleasure. And please let me know if I can help you look for anything else while you are here.

**Mr. Smith:** Thanks for your hospitality and great help.

**Frank:** You are welcome.

| | | | |
|---|---|---|---|
| souvenir | 纪念品 | handicraft | 手工艺品 |
| jade | 玉，翡翠 | | |

### Practice

1. You are the secretary to the general manager. Invite the visiting American

businessman to the general manager's house for a cocktail party and give some party details.

2. You are the general manager. Greet the American businessman and entertain him/her during the party. Express sincere wishes to further your cooperation in the future.

3. You are to pick up the visiting American businessman for some sightseeing and shopping. Make some introductions about the specialties in your city.

## C. Seeing off Clients

### Dialogue – Seeing off a client at the airport

Mr. Black sees Mr. Smith off at the airport.

**Mr. Smith**: Mr. Black, thank you very much for coming to the airport to see us off. Your great country and your company have left us a very deep impression and your working attitude and your way of doing business have changed my opinions of Chinese people.

**Mr. Black**: Thank you! I'm glad to hear that.

**Mr. Smith**: That's true. And this trip has been a very productive one for us.

**Mr. Black**: Thank you again for your visit. We are looking forward to any favorable reply from your side.

**Mr. Smith**: You can count on me, Mr. Black, I will try my best to promote this transaction.

**Mr. Black**: We are happy that we have established business relations. I really hope that we'll have more business to do and more opportunities to meet each other.

**Mr. Smith**: I'm sure we will have opportunities to meet each other in the future.

**Mr. Black**: Hope to see you again soon. OK, I think it's time for you to check in.

**Mr. Smith**: Yes, that's right. We have to say goodbye then. Thank you again for seeing us off.

**Mr. Black**: Have a safe and pleasant journey home!

**Mr. Smith**: I will, bye-bye!

### Practice

You are general manager of a company to see off your visiting client from the U.S. at the airport. Express your best wishes to him/her and expect a better cooperation in the future. The visiting client also expresses his/her gratitude to you and your company for the warm and thoughtful reception.

 Language Focus

## Welcoming Clients

- We appreciate very much that you have come to visit us in spite of the long and tiring journey.
- I'm delighted to make your acquaintance.
- Thank you for coming all the way to our company.
- It's a great pleasure to have you here with us.
- It's a great pleasure to have such an enthusiastic group to participate in our project.
- On behalf of the staff of Levien, I'd like to welcome you to our company.
- Can I get you something to drink?

## Entertaining Clients

| | |
|---|---|
| • We are going to give a dinner party at … this evening and would like to invite you all. | • Thank you very much for preparing such a splendid dinner especially for us. |
| • We'll meet you at the gate of the hotel at 6:00 this evening. | • I appreciate your hospitality. Thank you again for everything you've done for me. |
| • Make yourself at home. | |
| • I would like to propose a toast to your health! | |
| • I wish a brisk business for you all and a continued development in our business dealings! | |

## Seeing off Clients

| | |
|---|---|
| • I am confident that our cooperation will be a very successful one. | • Before I say goodbye, I'd like to say it has been a very pleasant and productive trip for me. |
| • I'm really happy for having worked with you for a few days. | • Your company has left me a very good impression, and I am deeply moved by your hospitality. |
| • I really hope to see you again some day and we are looking forward to hearing from you. | • Thank you for your hospitality. |
| • I hope you have enjoyed your stay. | |
| • Have a safe flight home. | |

## Role-play

### Task 1

**Student A：** You have just concluded a transaction with your client, Mr. Jenkins, after hard negotiation. Both of you feel you deserve a relaxation. Since this is Mr. Jenkins' first trip to your city, you are showing him the scenic spots and historical sites in and around your city. Introduce the places you visit.

**Student B：** You are Mr. Jenkins. You have just concluded a transaction with your partner after hard negotiation. Both of you feel you deserve a relaxation. Since this is your first trip to the city, you are very interested in seeing more of the city. Your partner offers to show you around.

### Task 2

**Student A：** You are Mr. Gao, the sales manager of your company. You are very excited about the deal that has nicely been reached. You then decide to invite Mr. Jefferson, the importer from Australia, to dinner. At dinner, you have an intimate talk with him about your interests, past experience in this business line, and your future plan.

**Student B：** You are an importer from Australia visiting Mr. Gao's company. After the deal is reached, you are invited to dinner with Mr. Gao. You share your interests and personal ideas on some business topics with your host.

### Task 3

Work in groups of 3 to work out a 4-day schedule.

**Student A：** You are Chen Hua, the Chinese host. Do your best to please your guests.

**Student B：** You are John Brown, the marketing manager of an American company. Your major concern is whether a new contract can be made during your visit. So you should see to it that enough time is given to the negotiations. As to other activities, you are quite open and flexible.

**Student C：** You are Mike Smith, the assistant to John Brown. This is your first visit to China. You'll listen to your boss when the arrangement for the negotiations is discussed. When it comes to recreation and other activities during your visit, tell your host what your interests are.

**Task 4**

**Group work**: Work in groups of 4. One of you represents the hosting company, treating two American business guests to some Chinese food. In the restaurant, the host asks the guests what they would like to have and recommends some local specialties, in addition, describes the features of the specialties. The fourth student will play the role of the waiter. During the meal, you recall what has been achieved during the visit, and look into the future.

## Discussion

### Topic 1

Do you think it is important to meet your guests at the airport or the railway station when they arrive and see them off when they leave? If yes, who do you think should be sent on this assignment? Explain your reasons.

### Topic 2

Do you usually have a schedule for your visiting relatives, friends or business acquaintances? If so, how is the schedule worked out? What items are usually included in the schedule? Are the schedules for your business acquaintances different from those for your relatives or friends?

### Topic 3

What should be taken into consideration when entertaining guests from a different cultural background? Are there any taboos?

 Related Information

## Hosting Visitors from Foreign Countries

The following factors should be considered when hosting the foreign visitors:

- Bring the visitors' background to your attention and prepare to meet the visitors on their arrival.
- Understand your visitors' objectives and their itinerary.
- Make valuable suggestions to help your visitors make best use of their time.
- Draft your reception plan.

- Arrange the interviews, meetings and field visits beforehand.

Entertaining clients is not as easy as it sounds. It's not just fine dining and attending enjoyable events. Entertaining clients means impressing them in a unique manner outside the office. Although you might not be in the office while entertaining a client, office-like behavior still applies.

### Things to Do

- Choose activities that are specifically targeted for individual clients. Customize what you do with your clients, depending on their interest. If you don't know what interests your clients, don't hesitate to ask. Therefore, both you and your client are able to participate in some activities you both enjoy.
- Use your manners.
- Prepare small talk conversation points.
- Send handwritten thank-you notes after the event or meeting.
- Establish a budget.
- Tend to the details and convey them to your clients.
- Always confirm with your clients 24 hours before the event.
- Know your clients' time constraints.
- Learn to listen.
- Always remember you are a reflection of your firm.

### Things Not to Do

- Don't forget to set up a meeting when you will see your client again. Make sure that you let your clients know you will see them again soon.
- Don't discuss the competition of you or your client. It's always better to take the high road and stay positive about your firm.
- Don't be late. Always give yourself plenty of time when meeting a client.
- Don't discuss controversial issues. Leave the taboo subjects such as politics and religion out of the discussion when meeting with clients.
- Don't drink heavily. Functions that involve drinking should not be perceived as a happy hour.
- Don't skimp on food quality or quantity.

| controversial | 引起争议的 | skimp | 节省；克扣 |
| --- | --- | --- | --- |

## Reception Desk Etiquette

The receptionist is the first point of contact for customers, investors and others who walk through the door of a business. As such, receptionists make the first impression on others. First impressions do count. To make that impression a positive one, receptionists must abide by an etiquette protocol that meets the company's standards. Remember, the visitor isn't interrupting your business, he is your business.

| abide by | 遵守；信守 | | protocol | 礼仪；协议 |
|---|---|---|---|---|

### Functions

Receptionists perform a variety of administrative support functions, such as answering the phone, greeting visitors, scheduling appointments and making sure the reception area is tidy and welcoming.

### Phone Etiquette

Receptionists should practice excellent telephone etiquette, because a large portion of their job relates to answering, screening or transferring phone calls. Practice proper phone etiquette by answering the phone by the third ring. Receptionists must speak clearly and slowly, and should not have food, beverages or gum in their mouths while speaking to callers. When they need to place callers on hold, they should ask the callers for permission to do this. Also, before transferring a call, the receptionist should inform the caller of what she is about to do.

### Phone Messages

Take detailed messages to ensure that the caller's information and needs will be passed to the relevant staff member. Note the caller's name, the company or department that he represents, the date and time of the call, an explanation of the call and the caller's phone number. Verify the information before you hang up the phone so that you can pass accurate information onto the intended recipient.

### Communication Etiquette

Whether the receptionist is on the phone or greeting visitors in person, she should follow standard communication etiquette. Receptionists should be patient with callers and visitors, no matter what the situation is. Even if callers or visitors express frustration or anger, the receptionist should remain calm and patient at all times.

### Dress Code

Since the receptionist is the first person to greet visitors as they come through the door, she should be well groomed and wear standard business attire which is set by the company. For example, a law firm likely will require its receptionist to wear a suit. A receptionist for a pediatric dentist, however, would be suitably dressed in tailored pants and a sweater in a bright, fun color. Avoid excessive makeup.

| pediatric | 小儿科的 |
|---|---|

### Reception Area

Part of having good etiquette entails maintaining an environment that is welcoming, clean and comfortable for others. This means the reception area should be neat and clean, and the receptionist should provide magazines for visitors to read while they wait, offer guests coffee or water, and greet people appropriately. Remember that the reception area promotes company image and should look professional.

| entail | 需要 |
|---|---|

### Questions

- What should a receptionist do when a guest has been waiting long?
- Do you think jeans and T-shirts are proper clothing for receptionists? What messages do they send?
- Suppose there are several visitors waiting in the reception area. Should the receptionist make small talk with each person or take the time for a lengthy conversation with one or two?

# Unit 4

# Companies and Products

 Learning Objectives

**In this unit, you will learn how to:**

- Guide a company tour
- Prepare for a new product launch
- Launch a new product

 Background Information

In business, you may need to present your company/product to visitors, potential investors or partners, or new suppliers and clients. What can you say about your company? How would you describe it? There are a number of things to consider, such as the company size, its employees, its branches, company history, culture, reputation, and future plans. Product presentations are an important part of selling your product to prospective customers. In many cases, this will be the customer's first impression on your company. First impressions are critical. There are also times when it is important to sell your product to the people inside your company as well as investors. Proper preparation is vital to presenting your product in the best light possible.

 Starting Up

**1. Are you familiar with the following famous companies and**

the products they make or services they offer? Please match the company information and talk about the ones that you know well.

| | | |
|---|---|---|
| 1. Nike Inc. | Britain | camera & photocopier |
| 2. Yum! | Sweden | wristwatch & timing device |
| 3. Canon | France | package delivery |
| 4. Electrolux | the United States | television broadcasting |
| 5. Alibaba | Italy | athletic shoes & apparel |
| 6. UPS | the United States | fragrance & makeup |
| 7. Ferrari | Switzerland | household appliance |
| 8. Chanel | the United States | online shopping |
| 9. Sky Inc. | Japan | sports car |
| 10. Longines | China | fast food |

2. **What industry does each of these companies belong to? Can you think of more companies that fall into the following categories?**

- Internet　＿＿＿＿＿＿＿＿＿＿＿＿＿＿＿＿＿＿＿＿＿
- Electronics　＿＿＿＿＿＿＿＿＿＿＿＿＿＿＿＿＿＿＿
- Automotive　＿＿＿＿＿＿＿＿＿＿＿＿＿＿＿＿＿＿＿
- Watch Manufacturing　＿＿＿＿＿＿＿＿＿＿＿＿＿＿
- Restaurants　＿＿＿＿＿＿＿＿＿＿＿＿＿＿＿＿＿＿＿
- Mass Media　＿＿＿＿＿＿＿＿＿＿＿＿＿＿＿＿＿＿＿
- Appliances　＿＿＿＿＿＿＿＿＿＿＿＿＿＿＿＿＿＿＿
- Fashion　＿＿＿＿＿＿＿＿＿＿＿＿＿＿＿＿＿＿＿＿＿
- Courier　＿＿＿＿＿＿＿＿＿＿＿＿＿＿＿＿＿＿＿＿＿
- Apparel & Accessories　＿＿＿＿＿＿＿＿＿＿＿＿＿＿

 Oral Workshop

## A. Leading a Company Tour

### Dialogue 1 – Taking a guided company tour

*Mr. Chang, the Production Manager shows the visitor Mr. Johnson around the factory.*

**Mr. Chang**：Good afternoon, Mr. Johnson. I'm David Chang, and I'm in charge of the

Production Department.

**Mr. Johnson**：Nice to meet you, Mr. Chang.

**Mr. Chang**：You too. Mr. Johnson, would you like to look around the factory first?

**Mr. Johnson**：Yes, that'd be great, thank you.

**Mr. Chang**：This is our office block. We have all the administrative departments here：Sales, Accounting, Personnel, R & D, and Production.

**Mr. Johnson**：What's that building opposite us?

**Mr. Chang**：That's the warehouse where the larger items of medical instruments are stored. We keep a stock of the fast-moving items so that urgent orders can be met quickly from stock.

**Mr. Johnson**：If I ordered an X-ray apparatus today, how long would I have to wait for the delivery in Thailand?

**Mr. Chang**：I think you'd better speak to Mr. Bell, he looks after shipping issues. You'll meet him when we go over to the workshop.

*(In the workshop)*

**Mr. Chang**：This is the smallest workshop of our three ones. This is the delivery bay.

**Mr. Johnson**：Oh, the smallest one is actually quite big, everything seems well-organized.

**Mr. Chang**：The steel sheets and bars come in, as you see, in different sizes and are unloaded onto the delivery bay here. We buy them in from a steel works in Germany. This is the new conveyor belt we had installed last year. We doubled our output in this department as a result.

**Mr. Johnson**：Oh, that's very impressive.

**Mr. Chang**：Shall we move to the assembly shop now?

**Mr. Johnson**：All right.

**Mr. Chang**：I hope the noise isn't bothering you.

**Mr. Johnson**：No, not at all. I'm accustomed to this sort of thing.

**Mr. Chang**：If there's some place you'd like to stop off, don't hesitate to ask.

**Mr. Johnson**：Thank you. I'll keep that in mind.

| stock | 库存 | apparatus | 仪器 |
| assembly | 装配 | | |

## Dialogue 2 – Introducing a company

*Mr. Brown introduces the company to Mr. Johnson.*

**Mr. Brown**：How do you do, Mr. Johnson? It's a pleasure to meet you.

**Mr. Johnson**：The pleasure's mine, Mr. Brown.

**Mr. Brown**：First of all, I'll show you a multimedia presentation about our company.

**Mr. Johnson**：That would be wonderful. Thank you.

**Mr. Brown**：If you have any questions during the presentation, please feel free to ask.

**Mr. Johnson**：That's very considerate of you. I will, Mr. Brown. I've heard your plant is phasing in robots.

**Mr. Brown**：Yes, we started last spring.

**Mr. Johnson**：These machines seem to be the latest models.

**Mr. Brown**：That's true. We believe that superior equipment will improve our productivity.

**Mr. Johnson**：When was this factory founded?

**Mr. Brown**：In 1976 with a capital of two million dollars.

**Mr. Johnson**：How many employees do you have?

**Mr. Brown**：There are about 1,200 in the plant, and 80 in the office.

**Mr. Johnson**：Are you expanding your plant?

**Mr. Brown**：Yes. Our new plant will start production next month.

**Mr. Johnson**：That will help to speed things up.

**Mr. Brown**：Of course.

**Mr. Johnson**：Thank you very much for your introduction, Mr. Brown.

**Mr. Brown**：You are more than welcome, Mr. Johnson.

| phase in | 逐步采用 | capital | 资本 |

## Practice

1. You are the general manager of Pramont Garment Company. Show a foreign visitor around your company and introduce your staff to the visitor during the company tour.

2. You are the general manager of Pramont Garment Company. You are giving a brief introduction of your company to a potential business partner from Britain.

## B. Preparing for a New Product Launch

### Dialogue 1 – Talking about a new product

*Andy, the marketing manager, is talking about the new product with his assistants Eddie and Sally.*

**Andy**：Eddie, what do you think of the RC510 cell phone?

**Eddie**：It's user-friendly with a number of smart functions. The games aren't bad, either.

**Andy**：OK. Now our agenda is to figure out the Four P's. I'd like to start with price and product. Sally, could you take notes?

**Sally**：Will do.

**Andy**：Now the price has been left to our discretion. We just have to keep in the RMB2,000 range. Any thoughts?

**Eddie**：It's a high-end phone, but I think we should keep it affordable.

**Sally**：Well, our costs are lower than that of our competitors, so we do have room to offer a lower price.

**Andy**：Let's make it RMB2,500, then. We can offer discounts later.

**Sally**：Now, how are we going to describe the product?

**Eddie**：We should make sure to mention that it has more features than any other phone on the market.

**Andy**：OK, that's good, but we should emphasize the most sought-after features first, like the build-in camera, the TFT display and digital audio capabilities…What else? Help me out here, folks.

**Eddie**：Essentially, it's a complete mini-office for professionals on the go.

**Sally**：How about a slogan "An Office at Your Fingertips", followed by a list of features in order of market appeal?

**Andy**：Now, we're getting somewhere. Let's put the finishing touches on our press release.

| discretion | 自行决定的自由 | sought-after | 广受欢迎的 |
| --- | --- | --- | --- |
| TFT | 薄膜晶体管 | on the go | 活跃，忙个不停 |
| appeal | 吸引力 | press release | 新闻稿 |

### Dialogue 2 – Talking about a new product launch

*Andy, the marketing manager, continues the discussion on the new product launch strategies with his assistants Eddie and Sally.*

**Andy**：Now, on to the next two P's：promotion and place. Remember, we have a limited budget.

**Eddie**：Why don't we start out with poster ads on buses and follow up with radio ads?

**Andy**：That sounds like it could be a cost-effective start. We can consider prime-time

TV commercials as we move on to the second phase.

**Sally：** How about a hip ad campaign on the Internet? We could use up-and-coming directors to put together exciting short clips.

**Eddie：** If they create a buzz, we would be able to differentiate ourselves from our competitors.

**Andy：** I think you might be on to something. Now, let's focus on place. How are we going to handle distribution?

**Eddie：** Since our initial target market is Asia, we'll need to start talking with IT resellers with whom we've had great success in the past.

**Sally：** We have already developed some key relationships with channel partners in Hong Kong and Macao.

**Andy：** But don't forget to get our distributors geared up. I want to find a different distributor for Japan. We've had some snags in negotiations with them recently.

**Sally：** Trade shows are starting to make a comeback.

**Eddie：** Which brings us to next week's product launch show. We need to work on our presentation.

**Sally：** Why don't we meet tomorrow afternoon at, say, 2:30? I'll book a conference room and email you confirmations.

**Eddie：** Of course you'll use the RC510 cell phone, right?

| | | | |
|---|---|---|---|
| prime-time | 黄金时间的 | commercial | 广告 |
| hip | 赶时髦的 | up-and-coming | 有前途的 |
| buzz | 时尚氛围 | differentiate | 区分 |
| gear up | 做好行动准备 | | |

## Practice

1. You are the Product Manager of New Century Computers Co., Ltd. Your company is going to launch a new laptop to the market. Talk about your new product features with your team members.

2. You are the Marketing Manager of New Century Computers Co., Ltd. Your company is going to launch a new laptop to the market. Prepare for the new product launch with your team.

# C. Launching a New Product

## Dialogue 1 – Presenting a new product

*Andy and his assistant Eddie are presenting their new product at the new product launch show.*

**Andy**: Hello. I'm proud to launch our first smart phone. It uses an open operating system and boasts more functions than any other phone on the market. We call it "An Office at Your Fingertips."

*(showing slides of the smart phone and its functions)*

As you can see, it's very sleek and compact. Particularly impressive is its ability to wirelessly connect with other devices. Now I'll let my colleague Eddie Crane provide you with specifics about RC510 cell phone.

**Eddie**: I'm here to tell you about some of the spectacular features of this phone.

*(showing a slide listing features of the smart phone)*

In addition to Wi-Fi Internet access, email integration, contact database, and instant messaging, it has digital music capabilities, and a build-in camera. Our phone's massive local storage greatly surpasses anything else on the market.

**Andy**: It's more than just a phone; it's a mobile office. In a single handheld unit, it offers everything a professional on the go needs to be on top of his or her game.

**Eddie**: Speaking of the games, the RC510 will have the greatest selection of games with the most advanced graphics.

**Andy**: Now we will take questions from the press.

| | | | |
|---|---|---|---|
| boast | 自夸，自负有…… | sleek | 时髦的 |
| compact | 小巧易携带的 | surpass | 优于 |

## Dialogue 2 – A Q&A session at a product launch

*Andy, Eddie and Sally are taking questions at the new product launch.*

**Reporter 1**: I have a question. Which telecom providers will you team up with?

**Andy**: Setcom will provide service in our greater Asia region. Bellflow and Televue will serve North America and Europe respectively.

**Reporter 2**: Will your new smart phone be able to support a range of different applications?

**Eddie：** Our goal is for the RC510 to be a must-have for professionals. In order to offer laptop functionality, we have integrated hard disk drives while not compromising battery life.

**Reporter 3：** What will you sell your smart phone for?

**Sally：** We have aggressively priced the RC510 RMB2,500. This is important because it prices a hard disk drive smart phone into the flash memory smart phone range. This will be a first for this market.

**Reporter 4：** You mentioned games. What types of games will your smart phone offer?

**Eddie：** We all welcome entertaining diversions, right? We have forged alliances with leading gaming software developers and will offer a full range of gaming options.

**Andy：** We thank you for coming to the product launch of the RC510. We expect that our customers will benefit greatly from our entry into the smart phone arena. Please visit our website for updates regarding our full product line.

## Practice

1. You are the Marketing Manager of New Century Computers Co., Ltd. At the launch show of your latest model of tablet, you and your team present your new product to the audience.

2. You are the Marketing Manager of New Century Computers Co., Ltd. After the new product presentation at the new tablet launch, you and your team answer the questions from the audience.

3. Search a company and one of its products from the Internet. Create a product presentation according to the following checklist:

- Identify objective
- Identify target audience
- Include positioning
- Include company overview
- Include product description
- Include benefits
- Include examples
- Identify and include closing

 Language Focus

## Talking about Companies

- We were founded/set up/established in ….
- We merged with X company in ….
- We set up a subsidiary in ….
- We floated on the stock exchange last year, and we are now listed on the London Stock Exchange.
- We make/produce/manufacture/supply ….
- We are developing new … for ….
- We make annual profits of … million.
- Our turnover is in excess of … million.
- The company is divided into different departments, each with its own director.
- We employ more than 2,000 people worldwide.

## Making a Company Tour

- Please stop me if you have any question.
- You'll know our products better after this visit.
- Maybe we could start with the Designing Department.
- What's your general impression, may I ask?

- I've been looking forward to visiting your factory.
- I hope my visit does not cause you too much trouble.
- I'm impressed by your approach to business.
- I think we may be able to work together in the future.

## Preparing for a New Product Launch

- The product gives us an edge over our competitors.
- No one can match us so far as quality is concerned.
- We are thinking of expanding into the overseas market.
- How will we differentiate our product from those of our competitors?
- After months of work, I'm so glad we've developed a product with a competitive advantage.
- Our product should meet the needs of our target market.
- Before we release the product, we need to …
- What are the selling points of our products?
- It seems that there's a fair market for the product at the moment.

## Launching a New Product

- Our new product will be available from …
- This new version improves on the previous version in terms of …
- The product's innovative features include …
- This product is superior to others on the market because …
- Our product takes less time to install and it's easy to operate.
- Our product is environmentally-friendly and user-friendly.
- This type of product is in great demand.
- The product is well thought of in America.
- This style is out of ordinary.
- To sum up, this product has excellent quality, reasonable price, distinctive features and a predicable large circulation.
- I hope you have a clearer picture of the product and its features, functions, distributions and pricing.

 Extended Activities

## Role-play

### Task 1

**Student A:** You are a Chinese CD player manufacturer. A Korean business person is very interested in your products. Introduce your CD player in terms of distinctive features, main functions, and competitive price.

**Student B:** You are a business person from Korea. You plan to import different models of CD players from a Chinese manufacturer. Talk with the Chinese to find out detailed information about the products.

### Task 2

**Student A:** You are the product manager of Lynch High Tech Company which makes anti-virus software. When a client from Japan comes to visit your company, show him around and present the latest software products.

**Student B:** You work for a Japanese company. You come to China to visit Lynch High Tech Company, seeking opportunities of cooperation. You wish to have a tour of the company and learn more about the company and its products.

## Task 3

**Student A**: You are Tony Wilson, an American client visiting Skyline Television Company. You would like to know more about the company.

**Student B**: You are Lucy, the secretary of Skyline Television Company. An American client, Tony Wilson, is coming to visit your company. Welcome the client and show him around your company.

**Student C**: You are Richard Brown, the general manager of Skyline Television Company. Introduce the company to Tony Wilson, the visitor from the United States.

## Task 4

**Group work**: Work in a group of 4. Two of the students represent the Sales Department of Lental Camera Company, which is going to launch the latest digital camera to the market. Discuss and figure out the details of the launch. The students are also supposed to give a brief presentation of the new product, including the features, the functions and the price, etc. The other two students are the clients attending the launch. Ask some questions about the new product.

# Discussion

## Topic 1

What makes a company and its product competitive in the market?

## Topic 2

What preparations should be made to make a product launch? Make a list of them according to the priorities.

## Topic 3

Think of some factors that may lead to failed company/product presentations.

# Related Information

## How to Create Successful Corporate Presentations

As compared to traditional forms of advertising, more and more companies are using corporate presentations to convey their message to their target audience. Corporate presentation is a unique way of communicating and building the brand image for a company. This effective tool can be used to promote a product, service or to simply tell something essential about your company.

- Decide the purpose behind developing a corporate presentation. Basically, corporate presentation is designed for internal office use or to showcase your achievements at trade fairs, conferences, mega events or shows.
- Be specific about the subject matter about the corporate presentation. Decide on who will be your audience and what message you would want to convey to them. These issues will serve as pointers towards the focus of your presentation.
- Choose the platform you would be using for designing the corporate presentations. You can use various platforms such as PowerPoint, Flash or Keynote.
- Avoid information overload while developing a corporate presentation. Too much information can be confusing for the audience.
- Put the message in a neatly laid out storyboard format. One point should lead effortlessly to the other. This will clearly and lucidly convey your message.
- Use more pictures in your presentation as a picture is worth a thousand words. Good pictures will increase the retention of your message.
- Make the presentation interactive by having options to include the audience at the end of the session. You can ask the feedback about the presentation what they think about it from the audience.
- Use relevant statistical data to make your corporate presentation effective and interpretative. Real time figures make a lot of difference of what you want to say to your audience.
- Use visual aids as transmitters of your message. With the help of visual aids you can easily present highly technical concepts before your audience without using too many words.
- For professional corporate presentations, you can look for a web development company to design and develop a presentation for you. A professionally designed corporate presentation helps in conveying the message succinctly and clearly.

 Supplements for Reflections

## How to Launch a New Product

The launch of a new product is often an indicator of its future success. Investors, executives and employees want to see the time and money spent in research and development pay off, so you need to strive for a successful product debut.

## Instructions

Start advertising the new product several weeks to a month before its launch. Depending on your target market, you may only need to alert your current customers to have a successful debut. Some items, like children's toys, should only be advertised once they are in stores so consumers can buy them shortly after seeing an advertisement.

Coordinate press releases to create a buzz in local and regional media. Journalists love quirky stories, so think about the news value of your product or company. For example, maybe you are the only security-scanner company in the area or are releasing a product that uses a very new technology.

Analyze the expected demand of your product so you don't over- or under-shoot your initial product run. Account for sales based on returning customers, media attention and advertising. With some new products, it is often beneficial to inform the public of how many units will be available at launch.

Hold a press conference to announce your new product and its release date. This marketing trick requires your product to create such a buzz that consumers and the media talk about it until the launch.

Create a website where the curious consumer can learn all about your product. The Internet can be a great place to post product specifications that look and feel out of place in an advertisement. Also, include an area where potential customers can post questions about the item.

Send out demo units of high-tech gadgets to large newspapers and trade magazines. A review will not only give you some free publicity, you'll also get some general feedback about problems that you may want to correct prior to the launch.

## Tips & Warnings

Hiring a public relations firm to handle your press releases and media inquiries can be a great help if you are a small business and don't have your own department of external communications.

Once you've launched your product, immediately start analyzing sales figures and data to figure out how to sustain the launch momentum.

Always go over any health and safety issues of your new product before the launch. A flawed or dangerous item could damage your company's reputation and affect the Product's Sales.

## Questions

- How long in advance should a company start advertising the product before its launch?
- How to make wise use of press to facilitate the product launch?
- What should a small business do with the launch if it does not have any internal department that has relevant expertise?

# Unit 5

# Marketing

##  Learning Objectives

**In this unit, you will learn how to：**

- Promote sales
- Advertise
- Conduct market research

## Background Information

Marketing is the process of telling consumers why they should choose your product or service over your competitors; if you are not doing that, you are not marketing. The key of marketing is finding the right method and defining the right message to use to educate and influence your consumers.

Companies make the mistake of thinking that marketing is just "one" thing, but in fact, marketing is everything that the consumer encounters when it comes to your business, from advertising to what they hear, to the customer service that they receive, to the follow-up care that you provide.

The activities of marketing are often confused with advertising and sales. However, it is important to realize that there is a difference between them. The best way to distinguish between advertising and marketing is to think of marketing as a pie, inside that pie you have slices of advertising, market research, media planning, public relations, product pricing, distribution, customer support, sales strategy, and community involvement. Advertising only equals one piece of the pie in the strategy. Marketing is everything that you do to reach and persuade prospects and the sales process is everything that you do to close the sale and get a signed agreement or contract.

 Starting Up

In order for businesses to win market share and stay relevant they need to consider many types of marketing strategies. Match the following frequently-used marketing strategies with the corresponding explanations and examples.

| Strategy | Explanation | Example |
| --- | --- | --- |
| 1.Cloud Marketing | A particular item is sold at low rates, or is given away free, to increase the sales of another complimentary item or service. | Catalogue Selling, Mail-order, Tele-calling and TV shopping. |
| 2.Digital Marketing | It is marketing through creating, maintaining and enhancing strong long-term relationships with customers to win their loyalty. | A restaurant can build relationships with customers by sending them discount offers on their birthdays. |
| 3.Direct Marketing | It uses various digital devices like smart phones, computers, or tablets to inform customers and business partners about its products. | Gillette mails disposable safety razors to young men near their 18th birthday, or sells razors at an artificially low price to create the market for the blades. |
| 4.Freebie Marketing | It takes place on the internet, where all the marketing resources and assets are transferred online. | Amazon.com sells tens of thousands of different products but has no physical stores. Customers receive notices about sales through their email. |
| 5.Free Sample Marketing | It interacts directly with consumers through (e)mail, texts, and fliers, calling for the consumers to make a direct response. | In Singapore, McDonald's offers dynamic display advertising to alert consumers to free breakfasts at local stores. |
| 6.Relationship Marketing | It refers to giving away a free sample of the product to influence the consumer to make the purchase. | In shopping malls or supermarkets, some companies handle out free samples of coffee, cookies, toothpaste, etc. |

 Oral Workshop

# A. Promoting Sales

## Dialogue 1 – Discussing promotion strategies

*Mr. Brown is having a meeting with his assistants Peter and Mary, discussing how to promote sales.*

**Mr. Brown**: Good morning, everyone. Today we will discuss the marketing plan for Q2 of this year. First of all, Peter is going to brief us the latest sales information of our palm PC.

**Peter**: Thank you, Mr. Brown. The sales of our palm PC decreased 30% in Q1 this year. The profits dropped by 60%. This mainly resulted from the heavy tax levied against Chinese electronic products in the US.

**Mary**: Yes. Because of the tax, Last year,China lost $2 billion. Our company is one of the many victims.

**Mr. Brown**: If we can't improve our sales in Q2, we'll have to reduce our labor force through layoffs, voluntary retirements and outsourcing, for the survival of the company and the plant.

**Peter**: This is the least thing we want to see. We need to promote the sales of our products at home.

**Mary**: I think the home market for our palm PC still has potential.

**Mr. Brown**: I agree. Thanks to our favorable economic environment, there are more and more would-be buyers. The problem is how to make more people, more companies and enterprises be aware of our products.

**Peter**: We could continue with our practice of having a display at the Exhibition Center.

**Mary**: Yes. And we need to enlarge our show counter at the Exhibition Center. Besides, perhaps we need to participate in PC exhibition shows held in other big cities.

**Mr. Brown**: That's a good idea. But we don't have enough staff for exhibition shows in other cities.

**Peter**: Do you think we could send brochures of our products to the PC exhibition organizers?

**Mary**: Sure. We could also send film or video recordings of our company and products directly to the organizers of the exhibitions. If this is workable, we can get our products known without much investment.

**Mr. Brown：** That's a brilliant idea.

**Peter：** And we will update our brochure, making it more attractive and impressive.

**Mr. Brown：** Absolutely. We also need to advertise our products on a national scale. We need the help of an advertising agency. Mary, will you please arrange a meeting for me with our advertising agency this week?

**Mary：** No problem. I'll make some phone calls right now.

---

| | | | |
|---|---|---|---|
| palm PC | 掌上电脑 | levy | 征税 |
| layoff | 临时解雇 | | |

---

## Dialogue 2 – Making a new brochure

*Mr. Brown, the marketing manager, is talking with Carol, the representative of an advertising company, about updating the product brochure.*

**Carol：** Nice to meet you, Mr. Brown.

**Mr. Brown：** Nice to meet you, Carol. I really need your help with our product brochure to meet the needs of the changing market.

**Carol：** It makes sense. I believe the brochure in use now is more than two years' old.

**Mr. Brown：** That's right. And it mainly targets the US market.

**Carol：** What would you like to have in the brochure this time?

**Mr. Brown：** I think the brochure should emphasize our price advantage and high quality of the product. Our lowest price for our palm PC is around ¥1,500, which is much lower than that of our competitors.

**Carol：** That's a good point.

**Mr. Brown：** Our new palm PCs not only have advantage in price, but they are also lighter and smaller. And the batteries are more durable.

**Carol：** We can emphasize these characteristics in the brochure with a new slogan.

**Mr. Brown：** Yes, but the slogan must be short and impressive.

**Carol：** OK, I'll talk it over with our team. Do you have any requirements for the photos and the color to be used in your brochure?

**Mr. Brown：** How about using black and red as the dominant colors? We want to convey a sense of speed and high-tech. As for photos, I will select some of the latest products for photography.

**Carol：** Shall I ask a photographer to take photos next week in your company? Do you have any idea about the design of the brochure?

**Mr. Brown：** Not at this moment. How about giving us some suggestions when we meet again next time?

**Carol：** Sure.

### Practice

1. You are the Marketing Manager of a household appliance company. The annual sales of automatic washing machines dropped dramatically last year. Discuss some strategies for sales promotion with your assistant at a weekly meeting.

2. You work for an advertising agency. One of your clients intends to replace the existing product brochure with a limited budget. You talk with your client and exchange ideas.

## B. Advertising

### Dialogue 1 – Advertising a new product

*Mary is discussing with Mr. Brown on how to advertise a new model of PC.*

**Mary：** Mr. Brown, I'm very happy to tell you that our new marketing strategy appears to be working. We're beginning to get more attention from domestic clients in various PC exhibitions. Everything is going smoothly as we initially planned.

**Mr. Brown：** That sounds pretty encouraging. Mary, I hope to see a robust recovery in our sales revenue.

**Mary：** Yes. I'd like that too. But we still need to find more other ways to promote sales in order to make our PC known to more potential customers.

**Mr. Brown：** Let's implement an advertising program with our local distributors. They are in good position to select the best ways to advertise in each of their local market places. In addition, our advertising funds will encourage them to spend more of their own money on advertising our PCs.

**Mary：** Good idea. Can we also resort to the mass media? It has much wider influence.

**Mr. Brown：** Of course. We could also try some less expensive means of advertising like online sales. Personally I prefer online sales. It's faster, cheaper and more convenient.

**Mary：** The Internet actually has become the fourth largest mass medium following newspaper, radio and TV. Nowadays people are more comfortable with searching information online.

**Mr. Brown**：Any ideas for the local market?

**Mary**：For the local market, we could also advertise our products in newspapers. The cost for newspaper ads has come down recently because several newspapers are competing for market share.

**Mr. Brown**：Right. Local newspapers enjoy a fairly large circulation. Almost every family reads one kind of local newspaper. Advertising our products on newspapers will surely promote our local sales.

**Mary**：Let's give it a try! I'll contact the advertising department of Evening News now.

---

robust　　强健的；坚定的　　　　　　　resort to　　求助于；凭借

circulation　发行量

## Dialogue 2 – Discussing forms of advertising

*Michael, the manager of Marketing Department, is explaining to a new employee Jason different types of advertising.*

**Jason**：I've heard the term "business advertising", but I'm not sure I understand what it means.

**Michael**：Well, broadly speaking, it can mean any kind of ads concerning business. In a narrow sense, it is one kind of ads classified by target audience.

**Jason**：What about the television, radio, newspaper, and magazine ads?

**Michael**：Classified by target audience, most of them are consumer advertisements.

**Jason**：So they are directed at the ultimate consumer.

**Michael**：Or at the person who will buy the product for someone else.

**Jason**：I see.

**Michael**：For example, an ad. for Coca-Cola may be aimed at both the purchaser and the consumer.

**Jason**：Well, it seems that the real business advertising is invisible.

**Michael**：That makes sense. The majority of advertising you see appears in mass consumer media. Business advertising, on the other hand, tends to be concentrated in specialized business publications or professional journals.

**Jason**：Then how many types of business advertising are there?

**Michael**：There are four distinct types：industrial, trade, professional, and agricultural.

**Jason**: What if a company wants to manage its reputation in the market place?

**Michael**: A company can use several types of corporate advertising, like public relations advertising, institutional advertising, corporate identity advertising and recruitment advertising.

**Jason**: What is the difference between PR advertising and institutional advertising?

**Michael**: Well, PR advertisements are designed to enhance a company's general community citizenship and to create public goodwill. Institutional advertising may be used for a variety of purposes — to report the company's record of accomplishment, to position the company competitively in the market, or to improve employee morale and so on.

**Jason**: When does a company employ corporate identity advertising?

**Michael**: For example, it is used when companies need to communicate a name or appearance changes.

**Jason**: I see. Thank you very much for your help.

**Michael**: You are very welcome.

| | |
|---|---|
| institutional advertising | 企业形象广告 |
| corporate identity advertising | 企业识别广告 morale 士气；精神面貌 |

### Practice

1. You are from the sales department of a television company and going to launch a new advertising campaign for your new digital TV. Discuss and decide what types of advertising you are going to use.

2. Your company has decided to launch a recently-developed Smartphone app to the market next month. This app helps people match clothes and colors, at a low price. Discuss with your partner and deicide how to advertise the new app.

## C. Conducting Market Research

### Dialogue 1 – Making plans for market research

*Michael Brown is the Marketing Manager. Cindy, a reporter from local newspaper, is interviewing him about his recent business plan.*

**Cindy**: Your new task is to reach $20 billion by the end of 2006. That's a magnificent task. How do you make sure you will accomplish it?

**Michael**: Well, in addition to improving the quality of our products, we need to open more international markets.

**Cindy:** As far as I know, you have many regular customers.

**Michael:** Yes, most trading companies have regular customers. But it is quite another story for those manufacturing enterprises that have just started exporting. They can't find certain distribution channels.

**Cindy:** Do you have any particular plan to help them to open up new markets?

**Michael:** Yes, we do. In order to help them build up marketing channels, we have decided to strengthen market research and gather more information from various resources, such as national trade statistics, trade journals and directories, international organizations and field investigations.

**Cindy:** I agree that a good marketing channel is important and indispensable to the success of exporting. Besides, as a friend of yours, I would suggest that you should be still more flexible in doing business.

**Michael:** Thank you for the suggestion! As a matter of fact, we need to make improvement in many areas.

**Cindy:** Yes, you said it.

---

| trade directory | 同业名录 | indispensable | 不可缺少的 |
| --- | --- | --- | --- |

## Dialogue 2 – Talking about market research

*Mr. Armod, the Marketing Manager, is talking about market research with David, a new employee of the Department.*

**David:** Mr. Armod, how do you define marketing?

**Mr. Armod:** Well, to put it in very simple terms, one of the objects of market research is to find out a market and serving it. But the concept of finding the needs of the consumers and satisfying them is the essence of marketing.

**David:** What do you think is the role of marketing in the management process?

**Mr. Armod:** I think marketing is not restricted to just buying and selling, or dealing with imports and exports. Actually it is closely involved in the management process.

**David:** Is there any difference between marketing research and market research?

**Mr. Armod:** I see them as different functions. Market research is an analysis of a specific market. For example, how many potential customers there are and where they are located. Marketing research is much broader than that and refers to collecting and analyzing data to identify a market for particular goods or services, and to answer more questions such as potential customers' purchasing power and buying habits, and the proper ways to promote sales.

**David:** Do you mean marketing research can be defined as gathering, recording, and analyzing all facts about problems related to merchandising?

**Mr. Armod:** Yes, this includes products planning, transport services and communication, too.

**David:** That's certainly a much broader concept than simply analyzing a particular market. Mr. Armed, who does this kind of job in our company?

**Mr. Armod:** Sometimes we carry out our own research, but for major products where development costs are likely to be high, we employ specialists.

**David:** As a salesperson, will I receive some special training for marketing research?

**Mr. Armod:** Yes, you will have initial training course later on, which includes product training.

**David:** What is that?

**Mr. Armod:** As a salesperson, you must fully understand the various applications, design features, special advantages and almost everything of the products we produce.

| essence | 本质；实质 |
|---------|-----------|

### Dialogue 3 – Doing market research

*A consumer is being interviewed by an employee from the Marketing Department of Luvious Company.*

**Employee:** Excuse me, sir. I'm from the Luvious Company. Here's my card. May I ask you a few questions?

**Consumer:** Why?

**Employee:** We are conducting a market research. We want to find out how many people have used our Luvious detergent. This information will help us with our marketing policy so that no risks are involved in production.

**Consumer:** Hmmm... All right.

**Employee**：Thank you. May I know your occupation, please?

**Consumer**：I'm a doctor.

**Employee**：I see. What detergent do you use?

**Consumer**：I like Rimo.

**Employee**：May I know why you've chosen Rimo? The price is higher than the others on the market.

**Consumer**：Well, let me see. Hmmm … it washes clothes clean. I needn't soak them for too long, you know. But as I tell my wife, what I really like about the brand is the smell. It is really nice.

**Employee**：Have you tried the Luvious detergent yet?

**Consumer**：Yes, once. It washed quite clean. Nevertheless, I can't stand the smell. It is really nauseating.

**Employee**：So, the smell is important to you.

**Consumer**：Yes. So long as your company's detergent has that smell, I won't buy it.

**Employee**：I see. Here's a sample for you so that you'll be able to try our latest detergent on the market. Please try it. It smells quite different from our previous detergent：it dissolves readily in water and washes clothes very cleanly in the shortest time ever.

**Consumer**：OK. Thank you.

**Employee**：Thank you for your time. Have a nice day.

| detergent | 洗涤剂 | soak | 浸泡 |
| nauseating | 令人恶心的 | dissolve | 溶解 |

### Practice

1. You are from the sales department of a cosmetics company. You are going to conduct a market research for your new product — a whitening essence. Find a customer and ask her some questions on using cosmetics.

2. After conducting the market research, discuss your result with the manager from sales department and analyze the result.

 Language Focus

| Promoting Sales |
| --- |

- Which promotional channels are we considering?
- We are considering national TV spots, print ads and product placement in movies.
- We should pick an effective spokesperson.
- Don't forget to incorporate an Internet and campaign.
- I think we should consider setting up counters in department stores.
- We do need to increase our visibility.
- My biggest concern is business promotion.

| Advertising |
| --- |

- The purpose of our advertising is to draw customers' interest and keep hold of their attention, so that they may do something in return.
- Advertising is an essential part of the entire process of marketing.
- Good advertising is vital to call attention to a product and introduce new products.
- Advertising can help build product recognition, but product itself builds image.

| Conducting Market Research |
| --- |

- You must first study the new product to be put on the market.
- We are making a closer study on the market conditions in your country.
- It'll pay you dollars for cents to do a lot of market research first.
- First of all, you've got to find out if there is any demand for your product, and what sort of competition you will meet.
- You also need to take local conditions and preferences into account.
- Will you show me some samples?
- What are the selling points of your products?

 Extended Activities

## Role-play

### Task 1

**Pair Work:** Your company is going to run a marketing campaign. Your partner and you are obliged to carry out it. Now communicate with each other to exchange your ideas. Information of 4Ps should be exchanged during your discussion.

### Task 2

**Group Work：** Shanghai successfully won the bid for hosting the 2010 Expo. Market opportunities for Chinese companies were immense. How could marketers cash in on the potential market for their businesses success? Work in groups of 4~5, search relevant information online, and try to create a marketing campaign and design the mission for the campaign.

### Task 3

**Group Work：** Work in groups of 4~5. Suppose you are the sales manager of a computer company and you are asked to open and develop overseas market for a new line of computers for different groups of consumers： teenagers, businessmen/businesswomen and parents who buy the products for their children. Consider the qualities of the computer that may attract these three groups. Choose one target group of customers and draft a memo outlining the objectives you propose for the computer's introduction and your reasons for them. Organize and make your sales presentation with your group members. Finally make a sales presentation.

## Discussion

### Topic 1

What questions are usually asked in a market research? Are there any taboo questions?

### Topic 2

Compare the main forms of mass media. Which form do you think is the best for food sales promotion? Why?

 Related Information

## How to Do Market Research —— The Basics

Marketing research can give a business a picture of what kinds of new products and services may bring a profit. For products and services already available, marketing research can tell companies whether they are meeting their customers' needs and expectations. By researching the answers to specific questions, small-business owners can learn whether they need to change their package design or tweak their delivery methods – and even whether they should consider offering additional services.

## Types of Market Research

**Primary Research:** The goal of primary research is to gather data from analyzing current sales and the effectiveness of current practices. Primary research also takes competitors' plans into account, giving you information about your competition.

Collecting primary research can include the following:

- Interviews (either by telephone or face-to-face)
- Surveys (online or by mail)
- Questionnaires (online or by mail)
- Focus groups gathering a sampling of potential clients or customers and getting their direct feedback

Some important questions might include the following:

- What factors do you consider when purchasing this product or service?
- What do you like or dislike about current products or services currently on the market?
- What areas would you suggest for improvement?
- What is the appropriate price for a product or service?

**Secondary Research:** The goal of secondary research is to analyze data that has already been published. With secondary data, you can identify competitors, establish benchmarks and identify target segments. Your segments are the people who fall into your targeted demographic—people who live a certain lifestyle, exhibit particular behavioral patterns or fall into a predetermined age group.

## Common Marketing Mistakes

- Using only secondary research. Relying on the published work of others doesn't give you the full picture. It can be a great place to start, of course, but the information you get from secondary research can be outdated. You can miss out on other factors relevant to your business.
- Using only web resources. When you use common search engines to gather information, you can only get data that are available to everyone and it may not be fully accurate. To perform deeper searches while staying within your budget, use the resources at your local library, college campus or small-business center.

- Surveying only the people you know. Small-business owners sometimes interview only family members and close colleagues when conducting research, but friends and family are often not the best survey subjects. To get the most useful and accurate information, you need to talk to real customers about their needs, wants and expectations.

## Supplements for Reflections

## 4Ps of Marketing

In the early 1960s, Professor Neil Borden at Harvard Business School identified a number of company performance actions that can influence the consumer decision to purchase goods or services. Borden suggested that all those actions of the company represented a "Marketing Mix". Professor E. Jerome McCarthy, also at the Harvard Business School in the early 1960s, suggested that the Marketing Mix contained four elements: product, price, place and promotion.

### Product

The product aspects of marketing deal with the specifications of the actual goods or services, and how it relates to the end-users' needs and wants. The scope of a product generally includes supporting elements such as warranties, guarantees and support.

### Pricing

This refers to the process of setting a price for a product, including discounts. The price need not to be monetary; it can simply be what is exchanged for the product or services, e.g. time, energy or attention.

### Placement (or distribution)

This refers to how the product gets to the customer, for example, point-of-sale placement or retailing. This third P has also sometimes been called Place, referring to the channel by which a product or service is sold (e.g. online vs. retail), to which geographic region or industry, to which segment (young adults, families, business people), etc. It also refers to how the environment in which the product is sold affects sales.

### Promotion

This includes advertising, sales promotion, publicity and personal selling, branding and refers to the various methods promoting the product, brand or company.

These four elements are often referred to as the marketing mix, which a marketer can use to craft a marketing plan.

The 4Ps model is most useful when marketing low value consumer products. Industrial products, services, high value consumer products require adjustments to this model. Services marketing must account for the unique nature of services.

## Questions

- Think of an example that the 4Ps model is successfully applied in its marketing strategy, and give your opinions.
- Do you think that they might be some limitations of the model in modern economy as marketing is more integrated into organizations with a wider variety of products and markets?

# 6 Unit

# Meetings

 Learning Objectives

**In this unit, you will learn how to:**

- Chair a meeting
- Ask for/give opinions
- Agree/disagree with opinions
- Make suggestions

 Background Information

Business meetings and conferences play a very important role in business world. Most business people come in contact with colleagues from both inside and outside the organization, and with both subordinates and superiors, formally and informally.

Meetings are held for different purposes. Some are to collect ideas; some are to discuss moves; some are to settle down differences; and some are to solve problems. Meetings may be conducted with great or little formality in their procedures. Generally the larger the number of people present, the greater the degree of formality. But more simply, it is obvious that when many people are present we need more rules for effective control than we do if two or three people are gathered around a table, which is not to say that small groups do not sometimes hold formally conducted meetings.

 Starting Up

**Read the following statements about meetings. Are they True (T) or False (F)?**

| Self–Assessment Test |
| --- |

☐ 1. The person who is in charge of the meeting is the person who takes the minutes.

☐ 2. The best way to call a meeting is to inform each participant individually by phone.

☐ 3. An agenda should outline the order and amount of time to spend on each item at the meeting.

☐ 4. Engaging in small talk throughout the meeting is an effective way to keep the focus.

☐ 5. When someone agrees with a motion it is "seconded".

☐ 6. The person who is speaking during a meeting is the person who "has the floor".

☐ **7.** A polite way to indicate that you want to make a comment during a meeting is to say: "If I could just come in here..."

☐ 8. When there is a tie vote, it is customary for the chairperson to ask one participant to reconsider his/her decision.

☐ 9. During the closing remarks, the person holding the meeting should introduce new staff members or guest speakers.

☐ 10. Reminders are typically announced after all of the items on the agenda have been covered.

 Oral Workshop

## A. Preparing a Meeting

### Dialogue 1 – Setting an agenda

*Mr. Lee is the General Manager. He is working on the business meeting agenda with his secretary Sophia.*

**Mr. Lee:** Sophia, is everything going well for tomorrow's meeting with the directors?

**Sophia:** Yes, Mr. Lee. Everyone has been told by external memo. I've also made sure of the meeting schedule with each presenter, personally.

**Mr. Lee:** Great. And what about the audio-visual aids? Are they all ready?

**Sophia:** Yes. There were a few bugs with the slide presentation, but they've all been taken care of.

**Mr. Lee**：You'd better double-check, just to make sure. We don't want any big problems.

**Sophia**：You're right. I'll get right on it. I'll spend the rest of the day proofreading all documentation.

**Mr. Lee**：Good. I'd like to set the meeting schedule now.

**Sophia**：OK. As usual, we'll start with a general introduction, then introductions of each presenter to the directors. After the introductions, Mr. Allen Smith will open with a 10-to-15-minute demonstration.

**Mr. Lee**：Tell him to make sure it doesn't go over fifteen minutes, unless the directors have a lot of questions.

**Sophia**：I'll keep that in mind. After that, each of the other presenters will follow as scheduled, no change there. And I'd like you to set up a lunch right after the meeting for the president.

**Mr. Lee**：No problem. Leave it to me.

| | | | |
|---|---|---|---|
| audio-visual aid | 视听设备 | bug | 瑕疵；故障 |
| proofread | 校对 | | |

## Dialogue 2 – Making bookings

*Stanley White works in International Trading. He is now booking a conference room with a hotel receptionist for the annual meeting of the company.*

**Stanley**：Good morning, I'm Stanley White with International Trading. I'd like to book a conference room here at your hotel.

**Receptionist**：I'm sure we can help with that. What kind of meeting is it?

**Stanley**：It's the annual meeting of our Association. We're expecting to have around 30 participants.

**Receptionist**：All right. What time did you have in mind?

**Stanley**：Next Friday morning from 9:00 to 11:00.

**Receptionist**：Well, the only one available that time is an auditorium which can accommodate 120 people.

**Stanley**：No, I don't think we need that much space. Then what about Friday afternoon? Do you have any rooms available?

**Receptionist**：Yes, we do. We have conference halls which can seat up to 60 people.

**Stanley**：Do you have any even smaller?

**Receptionist**: Yes, our meeting rooms normally hold 30. But they might be a bit too crowded just in case you may have one or two more.

**Stanley**: Yes, you're right. I'll have the conference hall then.

**Receptionist**: OK. All conference halls are equipped with podiums, microphones and computers. Anything else you'd like to have?

**Stanley**: Actually, I'm going to need a projector. Is that doable?

**Receptionist**: Yes, but the projector rents for $150 a day.

**Stanley**: That's fine. Can you please make seating arrangements for the meeting as well?

**Receptionist**: No problem. How would you like them?

**Stanley**: I need a podium in front, six tables, with six chairs at each table. And I'd like to have an aisle down the middle of the room.

**Receptionist**: That could be arranged. Is that everything?

**Stanley**: Oh, could you put two extra tables for some refreshments at the back?

**Receptionist**: Certainly!

| | | | |
|---|---|---|---|
| auditorium | 礼堂 | accommodate | 容纳 |
| podium | 表演台；讲台 | refreshments | 茶点 |

## Practice

1. You are an assistant to the general manager of a travel agency. A meeting will be held to discuss the cooperation with some other agencies regarding a new project. Go through the agenda with the manager to confirm everything.

2. At the end of a routine meeting, you inform the staff of the subject as well as the agenda for the next meeting. Your company is planning on an overseas trade fair. Things to be discussed may include anticipated expenses, air travel, schedule, accommodation, etc.

3. You are to book a conference room of your company for a 2-hour meeting this week. You will also need a projector and a whiteboard for the meeting.

4. You are to book a big function room for a press conference at a local hotel. Talk to the sales manager of the hotel and tell him/her the requirements you have. Decide on the time of the event, number of participants, equipment you need, and seating arrangements by yourself.

# B. Holding a Meeting

## Dialogue 1 – Opening a meeting

*Alan, the chairperson, opens the meeting and invites the Purchase Manager David to speak.*

**Alan:** Good morning, everyone. I believe we are all here. Please be seated and let's get started. Have you all got a copy of the agenda? Good. As you can see from the agenda, there are a couple of things we'll be looking at today. First of all, we're going to have a discussion on how to cut down our overheads. Secondly, we're going to talk over the possibility of opening a new branch in China. I'd like to keep each item to 25 minutes, and then we can finish by ten o'clock. Now, let's start with the first one regarding the overheads. As everyone is aware that our company is now experiencing the hardest time in history due to the global financial crisis; therefore, cutting down our daily expenses is obviously a must for the time being. David, you're the Purchase Manager. What do you have in mind?

**David:** I'd like to draw your attention to the stats of our monthly expenses …

**Alan:** Sorry to interrupt. Susan, would you please take the minutes? And David, go ahead please.

---

overheads    日常管理费用

---

## Dialogue 2 – Giving a presentation

*Mr. White, the chairperson, invites Mr. Brown to give a presentation at the meeting.*

**Mr. White:** Ladies and gentlemen, we're honored to have invited Mr. Brown to give us a presentation on effective internal communications. Mr. Brown is a respectable expert on HR management and has been delivering lectures and speeches in many of the Fortune 500 companies. Now let's welcome Mr. Brown.

**Mr. Brown:** Thank you. Mr. White. Ladies and gentlemen, thank you very much for coming along here today. I hope that my presentation isn't going to take too long and that you will find it interesting. The purpose of today's presentation is to discuss how we can improve internal communications within our company. Now let me begin by explaining that I'd like to talk about the business case for better communication; Next, I want to cover different styles and methods; and then I would like to finish off by talking about some of the basics we need to have in place to deliver good quality, consistent communications across the company. I'd be very happy to invite you to ask questions at the end of the session and I'm sure there'll be plenty of time for us to discuss some of the points that have been raised.

| respectable | 受人尊敬的 |
| --- | --- |

### Dialogue 3 – Concluding a meeting

*Alan, the chairperson, concludes the meeting after some discussions with other meeting attendees, Kevin and Peter.*

**Alan：** All right. I think that's probably about it, but anybody got anything else that they desperately want to raise before we wrap up? If not, I'd like to take a minute to sum up the main points we have agreed on. Firstly, we can't leave the product on the market, or we'll lose more money in the end. Secondly, we will put up a new model. Finally, we need a marketing plan for the new model. The ultimate goal is to recover the sales as well as the consumer confidence.

**Kevin：** Do we have deadlines for all these?

**Alan：** We'll take the product off the market this week. This should be done by Sunday. Peter, could you please see to it?

**Peter：** No problem.

**Alan：** Kevin, how is it going with the final testing of the new model?

**Kevin：** According to the schedule, the testing process takes two weeks. But since the whole thing is unexpected and really urgent, I'm sure we can speed it up and try to have it done by the end of this week.

**Alan：** That's great! Now, as for the marketing plan, I think we'll call a top-level management meeting for tomorrow to discuss.

**Kevin：** Okay.

**Peter：** All right.

**Alan：** If no one has anything else to add, then I guess we'll finish here.

| wrap up | 工作结束 |
| --- | --- |

**Practice**

1.  You chair a quick routine meeting. Open the meeting and state the following three items on the agenda: the news on the product re-launch, the office move, and other business.

2.  You are the manager of sales department. Chair a monthly meeting. You need to state the purpose of the meeting first, then set the agenda, and assign roles.

3.  Before you wrap up the meeting, first ask if there is anyone who wants to raise anything; then make a summary of what you have achieved at the meeting; finally, inform people of the time of next meeting.

## C. Attending a Meeting

### Dialogue 1 – Having a one-to-one meeting

*Andy is having an informal meeting with his colleague Carl.*

**Andy:** OK. Let's move on to the next point. That's the venue for the launching. Would you like to start, Peter?

**Carl:** I think we should use the Exhibition Center. It works well with all other products.

**Andy:** I'm afraid I don't quite agree with you. Look, this new series is going to be much more expensive than our other products, so, I don't think Exhibition Center is good enough.

**Carl:** I see what you mean, but the Exhibition Center is easy to book. We've been working with them for quite a long time, so there's no problem with the rent charge.

**Andy:** But I think what's really important is to go for a more up-market image. So, I suggest using a five-star hotel. You know, great atmosphere, great service. We could also attract some of the hotel guests.

**Carl:** Well, I'm not against it, but have you ever thought about the question of area? I mean, if we use a hotel, I'm afraid we won't be able to find a function room which is big enough for such a grand event. Otherwise, we have to strictly limit the number of our guests.

**Andy:** Well, perhaps I could get some information from all five-star hotels here.

**Carl:** Good point. And then we'll be able to make comparison and decide what to do.

**Andy:** Right.

## Dialogue 2 – Having a brainstorming meeting

*Alex chairs a brainstorming meeting with his colleagues Jenny, Carol, Leo and Sam.*

**Alex:** Good morning, everybody. It's time to begin. Would you please take the minutes of the meeting, Jenny?

**Jenny:** OK.

**Alex:** Today, we're going to talk over how to develop markets and increase sales in China next year. Any thoughts?

**Carol:** I think we should launch a new advertising campaign at the end of this year. If we want to enjoy a bigger market share in China, we shall first let more people know about our products. But timing is of great importance. Perhaps we could consider catching the Christmas season and the New Year. What's more important is to take advantage of the Chinese New year.

**Leo:** I quite agree with you, Carol. Apart from that, I think we need to run some more chain stores not only in large cities like Beijing and Shanghai, but also in some medium-sized cities, as competition is getting more severe there.

**Alex:** What are your views on that, Sam?

**Sam:** I agree to Carol's idea. But I'd like to point out that our products are priced a bit high, compared with other brands.

**Alex:** You mean we'll have to reduce our prices?

**Sam:** Well, I think it's a wise idea to reduce our prices by 10%. Perhaps we'll earn less profit at the beginning, but in the long run it will help with our market penetration and market occupancy.

**Carol:** Sorry, I don't go along with that. You know, we only make a small profit at current prices. I believe it's more important to improve product quality and after-sales service than to reduce prices.

**Alex:** This seems a constructive suggestion. Now, as we're running out of time, let me just briefly summarize all your ideas. First of all, we should do further advertising. At the same time, we should improve our after-sales service. And it's a good idea to open chain stores in some medium-sized cities. Are we all agreed? Jenny, please draft a proposal based on the minutes and give it to me tomorrow.

---

market penetration　　市场渗透　　　　　market occupancy　　市场占有率

## Dialogue 3 – Having a problem–solving meeting

*James chairs a problem-solving meeting with his colleagues Sophia, David and Sandy.*

**James:** Good morning, everyone. Right, shall we begin? As we all know, the company has a number of issues of concern at the moment. First, let me briefly explain to you the current situation we are facing. In the last two years, our market share has declined by almost 25%. There are several reasons for this. For example, consumers have become less loyal to our brands and are more willing to trade down to lower-priced products. Some supermarkets have been producing similar products under their own label, but at much lower prices. What's worse, the consumer surveys show that our brand no longer conveys a feeling of care, warmth, and enthusiasm. Therefore, the thing I want to look at with you is how we can halt the decline in the market share and increase our profits. Who would like to start the ball rolling? Sophia, what are your views on this?

**Sophia:** Obviously, I think we should reduce the price, by, say, 20% to 30% to make it more competitive. Consumers nowadays are very sensitive to prices, they always want to get the best value of what they pay for.

**David:** I go along with that. But this is not all about price, we have to work on advertising at the same time.

**James:** Could you be specific?

**David:** We can take advantage of the coming Easter and launch a new advertising campaign. Instead of our conventional marketing such as gift vouchers or free trial, we can switch to tie-in promotion or raffle sales.

**James:** I see your point, but the problem lies in our brand image as I mentioned just now.

**Sandy:** Could I just say something? I think we need to bring out a new product under the same brand. You know, to diversify our products, to offer our customers more choices, and more importantly to differentiate from our competitors.

**James:** Well, considering what you've suggested, I think maybe it's time for us to consider repositioning our products. We should change our image to appeal to a different market segment. Some changes should be made on packaging, logo as well as labeling. Now let's take a closer look at …

| | | | |
|---|---|---|---|
| halt | 使停止 | start the ball rolling | 使运行 |
| tie-in promotion | 搭配销售 | raffle sales | 抽奖销售 |

### Practice

1. Your company, a cosmetic company, is going to launch a new lotion. You and your partner are holding a meeting to discuss the packaging of the product.

2. You have called a colleague to have a one-to-one business meeting in your office. You two are to decide on the venue for your product launching ceremony coming next month.

3. Sales revenue have decreased in last season. To analyse the possible reasons. To make suggestions for improving your client's sales. To optomize the brand name in target consumers.

4. You receive quite a few complaints about the attitude and professionalism of the reception staff. As the general manager of the hotel, you hold an informal meeting to discuss the possible reasons and make suggestions to resolve the problem.

5. There is going to be a company picnic next month and everything has to be planned and organized in advance. Hold a meeting with department heads to discuss the issue.

 Language Focus

| Opening a Meeting |
| --- |
| • May I have your attention please? |
| • Now that everyone is here, I'd like to call the meeting to order. |
| • We're meeting today to discuss … |
| • There are a couple of things I'd like to look at. |
| • As you'll see from the agenda, we have … items for discussion. |
| • Could you take the minutes? |
| • This meeting should take about … |
| • The meeting is due to finish at … |
| • I'd like to keep each item to …, otherwise we'll never get through. |

| Controlling a Meeting |
| --- |
| • Shall we move on to the next item on the agenda? |
| • Whose turn is to take the floor? |
| • Would you wind up your statement? We're running out of time. |
| • I see your point, but can we please stick to the main subject here? |
| • I'm afraid we're getting a bit off the point. |
| • Please focus on the topic. |
| • We will come to that point later. |
| • Let's save this for another meeting. |

- You can discuss this among yourselves at another time.
- Has anyone got any objection to this proposal?
- Is there anything else to discuss?
- Let's put it to vote.
- I think we've spent enough time on this topic.
- We're running short on time, so let's move on.
- We're running behind schedule, so we'll have to skip the next item.
- We've spent too long on this issue, so we'll leave it for now.
- We could spend all day discussing this, but we have to get to the next item.

## Closing a Meeting

- OK, let's go over what we've agreed.
- In conclusion, we have discussed …
- Right, it looks as though we've covered the main points.
- I think that just about covers everything.
- It looks like we've run out of time, so I guess we'll finish here.
- I guess that will be all for today.
- It seems we've discussed everything, so we can draw the meeting to a close.
- If no one has anything else to add, then I think we'll wrap this up.

## Giving Reminders & Follow–up

- Oh, before you leave, please make sure to sign the attendance sheet.
- Don't forget to put your ballot in the box on your way out.
- If I didn't already say this, please remember to introduce yourself to the new trainees.
- Could I have your attention again? I neglected to mention that …
- If you could all return your chair to Room 7 that would be appreciated.
- Please take all of your papers with you and throw out any garbage on your way out.
- We'll meet again on the first of next month.
- If anyone has any questions about anything we discussed today, feel free to send me an e-mail.
- The minutes from today's meeting will be posted as of tomorrow afternoon.
- I'll send out a group e-mail with the voting results.

## Expressing & Soliciting Opinions

- It is quite clear that …
- Personally, I don't think …
- How do you think we should deal with the matter?
- What are your views on this?
- I understand you very well, but I have to disagree.

| **Interrupting** |
| --- |
| • May I get in a word? |
| • Sorry to interrupt you, but I'd just like to say that … |
| • I don't want to interrupt you, but could you give me an example? |
| • Could I just make a point here? |

 Extended Activities

## Role-play

### Task 1

**Group work：** You will be having a meeting to gather some information about your main competitor. Your team will include：a chairperson – Managing Director, a marketing manager, an R & D (Research and Development) manager, a market research expert and a secretary.

### Task 2

**Group work：** Recently, most of the staff are not satisfied with the business lunches in your company. There have been a few choices for the food, and the taste is getting worse. However, the food was not this way before, and it used to be very good. Hold a meeting to solve the problem. Below are the procedures for holding a problem-solving meeting.
- The chairperson provides the background.
- The chairperson defines the problems to be discussed.
- Participants and the chairperson provide their solutions.
- The chairperson and participants comment on the solutions.
- The chairperson chooses the proper solutions.
- The chairperson allocates tasks.

### Task 3

Form a group of 4. You are having a meeting in order to find ways of effectively cutting costs of your company.

**Student A：** You find the sales people always travel first class and stay in five-star hotels.

**Student B：** You think costs should be cut down in the Marketing Department, as clients are frequently invited to dinners, and expensive gifts are given away very often.

**Student C:** You find that every department manager has a car allotted by the company.

**Student D:** You think the overheads should be cut down. Currently, cleaners stay in the company all day long and air conditioners are turned on all year round.

### Task 4

**Situation:** Mr. Head, the general manager of the company, is having a meeting with the heads of department discussing a proposal to introduce flexible working hours to your company.

### Task 5

**Situation:** Suppose a large, influential customer continually pays late. The sales manager and credit controller have politely and repeatedly complained to the client but this hasn't made any difference. The time has come to decide what to do about this.

## Discussion

### Topic 1

How do you define the role of a chairperson? Work with your partners and make a list of chairperson duties.

### Topic 2

What is brainstorming? What is the proper length of a brainstorming session? What should be the best composition of the participants? What to do with all the ideas and opinions raised?

 Related Information

## How to Take the Minutes?

Anyone, including you, may be assigned to take the minutes at a meeting. Often someone who is not participating in the meeting will be called upon to be the minute-taker. Before a meeting the minute-taker should review the following:

- The minutes from previous meeting
- All of the names of the attendees (if possible)

- The items on the agenda

It also helps to create an outline before going to the meeting. An outline should include the following:

- A title for the meeting
- The location of the meeting
- A blank spot to write the time the meeting started and ended
- The name of the chairperson
- A list of attendees that can be checked off (or a blank list for attendees to sign)
- A blank spot for any attendees who arrive late or leave early

The minute-taker can use a pen and paper or a laptop computer to take notes and does not need to include every word that is spoken. It is necessary to include important points and any votes and results. Indicating who said what is also necessary, which is why the minute-taker should make sure to know the names of the attendees. If you cannot remember someone's name, take a brief note of their seating position and find out their name after the meeting. A minute-taker should type out the minutes immediately after the meeting so that nothing is forgotten.

 Supplements for Reflections

## How to Deal with Ineffective or Inefficient Meetings?

Meetings dominate the way in which we do business today. In fact, approximately 11 million meetings are said to occur in the U.S. each and every day. Most professionals attend a total of 61.8 meetings per month and research indicates that over 50% of this meeting time is wasted. Survey reveals that most professionals who meet on a regular basis admit to daydreaming (91%), missing meetings (96%) or missing parts of meetings (95%). A large percentage (73%) say they have brought other work to meetings and 39% say they have dozed during meetings. How seriously do these inefficiencies affect participants and the organization? Some direct effects of unproductive meetings include the following:

- Meetings are longer, less efficient and generate fewer results.
- More meetings are needed to accomplish objectives.
- With so much time spent in ineffective meetings, employees have less time to get their own work done.
- Ineffective meetings create frustration at all staff levels.
- Information generated in unproductive meetings usually isn't managed properly.

• Inefficient meetings cost organizations billions of dollars each year.

The following suggests something for improvements.

### Reduce the Number of Meetings You Schedule

If you're having too many meetings that fail to actually accomplish anything, you need to cut the meetings back. Before you schedule another meeting, there are a couple of considerations. Firstly, set a goal for the meeting. Never have a meeting without a specific purpose. Secondly, create and distribute an agenda to participants a few days before the meeting. Thirdly, make sure appropriate people will be able to attend. If relevant decision-makers are unable to attend, it is not likely to make real progress. Finally, if the purpose of the meeting is sharing information or giving updates, send a memo or email instead.

### Create an Agenda Every Time

Creating an effective agenda is one of the most important elements for a productive meeting. The agenda tells participants which topics will be discussed, who will be presenting each topic and the time allocated to each section. It's essential to prepare and distribute an agenda before the meeting, so participants have enough time to prepare.

### Keep Your Meeting on Track

Once the agenda is prepared, the next step is to actually stick to it. Make sure you stick with the allocated time limit for each topic. If you start to go over, wrap it up and move onto the next topic. You can always schedule another meeting if there's more to discuss, but if people are just debating for the sake of it, a firm time limit can force people to make a decision.

### Conduct a Meeting Cost Analysis

If you really need help breaking an excessive meeting habit, try calculating the cost of your meeting. Once you've seen how much money is wasted during an ineffective meeting, you'll be reluctant to ramble on for three or four hours at a time!

### Questions

• What items should be covered in an agenda?

• To what extent is the venue of a meeting or conference important? How should the room be equipped? Should seating arrangements receive proper attention?

• A mini case study: Consider the following situation. What are the problems with the meetings? What do you suggest to improve?

The CFO is a meeting addict. He calls meetings 2 ~ 3 times per week which often last for hours due to lots of participants and the lack of formal agenda. Even if there is an agenda, they somehow get way off track. His group is starting to dread a meeting before it starts for fear of missing lunch and even dinner. How can I help him be more organized?

# Unit 7

# Recruitment

 ## Learning Objectives

**In this unit, you will learn how to：**

- Describe job duties
- Conduct a job interview
- Introduce and learn about a company

 ## Background Information

Recruitment refers to the process of screening, and selecting qualified people for a job at an organization or a firm, or for a vacancy in a volunteer-based organization or a community group. While generalist managers or administrators can undertake some components of the recruitment process, mid- and large-sized organizations and companies often retain professional recruiters or outsource some of the process to recruitment agencies. External recruitment is the process of attracting and selecting employees from outside the organization.

The recruitment industry has four main types of agencies： employment agencies, recruitment websites and job search engines, "headhunters" for executive and professional recruitment, and in-house recruitment. The stages in recruitment include sourcing candidates by advertising or other methods, and screening and selecting potential candidates using tests or interviews.

 Starting Up

Human resources recruitment methods vary according to staffing needs, company size, recruiting staff expertise and budget for advertising. Discuss the pros & cons of each of the following commonly used methods.

| HR Recruitment Methods | Pros | Cons |
|---|---|---|
| Newspaper Advertising | | |
| Internet Job Boards | | |
| Employee Referral | | |
| College Recruiting | | |
| Job Fairs | | |

 Oral Workshop

## A. Preparing for New Recruitment

### Dialogue 1 – Preparing job description

*Jack, the Sales Manager is talking with his assistant Tim on job description.*

**Jack:** We need a clear idea of what we want everyone to concentrate on.

**Tim:** Well, I've been working on these information packs for all the new recruits.

**Jack**: Let's have a look. I see, so you've written out everyone's job description in full.

**Tim**: Then there can't be any confusion that way.

**Jack**: You might want to add in some information about salary and commission, just to make it all absolutely clear.

**Tim**: That's not a bad idea. Have you decided what you're going to offer them yet?

**Jack**: Yes, it's RMB 4,000 per month basic salary plus an extra RMB 5,000 if they meet their sales targets.

**Tim**: I suppose the next thing we need to do is to give everybody specific geographic areas to focus on.

**Jack**: Well, half of the team will be working closely with you and concentrating on the Chinese market.

**Tim**: And the rest will be covering overseas business with you, right?

**Jack**: Yes. How you want to allocate individual countries is up to you.

**Tim**: OK, we also need to get everyone to submit their own action plans to us by the end of the first week.

**Jack**: The end of the first week might be a bit of a tall order – maybe give them a few extra days.

**Tim**: Fair enough. But I think each person needs to draw up a list of, say, the top 50 target customers within their geographic area.

**Jack**: Right. I've already got a pretty comprehensive contact list that I'll be distributing to everybody.

**Tim**: They'll still have to do quite a lot of research to get a list of 50 together, though.

**Jack**: Yes, but it shouldn't be anything they can't handle.

**Tim**: After that it will just be a case of getting on the phones and introducing our company to the potential customers.

**Jack**: Well, I'm going to do a session with everybody about how to present the company properly.

**Tim**: Well, let me know when you're going to do it.

## Dialogue 2 – Talking about recruitment

*Andrew and Stanley are talking about job recruitment for the marketing department.*

**Andrew**: Well, let me give you the bad news first of all.

**Stanley**: Don't tell me we can't take on as many people as we wanted.

**Andrew**: I'm afraid not. We can only hire three full-time marketing assistants.

**Stanley**: That isn't too bad, I suppose, although four or five would have been ideal.

**Andrew:** If we find we can't manage, then we'll have a strong case for hiring another one.

**Stanley:** Anyway, let's talk about the job recruitments.

**Andrew:** I think the minimum requirements should be a marketing-related degree or two years' work experience in a marketing.

**Stanley:** Definitely. We haven't got time to offer much in the way of training.

**Andrew:** But you're happy to consider new graduates?

**Stanley:** I think so, as long as they've at least had some sort of proper work experiences.

**Andrew:** I'm pleased about that. I always think new graduates are worth considering.

**Stanley:** Yes. They're often more driven and more hardworking.

**Andrew:** And let's face it; you don't have to pay a new graduate as much as someone with a few years' experience.

**Stanley:** Well that's true, I suppose. So where do you think we should advertise?

**Andrew:** Marketing Week would be the best place to start – most marketers read that these days.

**Stanley:** And what about people who are leaving university?

**Andrew:** Well, we need to call a few university career centers and find out what their procedures are.

**Stanley:** And what salary are you going to start them on?

**Andrew:** RMB 3,000 per month – I think that's reasonable.

**Stanley:** And we mustn't forget to include information about other benefits.

Practice

1.  You work for the HR department of Elean Company. Your company is going to recruit a receptionist. Discuss with the HR manager to work out the job advertisement that is to be put up on the newspaper.

2.  You are the General Manager of Elean Company. You need a new assistant and talk about the requirements with the HR manager.

# B. Conducting a Job Interview

### Dialogue 1 – Talking about personality

*Mr. Brown, the personnel manager, is interviewing Peter White.*

**Mr. Brown:** Tell me a little bit about yourself.

**Peter White:** My name is Peter Williams. I was born in 1982. My major in college was electrical engineering.

**Mr. Brown:** What kind of personality do you think you have?

**Peter White:** Well, I approach things very enthusiastically, I think, and I don't like to leave things half-done. I'm very organized and extremely capable.

**Mr. Brown:** What are your great strengths?

**Peter White:** Well, I am a hard-working and persistent person. And I'm quite a fast-learner.

**Mr. Brown:** Then what would you say about your weaknesses?

**Peter White:** Well, I'm a quiet person, however I'm fully aware of this, so I've been studying how to be more active to express myself in public.

**Mr. Brown:** How do you relate to others?

**Peter White:** I'm very co-operative and have good teamwork spirit.

| | | | |
|---|---|---|---|
| approach | 着手处理 | persistent | 坚持不懈的 |

## Dialogue 2 – Talking about experience and qualifications

*Mr. Brown, the personnel manager, is interviewing Peter White.*

**Mr. Brown:** What is your work experience?

**Peter White:** I have worked for IBM for three years.

**Mr. Brown:** How will your experiences benefit this company?

**Peter White:** I know the marketing from top to bottom and I can develop a new market for you. That will increase your profit margin and keep the shareholders satisfied.

**Mr. Brown:** Are you aware of the aspects of this position and do you feel you are qualified?

**Peter White:** Yes, I understand my qualification and your needs by researching your company.

**Mr. Brown:** Do you have any licenses or certificates?

**Peter White:** I have a driver's license, and I am a CPA.

**Mr. Brown:** If you are hired, what section would you like to join?

**Peter White:** If possible, I'd like to be positioned in the International Trade Department.

**Mr. Brown:** What are your salary expectations?

**Peter White:** I would expect the standard rate of pay at your company for a person with my experiences and educational background.

### Dialogue 3 – Talking about seeking new employment

*Mr. Brown, the personnel manager, is interviewing Peter White.*

**Mr. Brown：** Why are you interested in working for our company?

**Peter White：** Because your operations are global, and I feel I can gain the most from working in this kind of environment. Besides, I think my major is closely related to the position.

**Mr. Brown：** Tell me what you know about our company, please.

**Peter White：** Well, the company was founded in Chicago in 1960 by Samuel Derick, who was the first president. It has 2 billion dollars in capital; it employs 6,000 people, and it is the largest company in its field in the States.

**Mr. Brown：** What do you know about our major products and market share?

**Peter White：** Your company's products are mostly marketed in Europe and the United States, but particularly are sold very well here in China. So I think in the future you'll find China a profitable market as well.

**Mr. Brown：** What has made you decide to change your job?

**Peter White：** I would like to get a job in which I can further develop my career.

**Mr. Brown：** May I ask you why you left your previous job?

**Peter White：** Basically I want to seek new challenges.

### Practice

1. You have applied for the position of secretary of Elean Company. Now you are being interviewed by the HR Manager of the company. Make a brief introduction about your educational background and work experience.

2. You have applied for the position of secretary of Elean Company. Now you are being interviewed by the HR Manager of the company. Ask the interviewer about the working hours, salary, holiday and benefits of the company.

## C. Getting to Know the Company

### Dialogue 1 – Showing a new employee around the company

*Jenny is the personnel manager. She is showing the new employee Michael around the company.*

**Jenny**: Michael, this way please. Can you see the window at the far end of the corridor?

**Michael**: Yes.

**Jenny**: Peter Wilson's office is just to the right of that window. Mr. Wilson is our CEO. Let's walk down the corridor and start from Mr. Wilson's office.

**Michael**: OK.

**Jenny**: Opposite to Mr. Wilson's office is the Accounting Department. And the Personnel Department is next to it.

**Michael**: I see. What is this room for? I hear someone's voice coming from it.

**Jenny**: This is our conference room. There is a meeting going on at present.

**Michael**: Alright. Jenny, is there going to be an orientation for the new employees in this conference room?

**Jenny**: Yes. Please come on time for the orientation.

**Michael**: I will. Where is the Sales Department where I work?

**Jenny**: Let's go downstairs. It's on the first floor. Here we are. The Sales Department is located between the Purchasing Department and the Marketing Department. Mr. Smith will introduce the co-workers to you.

**Michael**: Jenny, thank you very much for showing me around.

**Jenny**: My pleasure. Oh, I forget to tell you that coffee and tea are served behind the reception area.

**Michael**: Great. I'd like a cup of coffee during the break. Thank you.

---

orientation 任职培训

---

## Dialogue 2 – Introducing the company to a new employee

*Sarah is introducing the company to one of the new employees, Robert.*

**Sarah**: We are so glad to have some employees here this year. The company grows larger and larger every year.

**Robert**: And I am so excited to join such a great company. Sarah, there is still so much I don't know about our company. Would you mind telling me a bit more?

**Sarah**: Sure. That's what people do at orientations, isn't it? What would you like to know?

**Robert**: Quite a lot. Firstly, I've already learned that the Sales Department is the largest of its kind here in Beijing. Does it mean that trading is its main activity?

**Sarah：** Yes, you are right. The ABC Company Beijing Branch is mostly in charge of sales. It has two major functions：market research and sales. Mr. Brown can tell you more later on. He is the sales manager.

**Robert：** Thanks. Who is in charge of our products supply? I mean who is making the products we are selling now.

**Sarah：** That's the responsibility of ABC Company Shanghai Branch, where several big factories are located.

**Robert：** Oh, I see. A lot of companies have their manufacturing bases in Shanghai. It is an important industrial zone.

**Sarah：** It is indeed. The ABC Company has 6 branch offices in the United States.

**Robert：** Well, I guest I am lucky to be part of the company. And I really did learn a lot from you today. Thanks, Sarah.

**Sarah：** I am glad to be of help. You are always welcome to ask any questions.

### Practice

1. You are the HR assistant of Elean Company. On the first day of a new employee, show him/her around the company and introduce him/her to the department manager.

2. You are the HR manager of Elean Company. At the orientation, introduce the company and answer the questions raised by the new employees.

 Language Focus

| Getting to Know More about the Job |
| --- |
| • What kind of job is it? |
| • What are the responsibilities of the job? |
| • Does the job involve much travel? |
| • What are the working hours? |
| • Do people often work overtime? |
| • How many positions are you filling at this time? |
| • Your ad. didn't specify the type of opening. Could you tell me a little about it? |

## Getting to Know More about the Interviewee

- Tell me about yourself.
- What do you know about our company?
- What do you know about this industry?
- What are you looking for in terms of career development?
- What were the responsibilities of your last position?
- Why are you leaving your present job?
- What salary are you seeking?
- How would you evaluate your present firm?
- What is your greatest failure, and what did you learn from it?
- What can you do for us that other candidates can't?
- How long will it take for you to make a meaningful contribution?

## Stating Qualifications, Experiences and Intentions

- I've just graduated from college.
- I got a degree in … and took a course in …
- I've been doing … for … years.
- For the past three years, I've been working for …
- Actually I was trained for that sort of job.
- I think with my experience and special training I have the ability to do the job.

## Stating Your Reasons for Applying the Job

- I've always wanted a steady job.
- Your company has a good reputation.
- I prefer working in a multinational company.
- Working for your company, I believe I would be able to develop my abilities.
- I'd like to get more challenging opportunities.
- I don't think my precious job suits me.

## Showing Someone around the Company

- Up ahead and to your left, you will see …
- As we turn the corner here, you will see …
- In a few moments, we'll be passing …
- Over there is …
- You may have noticed that we came past a large blue-coloured machine. That was …
- Shall we now walk over here?
- If you have any questions, please feel free to ask at any time during the tour.

 Extended Activities

## Role-play

### Task 1

**Student A:** You are Patrick Miller. You have applied for the vacancy of Software Programmer of Morgan Co. Ltd. You are going to be interviewed by the personnel manager of the company. Answer the interviewer's questions and ask some questions about the company. (Tip: DO NOT ask silly questions!)

**Student B:** You are Kevin Wilson, the personnel manager of Morgan Co. Ltd. You are going to interview a candidate who applies for the position of software programmer. Ask the interviewee about his educational background and expectations for working in the company. You should also give some information about the company.

### Task 2

**Student A:** You are a career advisor working at the University Careers Development Center. Your job is to offer graduate students advice on job hunting and interviews. Ask questions to learn about the student before giving any specific suggestions. The questions may cover: major, interests, performance, abilities, personality, experience, and accomplishments.

**Student B:** You are about to graduate from university very soon. Now you are at the University Careers Development Center seeking some information and advice from the careers advisor. Be prepared to answer the questions from the career advisor.

### Task 3

**Group work:** Work in a group of 3~4. Brainstorm the questions that you cannot ask an employer during a job interview and explain the reason. Compare your questions with those of other groups.

### Task 4

**A Survey**

Learning about the organization is important because it can help you relate your qualifications to the organization. Have you ever thought about a company that you would like to work in? Follow the steps and complete the task listed below.

1.  Select a company that you might like to apply for a job.

2.  Use the Internet to conduct some preliminary research about the company. You may want to ask yourself the following questions.

- What Internet sources did you use to obtain this information?
- What did you learn about the company that would help you with a job interview?
- What makes you qualified for the position in the company?
- What aspects of the company appeal to you?

3.  Work in groups of 4~5, and share your research results with the group members. Why do you have different interests or preferences in career choices? What are your main concerns in job hunting?

# Discussion

### Topic 1

Would you like to have a steady office job? Why?

### Topic 2

What do you think of being self-employed? What are the advantages and disadvantages of being self-employed?

### Topic 3

Do you think it is proper to ask about salary in a job interview? If yes, when and in what way can you bring up the question?

 Related Information

## Guide to Successful Job Interviews

**General rules about job interview success**

1.  People decide about you in the first 10 seconds.
2.  You have to make a good first impression.
3.  Always ask insightful job interview questions.
4.  Learn as much as you can about the company.
5.  They'll probably ask interview questions designed to trip you up.
6.  Have some quick answers to interview questions at the ready.

Some of them make perfect sense, but getting the job you want isn't about following rules or giving the "right" interview answer. It's about presenting yourself in the most authentic way that takes care of you and the interviewers at the same time.

At the end of your interview, if you haven't been advised, ask when they think they'll be making their decision. At least then you'll know how long you'll have to wait before you are informed. Many companies don't automatically let people know if they haven't got the job, so one follow-up call is allowable.

No matter how bad you think the interview went, if you want the job, always send a follow-up interview thank you letter. Since most of us think of clever things to say after the fact, include one or two of the following phrases, referring to something specific from the interview.

"I've given a lot of thoughts to our interview and …"

"Something you mentioned got me thinking …"

"What you said about … really struck bomb."

If you don't get the job and you're curious, why not phone up and get some feedback? It may help you for the next interview.

## Do's and Don'ts for a successful interview

**Don'ts —**

1. Don't chatter. Be brief and clear.

2. Don't be shy. Be self-confident and courageous.

3. Don't appear humble or haughty. Be enthusiastic but polite.

4. Don't brag or boast. Be frank and truthful.

5. Don't claim kinship or personal connections to anyone known to the interviewer. Proclaim your own competence and qualifications.

6. Don't be choosy. Be realistic.

7. Don't ask about pay unless you know how to do it tactfully.

8. Don't fidget. But do use your facial expressions and gestures.

9. Don't dress like a queen or a dandy. Make yourself look firm and reliable.

10. Don't be late. Be on time.

**Do's —**

1. Do be observant.

2. Do show that you can listen.

3. Do consider why the interviewer is asking such questions.

4. Do be alert to signals.

5. Do encourage your interviewer to do some of the talking.

## 📖 Supplements for Reflections

## Resume-writing

Resumes serve two purposes including the following:

- to present important information; and
- to present that information succinctly.

When writing a resume, as when writing anything, think of your reader: The person reading your resume first will probably be a hiring manager. She or he will read through dozens – perhaps hundreds – of resumes, before inviting a handful of people in to interview for a job. Think of your resume as a first step. Along with a strong cover letter, it can get you in for a solid face-to-face talk that lands you your desired job – or, at least, another interview. It's very rarely that people are hired on resumes alone. However, resumes are first impressions, and there's some truth to the saying that "first impressions are everything."

Try to follow the following format when writing your resume:

### Personal information

Name

Address

Cell phone

Email

Then, in separate sections:

### Education

Put this after your name and contact information if you're a recent graduate; otherwise, education can follow work experience. The lengthier your work history, the less important your education is generally considered to be. Typically, employers are most concerned with what you've been doing recently. Education is always important, but if you completed college 15 or 20 years ago, it probably doesn't make sense to place your collegiate credentials at the top of your resume.

| collegiate | 大学的 | credentials | 证书 |

### Work experience

List your professional experience from most to least recent. Include the name of your employer, your title, the location of your workplace (e.g. city, state), and the dates between which you held each position. Provide a brief description of the duties you performed, taking care to highlight the skills and experiences that are most important to your potential employer. Do not, however, point out in your resume that these skills are important or relevant. This can be done in a cover letter, and in any case, your qualifications should speak for themselves.

A word of caution: Do not provide too lengthy descriptions. Resumes should be, at most, two pages – but ideally one page. To limit the length of your resume, consider excluding experience that is not recent enough to be relevant (e.g. the job you worked in high school) or experience that is not qualitatively relevant to your potential position (e.g. don't include a retail job if you're applying to an engineer position).

### Volunteer experience

Volunteering shows commitment and, in some cases, social awareness. List your volunteer experiences as you do your paid experiences – in order of most to least recent. Also, include the names of the organizations you assisted, the locations of these organizations, the dates of your involvement, and the nature of your responsibilities.

### Skills

Use this section to highlight abilities not covered elsewhere. Do not list generic, abstract skills (e.g. communication skills, organizational ability). Rather, focus on specific, concrete skills, such as language proficiency (indicate both language and level of facility) and computer training (e.g. knowledge of certain operating systems or software).

### Interests

A brief list of interests (e.g. hiking, photography) reveals more about you as an individual. Many employers recognize that non-work interests and accomplishments positively affect work performance, and some employers would rather not hire people who don't have "balanced" interests (i.e. interests outside work).

### A word about formatting

Keep your margins at 1 inch and your font at 11 or 12 point.

Do not use multiple fonts; use fonts of multiple colors or sizes; use underlining, bold, and/or italics to excess or inconsistently (they may be used in moderation and so long as their use follows a predictable pattern).

Also, pay attention to verb tenses. If you currently hold a position, use the present tense to describe your activities. If you no longer hold a position, be sure to use the past tense.

The bottom line is to make your resume easily readable. Could a hiring manager scan it in less than a minute, without rereading it; glean your strengths; and make a decision?

| | | | |
|---|---|---|---|
| font | 字体 | bold | 粗体字 |
| italics | 斜体字 | glean | 收集 |

## Questions

- Is writing a resume in English similar to writing in your native tongue? Is a resume in English simply an English translated version of your Chinese resume?
- What makes an eye-catching resume and how do you leave a good impression on the interviewer?

# Trade Fairs

## Learning Objectives

**In this unit, you will learn how to：**

- Talk about fairs in detail
- Book a stand
- Develop talks at fair

## Background Information

A trade fair (trade show or expo) is an exhibition organized at which companies in a specific industry can showcase and demonstrate their latest products, service, study activities of rivals and examine recent trends and opportunities. Some trade fairs are open to the public, while others can only be attended by company representatives (members of the trade) and members of the press, therefore trade shows are classified as either "Public" or "Trade Only". They are held on a continuing basis in virtually all markets and normally attract companies from around the globe. These events range in size, varying from a small group of exhibitors in a hotel ballroom to large-scale affairs in a convention center.

Trade fairs often involve a considerable marketing investment by participating companies. Costs include space rental, design and construction of trade show displays, telecommunications and networking, travel, accommodations, and promotional literature and items to give to attendees. In addition, costs are incurred at the show for services such as electrical, booth cleaning, Internet services, and drayage (also known as material handling).

An increasing number of trade fairs are happening online, and these events are called virtual tradeshows. They are increasing in popularity due to their relatively low cost and no need to travel for companies both attending and exhibiting at trade fairs.

 Starting Up

Participation in trade fairs takes an extreme amount of planning and organizing. The following are some of the must–dos for exhibitors to make most of the trade shows. Please arrange them in sequential order and decide when they should be completed.

1. Advertise your show participation.
2. Verify dismantling and shipping arrangements for returning your exhibit.
3. Conduct daily meetings to assess progress, process paperwork, and adjust sales activities and schedules.
4. Confirm arrivals of exhibit, equipment and services, and supervise booth setup.
5. Reserve next year's space.
6. Determine exhibit objectives.
7. Supervise the dismantling process.
8. Evaluate and select show(s).
9. Evaluate your company's performance at the show.
10. Finalize shipping information and provide to vendors.
11. Distribute sales leads and orders as soon as possible.
12. Rough out a basic plan.

| | |
|---|---|
| Before the show | |
| During the show | |
| After the show | |

# A. Making Preparations

### Dialogue 1 – Talking about a fair

*David intends to promote the products of his company. Bruce suggests attending a trade fair.*

**Bruce:** Hello, David. How have you been?

**David:** Hi, Bruce. I've been really busy these days. Our company has decided to promote the products to the United States. And I'm responsible for the marketing program.

**Bruce:** Have you ever thought of attending a fair in the U.S.? It helps to publicize your products in the local markets.

**David:** Yes, you're right. Do you know any good fairs that would be most beneficial for us to attend?

**Bruce:** Yes. The Annual Miami International Wine Fair is one of the largest wine trade shows in the States. The fair attracts hundreds of renowned importers, distributors, retailers and buyers to participate every year. Therefore, exhibitors can be guaranteed to meet with relevant potential buyers from not only 50 states of the U.S., but also from Canada, Mexico and the Caribbean.

**David:** That's very impressive. Does it enjoy much popularity among consumers?

**Bruce:** Absolutely! Take last year for example. More than 2,000 consumers and 4,000 trade professionals flocked to the Center during the fair days.

**David:** That sounds terrific. When is it scheduled for 2018?

**Bruce:** It's going to be held from September 14th to 16th at the Miami Beach Convention Center.

**David:** How big is the exhibition area?

**Bruce:** The exhibit space is over 85,000 sqft. Guests will have the opportunity to taste more than 1,800 different wines from 20 countries.

**David:** How come you know so well about the fair? Have you been there before?

**Bruce:** Yes. I go there every year in recent four years. The best part I like about the fair is that I can spend all day tasting top-class wine from around the world.

**David:** That's how you learn about the fair firsthand?

**Bruce:** No. Actually, my wife works there.

**David:** That's no wonder!

## Dialogue 2 – Arranging an exhibition

*Ms. Lee, an exhibition organizer, is talking with Peter from ABC Electronics, one of the exhibitors.*

**Peter**：Good morning, Ms. Lee. I'm Peter Bryant from ABC Electronics.

**Ms. Lee**：Good morning, Mr. Bryant. Nice to meet you!

**Peter**：Nice to meet you too. I'm sure you have received the enquiry and the outline we sent to you for the coming exhibition. And I'd like to confirm with you the date and a couple of other issues.

**Ms. Lee**：All right. The exhibition is to be held from 21st to 23rd, for 3 days. Is that right?

**Peter**：Yes. What's the capacity of your exhibition hall? We are expecting an attendance of 500 at a time.

**Ms. Lee**：I don't think there is any problem. You can actually choose between Hall A01 and B03.

**Peter**：How are they different?

**Ms. Lee**：They are of about the same size, and both can hold up to 800 people. But Hall A01 is with anti-skid flooring, whereas B03 with concrete trowel flooring.

**Peter**：I see. I think A01 will do.

**Ms. Lee**：All right. Do you have any special requirements?

**Peter**：Yes, that'll be the temperature. I think the hall should be under 18℃ , because this is a hi-tech products show, you know.

**Ms. Lee**：Yes, I see. I'll see to it. By the way, do you need an aisle carpet?

**Peter**：Absolutely, that'd be very necessary. The people coming to this show are all very important people from some major international organizations. So, red carpet is a must.

**Ms. Lee**：Then I guess you also need some flowers and plants?

**Peter**：Oh, yes. You've been very thoughtful. Thank you. But please make sure the flowers are fresh and fragrant.

**Ms. Lee**：No problem.

### Dialogue 3 – Discussing stand location

*Mary Martin is discussing the stand location with John Williams, an exhibition organizer.*

**Mary:** Where do you think it would be good for us to set up our booth, Mr. Williams?

**John:** Here's the map of the layout. Look, here, I still have several prime spots in high-traffic areas. But they're going really quickly. How about this corner booth? It's close to main entrance.

**Mary:** It must be expensive, I believe. We just need to be close to our major competitors. Where are they?

**John:** Some haven't confirmed yet, but they're mostly in this blue area.

**Mary:** Booth B225 looks like a good spot, doesn't it?

**John:** Yes, it's close to the restrooms. Lots of traffic.

**Mary:** How much is it going to cost us?

**John:** It's cheap. Only 2,000 dollars.

**Mary:** But, you know, we paid about half that last year.

**John:** Well, Ms. Martin, we're running on a flat-fee basis this year to make everyone's lives easier. And we're also expecting a fifteen percent increase in attendance.

**Mary:** So, commissions and entrance fee distributions are no longer part of the package?

**John:** You said it.

**Mary:** What about credit card payment machines and Internet connection?

**John:** The same as last year, an additional 50 dollars.

**Mary:** All right. I'll go with booth B225.

### Practice

1. In order to better promote your products – electric toys, your company decides to attend a fair. You are assigned to consult someone about some major international fairs in Europe.

2. You want to book a stand at the International Exhibition Center. You visit the center and talk with a clerk to find out detailed information.

3. You are to book a booth at an international fair. You require a medium-sized one close to escalator with good traffic.

# B. Attending Fairs

## Dialogue 1 – Setting up a booth

*Jason and Cindy are setting up a booth at an exposition.*

**Jason:** Is this your first time to a trade show, Cindy?

**Cindy:** No. I was helping last year at the Expo. But for setting up a stand, yes, it's my first time.

**Jason:** Here are the books we'll be selling. Could please put them up on the shelf?

**Cindy:** Sure. What shall we do to make our exhibit booth stand out from the rest, especially our competitors?

**Jason:** We have designed some attractive and informative brochures. And look, these are the postcards we brought back from the resorts. The visitors can have them for free later.

**Cindy:** Do you think we have to do something with this boring wall?

**Jason:** That's what these posters are for.

**Cindy:** I see they feature the Northern Europe region.

**Jason:** Yes. And that ties into our drawing for a 5-day free trip to Norway for two.

**Cindy:** That's very tempting. But I think we still need something else that would really get people's attention.

**Jason:** That really reminds me. Here.

**Cindy:** What do we do with these DVDs?

**Jason:** Obviously we sell them. We also play them here. Can you give me a hand with the TV and the DVD player in that box?

**Cindy:** Do they go to the table in the corner?

**Jason:** Exactly. It seems everything's done. Let's take a break.

## Dialogue 2 – Introducing products

*Frank is introducing the products to a customer at the exhibition.*

**Frank:** Good morning. Can I help you?

**Robert:** Good morning. I'm just looking at the moment.

**Frank:** Yes, please do. Have you come across our products before?

**Robert:** I think I've heard of them.

**Frank:** We are relatively new but Healthy Life is acquiring a reputation very quickly. We enjoy a very big market share in the European market.

**Robert:** Really? Well, actually I'm quite interested in the running machines. Could you tell me what the prices are in this range?

**Frank**： Of course. The prices start at $199 and they go up to $1,299.

**Robert**： Did you say $1,299?

**Frank**： Yes, that's right. This Horizon range is designed for health club and gym.

**Robert**： I'm sure this is a real state-of-the-art when it comes to professional machines.

**Frank**： Absolutely! Perhaps you'll be interested in looking at our running machines for home use. Can I show you some?

**Robert**： Yes, please.

**Frank**： Over here, Beny offer an excellent value range of relatively inexpensive motorized running machines for home use. They avoid gimmicks while incorporating useful functional features in all their running machine. And this one, T1R-08 with speed of 1-10mph, gives feedback about calories, speed, incline, heart rate, distance, as well as time.

**Robert**： What's the price?

**Frank**： It's on special at the fair, only $359.00 instead of the regular price $499.00. Very reasonable price I think you'll agree.

**Robert**： Mmm, not bad. Do you have some information about the warranty?

**Frank**： Of course. We provide a lifetime warranty for frame, 5 years for motor.

**Robert**： Right. How much weight is it able to bear? You know, I'm of big size.

**Frank**： Oh, you needn't worry about that. The maximum user weight allowed is 110kg. Would you like to try one out in the practice area?

**Robert**： Er, no, thank you. I'm afraid I don't have time at the moment. But I would like to read some more about your products.

**Frank**： Sure. Here are some of our latest brochures with up-to-date information on the full ranges. And also my card.

**Robert**： Thank you.

**Frank**： Please contact me if you need any more information.

| state-of-the-art | 使用最先进技术的产品 | | |
| --- | --- | --- | --- |
| gimmick | 花招，诡计 | incline | 坡度 |

## Dialogue 3 – Discussing discounts

*Tony is interested in the fax machines made by Five Star Fax Machine. Now he is discussing discounts with Grace.*

**Grace**： Good morning. I'm Grace Henderson with Five Star Fax Machine. What can I do for you?

**Tony：** Good morning. My name's Tony Ford. Nice to meet you.

**Grace：** Nice to meet you too, Mr. Ford.

**Tony：** I'd like to ask you about your fax machines you have here.

**Grace：** Ah, yes, you mean S89.

**Tony：** Yes, that's right, the S89. Now I want to know whether it can deal with high-quality B3 paper.

**Grace：** Certainly. That's no problem at all.

**Tony：** Fine. You see we're looking for replacements for our fifteen-year-old machines. So we need the latest technology. Now, if we were interested in making a firm order, how quickly could you deliver the machines?

**Grace：** Well, I can't give you a firm delivery date myself at this moment. But we can deliver pretty quickly.

**Tony：** Our company would be interested in 20 machines.

**Grace：** That's very good.

**Tony：** So I was wondering, could we get a 16% discount on an order of that size?

**Grace：** Well, as you can see from our catalogue here, we normally offer 13% on an order of that kind.

**Tony：** Yes, but HBC down there, they are willing to give me 16%.

**Grace：** Well, of course, we'd be very glad to do business with you, Mr. Ford. And I'd like to draw your attention to the latest Super 5 technology, which our S89 contains.

**Tony：** Yes, that's true. But you know the discount is also important.

**Grace：** Look. If you'd like to wait just a few minutes, I can get through to my head office and I'll inquire about any special arrangements, which we might be able to make for you.

**Tony：** No, no, please don't bother about that just now. There's not that much of a hurry. I still have to report back to our Purchasing Manager. Here is my card. It'll be quite enough, if you just drop me a line about things like the discount by the end of next week.

**Grace：** Yes, of course, very well Mr. Ford. I hope to see you soon, Mr. Ford.

**Tony：** Goodbye.

## Practice

1. You are introducing your digital cameras to a potential customer at a trade fair.

2. You are at the International Trade Show representing Pacific Hi-Tech. A customer comes to your stand and shows great interest in your latest models. You introduce your products as well as deal with all the questions he/she asks.

3. A Japanese customer at a textile fair is very interested in your products. You are talking with him/her about the prices and discounts.

 Language Focus

| General Questions at Trade Fairs |
| --- |
| • Can you tell me something about your products?<br>• Is there anything else worth mentioning about your products?<br>• Are there any other benefits?<br>• Do you provide … service? |

| Talking about Quality | |
| --- | --- |
| • What about the quality?<br>• I'd like to know more about the quality.<br>• Would you please describe your product quality? | • Our products are famous for their superior quality.<br>• Our goods are well received in … |

| Talking about Price and Discounts | |
| --- | --- |
| • What are your terms of payment?<br>• Your price is not competitive compared with what is quoted by other suppliers. Can you lower it a bit?<br>• Can you offer us a discount? | • We think our price is acceptable/reasonable.<br>• Our price has already been at its lowest level.<br>• In order to encourage business, we are prepared to make a reduction.<br>• For the sake of establishing business relations between us, we may consider allowing you a quantity discount. |

| Talking about the Supply and Shipment | |
| --- | --- |
| • When can you deliver?<br>• How soon can you make the delivery? | • We can meet your deadline in …<br>• Actually, the goods are in short supply.<br>• There is no stock at the moment. The production was behind schedule.<br>• We are running short of stock. The goods are in high demand. |

- For more details, please contact us as soon as possible.
- We should be grateful if you would cooperate with us.
- We would greatly appreciate it if you could send us your latest catalogue.

 Extended Activities

## Role-play

### Task 1

**Student A:** You are introducing your leather jackets to a customer from Germany at an international toy fair. Show him/her the catalogue and explain the features, off your prices.

**Student B:** You are a businessman from Germany. You are visiting Canton Fair in China. You stop at a stand and show great interest in the leather jackets. Learn more about the products.

### Task 2

**Student A:** You are the owner of a well-established printing company, which enjoys a reputation for top-quality printing at competitive prices. You are visiting a potential customer you have met previously at a trade fair to discuss a new printing contract. You have the following information about the customer.
- Name: Daniel Laurence
- Business: Architects
- Print requirements: standard office stationery, plus architectural stationery

**Student B:** You represent a firm of architects. You have arranged to see the owner of a small local printing company you have learned about at a trade fair. You want a quotation for taking over the annual printing needs of your firm, which includes the following:
- Letterheads: 1,500
- Compliment slips: 3,000
- Envelopes: 5,000
- Architectural: 5,000 of A2, plus assorted

• Drawing paper: special orders

## Task 3

**Group work:** Many entrepreneurs or business owners frequently ask a question: Is the participation in a trade fair or convention by a business worth all the trouble and will it bring in new orders? Work in groups and brainstorm reasons for your attending or rejecting a trade fair.

## Task 4

**Group work:** On behalf of your company, you are exhibiting your company's products at a trade fair, where you meet customers from home and abroad. Keep a record of those prospective buyers you have talked with. Then, prepare a presentation about your achievements at the fair and perform it in class.

**Procedures:**

• Form a group of 4~5. Half of the group members are from the exhibiting side and the other half from the purchasing side.

• Two sides conduct a trade talk concerning the following aspects: model, price, discount, quality, quantity, features, product performance, delivery, maintenance, money back guarantee and other terms.

• Work together to prepare an outline of a presentation, which should include the information about at least three buyers as well as the agreement reached with them.

• Choose a group member to make the presentation.

## Task 5

**Group work:** Form a group of 4~5. You are to attend an international toy fair next month in Beijing. The group members need to work together to fulfill different tasks. The tasks may include booking flight tickets and accommodations, booking a stand, as well as stand design. Have one representative from your group present what you have come up with.

# Discussion

## Topic 1

Think of some local, national and international exhibitions and fairs. What do they specialize in? What are their scales? What influences do they have? Compare the ones of the same category.

### Topic 2

Suppose you are attending an exhibition overseas, what should be arranged? What factors should you be aware of in planning schedules?

### Topic 3

Is the location of a stand important? In what ways does it facilitate or hinder the promotion of products?

 Related Information

## The Purpose of Trade Fairs

Promotion, being one of the components of the marketing mix, is comprised of different elements. Although products can be boosted through different types of promotional activities, trade fair is an important tool, as it involves face-to-face communication. It is a means of displaying products to persuade and remind prospective buyers about the enterprise. Companies from around the world have been reaping the benefits of participating in trade fairs, which is an excellent way of generating new business for both large and small companies.

It offers companies many advantages, such as obtaining sales leads and competitor intelligence, and learning more about industry developments and trends. It also offers companies outstanding exposure, and chances to capture their share of the global market.

It provides a place for sellers to display their goods and make them known to buyers. It is a very common means for sellers to promote their goods and for buyers to choose goods from the vast variety on offer. It's a marketplace filled with qualified buyers, joint venture partners, distributor and partners – all in one place.

It is an ideal and highly effective platform for new product launches. Research shows that a large percentage of visitors are attracted to exhibitions by new products and technology. As for buyers, they can see a large variety of goods at the same time in a trade fair. They can compare goods of different brands, examine the goods and ask the exhibitors to show them how to use the products. They can also place orders at the fair, or just get the information they need and make a decision later.

By taking part in a trade fair sellers needn't bother to travel to many places to promote their goods, and buyers don't have to travel too much to look for the goods they want. It should be seen as an integral element of an overall sales and marketing campaign.

## Trade Fair Booth Display & Setup

Your booth display and setup at fairs should create a consistent image that connects with your target customers. Whatever type of trade show your booth is at, your goal will be the same: to attract visitors. Therefore, your booth setup should complement your products, and reflect the tastes and expectations of your customers. Customers are savvy shoppers with high expectations, so even though you may be sitting under a canopy in a park, customers still expect and respond to a great show booth display. How do you make sure your exhibit or display booth stands out and gets noticed? Here are some ideas to make sure your display booth does not get lost in the crowds, but instead attracts the visitors you want at the trade show.

- Register your display booth early. Registering early at the trade show assures that your exhibit gets a good spot in a prime location with lots of traffic.
- Design your display booth to be well-lit, have a theme consistent with your product, and have bright, noticeable colors. To determine what colors are noticeable, attend other trade shows of the sort you're going to display at and see what colors are used the most and what are used the least.
- Use color to set the tone. Take some time to determine the color(s) you'll use in your booth; color can send a powerful message and cause your target customers to head straight to your booth or walk right on past. The right color should grab customers' eyes and draw them into the booth, and yet, disappear into the background as customers draw closer. Therefore, your work, not your booth display is what gets the attention once customers are in the booth.
- Figure out what your target market and visitor will want at the trade show. Aim your convention freebies and giveaways at that market.
- Don't try to be something to everyone. This guiding principle can be applied across the board from product design to booth display. Find a theme in your work, determine your unique voice or image and carry that theme or image through all aspects of your booth display.
- Unless your display booth involves many interactive exhibits and you want to encourage many attendees to linger in a bunch, plan your trade show booth to be linear, allowing attendees to go along the display booth and then on their merry way, your business card, product, or giveaway in hand.

- Make your booth look like a store with a focused image that matches with the style of your products. Your booth has to function as a traveling store, so you'll have to take some practical considerations into account, but do notice fresh and creative ways to display products.

- As you make choices for your booth setup, always come back to the style of your work, and the tastes and expectations of your target customers. If you consistently choose display ideas that meet and exceed your customers' expectations and show off your work in its best possible light, you will create a winning booth display.

## Questions

- Which colors stand out best at the convention – including black and white?
- How do you make your choice of exhibits at a fair?
- How is the design or setup for a book stand different from that for a clothes stand?
- If you're exhibiting at a sports show and you aim to attract visitors who are sports hobbyists, what appropriate giveaways would you offer?
- Suppose you are attending the cosmetics fair. Work out a booth setup plan with your partners.

# Inquiries and Offers

 Learning Objectives

**In this unit, you will learn how to:**

- Make inquiries
- Make quotations
- Make offers

## Background Information

When a businessman intends to import some products, he may send out an inquiry to an exporter, inviting a quotation or an offer for the goods he wishes to buy or simply asking for some general information about these goods.

An inquiry is a request for business information, such as price lists, catalogues, samples, and details about the goods or trade terms. On receiving the inquiry, the exporter should reply to it without delaying to start the negotiation.

A quotation is a promise to supply goods on the terms stated, while an offer is a formal presentation of the goods to be supplied on the terms specified for the buyer's acceptance. An offer is actually a proposal of certain trade terms and an expression of a willingness to make a contract according to the terms proposed. These terms mainly include name of commodity, brand, specifications, quantity, price, packaging, payment and shipment, etc.

In order to expand export trade, sometimes sellers may take the initiative to make offers or quotations according to the conditions called for, even though no inquiries are received from foreign customers.

##  Starting Up

**Read the following statements about inquiries. Are they True (T) or False (F)?**

| True or False? |
|---|
| ☐ 1. Inquiries are usually made by sellers in international trade. |
| ☐ 2. In response to an inquiry, a quotation may be sent. |
| ☐ 3. In reply to an inquiry, you can provide more than what are asked for. |
| ☐ 4. There is no need to reply if you have no interest in the inquiry. |
| ☐ 5. A quotation is an indication of price without obligation. |

##  Oral Workshop

## A. Making an Inquiry

### Dialogue 1 – Making an inquiry for table cloth

*Lia works as a sales person. She is receiving Mr. Black, a foreign customer, in the sample room.*

**Lia:** Mr. Black, here's our sample room. Most of the commodities we handle are displayed here.

**Mr. Black:** You certainly have a large collection of samples here.

**Lia:** Then what particular items are you interested in?

**Mr. Black:** I've gone through your catalog and seen your samples. I'm particularly interested in Cotton Table Cloth Art. No.105 and 106.

**Lia:** What are your specific requirements?

**Mr. Black:** We'll be pleased if you will quote us the lowest price in pounds sterling, CIF Lagos.

**Lia:** No problem. We'll make out the quotation in a couple of days.

**Mr. Black:** I'd also like to know the quantities of the various sizes that you can supply for prompt delivery. If your prices are reasonable and quality satisfactory, we'll place a large order.

**Lia**：You may be assured that our goods are superior in quality and favorable in price. We'll make you our most favorable quotation soon.

**Mr. Black**：OK. I'll be looking forward to that.

---

inquiry 询价，询盘                Lagos  拉各斯（尼日利亚首都）
quotation 报价

---

### Dialogue 2 – Asking for a quotation

*Mr. Huang is a sales representative. Mr. Smith is asking him for a quotation.*

**Mr. Huang**：Hello, Mr. Smith. I understand that you're interested in our machine tools.

**Mr. Smith**：Yes, Mr. Huang. We'd like to know what you can offer in this line as well as your sales terms.

**Mr. Huang**：As you know, we supply machine tools of all types and sizes. We have years of experience in handling this line.

**Mr. Smith**：We've read about this in your sales literature. Could you give us some idea of your prices?

**Mr. Huang**：Our prices compare favorably with those offered by other suppliers. Here is our latest price list.

**Mr. Smith**：Erh… How long does it usually take you to deliver the goods?

**Mr. Huang**：As a rule, we deliver all our goods within one month after receiving the covering L/C.

**Mr. Smith**：OK. One more thing, all your prices are on C.I.F. basis. We'd rather you quote us on F.O.B. basis.

**Mr. Huang**：No problem. That can be arranged.

**Mr. Smith**：Thank you.

---

line    行业；商品的一类

---

### Practice

1. You are Mr. Wang, the president of Tianjin Machine Tools Corporation. You are having a general discussion with a Canadian importer Mr. Black about a certain kind of machine tools.

2. You are a representative of a cosmetics company. You are selling fat-reducing soap which is very popular in China. Your customer wants to place a trial order with you.

# B. Making a Quotation

### Dialogue 1 – Talking abut a quotation for carpets

*Wang Lin, a sales representative, is talking about the quotation for carpets with Mr. Smith.*

**Wang Lin**：Welcome to China, Mr. Smith.

**Mr. Smith**：I'm very glad to have the chance to visit your company. I hope we can do business together.

**Wang Lin**：It's a great pleasure to meet you. Let's get down to business. Which items do you think might have a chance in your market?

**Mr. Smith**：Some China-made carpets, tapestries, and so on, I guess.

**Wang Lin**：Well, that definitely falls within our business scope. We can easily supply you with them. Our manufacturers guarantee world-standard quality so our products have a solid reputation both at home and abroad. I'll show you around our sample room later if you like.

**Mr. Smith**：I'd like to go over some of your brochures first.

**Wang Lin**：Okay, and a price list, here you are. The price list will give you indicative prices for all our export products.

**Mr. Smith**：Good, now I'd like to have a look at the samples.

**Wang Lin**：OK, the sample room is in this way. Follow me, please.

(in the sample room)

**Wang Lin**：So what do you think, Mr. Smith? Are you interested in our products?

**Mr. Smith**：Yes. There's really a rich assortment to choose from, and I'm interested in some of the items. Look at these hand-made woven ones. They look very nice and attractive. Can you supply them now?

**Wang Lin**：Yes, they're in stock.

**Mr. Smith**：I think they'll find a good market in my region.

**Wang Lin**：Good. We'll make you a quotation once you make a specific inquiry.

**Mr. Smith**：OK, I'll make an inquiry soon.

| scope | 范围，领域 | at home and abroad | 国内外 |
|---|---|---|---|
| indicative price | 参考价格 | specific inquiry | 详细询盘 |

### Dialogue 2 – Supplying from stock

*Grace is a sales representative. Mr. Black is the buyer from Rotterdam. They are trying to establish relationship with each other.*

**Grace**：Good morning, Mr. Black. Would you tell me which items you are keen on?

**Mr. Black**：All of your products are fantastic. I'm especially interested in Art. No. 51. How is the supply position?

**Grace**：All the articles displayed here are available. Generally speaking, we can supply from stock.

**Mr. Black**：I should say that we think highly of your products.

**Grace**：I'm very glad to hear that. We are very confident that our products will find a good market in your country.

**Mr. Black**：There's no problem about it. Here is our inquiry note. Please quote us your lowest price, CIF Rotterdam.

**Grace**：I'll look into your requirements first and let you have our quotation tomorrow. You'll surely find our price favorable.

**Mr. Black**：I hope so.

**Grace**：How soon do you want your goods to be delivered?

**Mr. Black**：Is it possible for you to make prompt shipment?

**Grace**：No problem. As I mentioned, we can supply from stock. See you tomorrow then.

### Practice

1. You are Mr. Wang, the sales manager of Tianjin Home Textiles Corporation. Your products include towels, bedclothes and curtains. You are now having a talk with an American businessman concerning your company and the line of business, trying to persuade him to buy your products.

2. You are Mr. Anderson, an American businessman. You are visiting an exhibition and interested in a new product, a kind of "air cushioned" shoes manufactured by a small business. You ask Mr. Zhang for a quotation.

## C. Making Offers

### Dialogue 1 – Making an offer for microwave ovens

*Allan, a buyer, comes for an offer. Tracy is receiving him.*

**Allan**：I've come for your offer for your "Good Wife" brand microwave ovens, Tracy.

**Tracy**： Oh, yes. We have the offer ready for you now. You are inquiring for 3,000 sets of "Good wife" brand microwave ovens and the Article number is KS-100Z, is that right?

**Allan**： Yes, and we'd like you to offer us the goods on FOB basis.

**Tracy**： We've worked it out. The price for KS-100Z is USD 125 per set, FOB Xingang, Tianjin.

**Allan**： I see. Do you allow any discount?

**Tracy**： According to our usual practice, we don't allow any discount for goods like this. But if the quantity you inquire for is large enough, we can give it a special consideration.

**Allan**： OK, we'll think about the price and the discount later. What about delivery?

**Tracy**： Shipment will be made during April, 2009. We'll arrange to book the shipping space as soon as you accept our offer. After the goods are shipped on board, we'll fax you a shipping advice so that you can cover insurance in time.

**Allan**： That's good. Is this an offer with engagement?

**Tracy**： Yes, it remains valid for three days. That is to say, you should give us a definite answer within three days.

**Allan**： OK, I'll study all the details of the offer and give you an answer as soon as possible.

**Tracy**： All right. We look forward to your favorable reply. See you then.

| | | | |
|---|---|---|---|
| FOB(Free on Board) | 离岸价 | shipping space | 舱位 |
| shipping advice | 装船通知 | cover insurance | 投保 |
| valid | 有效的 | | |

## Dialogue 2 – Making an offer to an old client

*Coco, a sales representative, is talking with an old client for further cooperation.*

**Coco**： Good morning. How's everything?

**Hans**： Fine, thank you. I've come to hear about your offer for Men's Shirts.

**Coco**： As you already know, our cotton shirts are exquisitely made and moderately priced. Here's a wide range of samples in our showroom. Some of them are the latest style this autumn. Which items are you particularly interested in this time?

**Hans**： We have a great interest in Art. Nos.22 and 23.

**Coco**： What's the quantity you are likely to take?

**Hans**：800 dozen. I hope you'll quote us on your best terms. The other requirements are in this inquiry note.

**Coco**：Wait a moment, I'll check it out for you. OK, now we are pleased to offer you 800 dozen Seagull Brand Men's Shirts, Art. Nos.22 and 23, at $240 per dozen CIF New York. The shirts will be packed in one plastic bag each, every 5 dozen to a cardboard box. Shipment will be made in July.

**Hans**：Thank you very much for your offer. We'll give it serious consideration. And we will let you know once we get the result. One more thing, since this is not the first time we do business together, is it possible for us to make payment on easier term?

**Coco**：I can't give you an answer right now. I'll go back to consult my boss and give you an answer as soon as possible.

**Hans**：Fine. We'll be waiting for your reply. See you then.

| | |
|---|---|
| Art. No.(artide No.) | 货号 |
| CIF( Cost, Insurance and Freight) | 到岸价 |

### Practice

1. You, the representative from × × × Textiles Imp. & Exp. Corp., are talking with Mr. Simpson, a Canadian businessman, who is interested in Chinese cotton piece goods. Mr. Simpson is not quite satisfied with the designs and asks you to produce according to patterns provided by him. You agree to make him a favorable offer provided he increases the quantity for each design to 5,000 yards.

2. You are a Japanese businesswoman visiting the Tianjin Fair in China. You are interested in Chinese Green Tea. You make an inquiry. The seller makes you an offer at USD 65 per kilo. You discuss and settle the price and date of delivery with him.

 Language Focus

### Technical Terms

| | |
|---|---|
| inquire | 询价，询盘 |
| make an inquiry for… | 询购 |
| quote | 报价 |
| make a quotation | 报价 |
| negotiation | 洽谈，磋商 |
| consumer product | 消费品 |

| style | 式样 |
|---|---|
| design | 款式 |
| pattern | 图案 |
| model | 型号 |
| workmanship | 工艺 |
| specifications | 规格 |
| catalog | 商品目录 |
| terms and conditions | 条款；条件 |
| usual practice | 惯例 |
| invitation to offer | 邀盘 |
| offer with engagement | 有约束力的报盘 |
| offer without engagement | 无约束力的报盘 |
| subject to our confirmation | 以我方确认为准 |
| under offer | 在出售中 |
| European Main Ports | 欧洲主要口岸 |
| bid | 递价，出价 |

## Functional Expressions

### Making an Inquiry

- We are interested in your printed pure silk scarves; could you give us an idea of your price?
- Please quote us your lowest price as soon as we make you an inquiry.
- We are looking forward to your reply to our inquiry.
- Would you please quote us a price on your reversible wool blankets of 15% wool and 85% cotton?
- As our buyers are unwilling to make a bid, you'd better make an offer as soon as possible.
- If you can supply goods of the type and quality according to the requirements, please make us an offer and quote your lowest unit prices.
- We shall be very glad to receive an offer from you on this brand of bikes.

### Making a Quotation

- We will make you our most favorable quotation as soon as we receive your specific inquiry.
- As requested, we shall submit our quotation and shall appreciate your placing the order with us as early as possible.
- Your inquiry of June 5 has been passed on to us for our attention.
- At your request, we are now making you a firm offer for 2,000 sets LCD of Type 112.
- We are making you an offer subject to our final confirmation.
- Against your inquiry, we are making you a special offer as follows.
- Please tell us the quantity you require so that we can work out the offer.

| Stating Validity |
| --- |
| ● This offer will expire on March 30. We look forward to your immediate reply by fax. Our offer is firm until the 15th next month. <br> ● We keep the offer open till the end of this week. |

| subject to | 以……为准；以……为有效 | open | 有效的 |
| --- | --- | --- | --- |

 Extended Activities

## Role-play

**Task 1**

**Student A：** You are a food importer in Australia. You are interested in the canned fruits of Shanghai Foodstuffs Imp. & Exp. Corporation. Make an inquiry about the price, the packaging, the size and so on.

**Student B：** You are a sales representative of the canned fruits of Shanghai Foodstuffs Imp. & Exp. Corporation. You are receiving a potential customer from Australia. Make a quotation according to his requirement.

**Task 2**

**Student A：** You are Mr. Wang from Guangzhou Yuehua Import & Export Corporation. You are having a business talk about Toy trains with one of your customers and make the offer.

**Student B：** You are Mr. White from Australian Johnson & Son Trading Corporation. You are in the market for 3,000 pieces of Art. No. SMF145 and 5,000 pieces of Art. No. SMF344. The price offered by Mr. Wang is USD 2.5/PC CIF Sydney and you ask for payment by D/P at sight.

| D/P ( Documents against payment ) | 付款交单 |
| --- | --- |

**Task 3**

**Student A：** You are Mr. White from California Trading Corporation. You are interested in the Canned Yellow Peach, and intend to buy 1,000 cartons at USD 145/

CIF San Francisco.

**Student B:** You are Miss Zhang from Tianhong Foodstuffs Co., Ltd. Now you are having a business talk with Mr. White. Finally, you settle the price at USD 150 per carton and agree to effect payment by irrevocable L/C at sight.

L/C (Letter of Credit)　　　信用证

### Task 4

**Student A:** You are Mr. Burns. You are interested in the carpets that Mr. Zhang's Company handles and you inquire for 500 pieces of Art. No. S008 for prompt shipment.

**Student B:** You are Mr. Zhang. Since the article Mr. Burns has inquired is out of stock, you recommend Art. No. S009 as a substitute and assures Mr. Burns of the same quality and even better price.

### Task 5

**Presentation:** Give a 2~3 minute presentation on the topic: What should be taken into consideration before making an offer? You may want to cover the following:

- proper price terms and other terms as well as conditions that may affect the price;
- the cost of goods and other export charges;
- marketing situation.

## Discussion

### Topic 1

What does an offer usually include?

### Topic 2

What are the differences between FOB prices and CIF prices?

### Topic 3

What are the differences between a firm offer and a non-firm offer?

## Business Negotiation

Business negotiation is an important part of conducting an export transaction. It is the dealing between seller or exporter and buyer or importer in order to reach an agreement on the price, quantity, quality, payment and other terms or conditions of a sale. Evidently, the conclusion of a sales contract results from the business negotiation to the satisfaction of both parties.

No matter in what way the negotiations are held, generally speaking, they consist of the following parts：inquiry, offer, counter-offer, acceptance and conclusion of sales contract. Among them, offer and acceptance are two indispensable links for reaching an agreement and concluding a contract.

Business negotiations are carried out either verbally or in writing. In the latter case, traders talk about the terms or conditions of a sale with each other in person or by telephone. The foreign merchant may call on the domestic trader upon invitation, or the exporter will make a visit to an overseas importer on his own account. Business talks are also held at international fairs where businessmen all over the world can negotiate with one another over export and import trading. Through verbal negotiations, trading transactions between Chinese and foreign merchants are concluded in large amounts at the China Export Commodities Fair in Guangzhou which be held twice a year.

| business negotiation | 商务谈判；交易磋商 | transaction | 交易 |

## Supplements for Reflections

## WTO Raises 2014 Global Trade Growth Forecast to 4.7 Percent

The World Trade Organization (WTO) on Monday raised its forecast for global trade growth in 2014 to 4.7 percent, from its previous prediction of 4.5 percent.

The predicted growth is more than double the rate of 2.1 percent in 2013 but remains below the 20-year average of 5.3 percent and well below the pre-crisis trend of 6 percent (1990 — 2008), said WTO in a report.

The 2014 global trade forecast was based on an assumed 3 percent growth in world gross domestic production (GDP) at market exchange rates, said the watchdog of international trade.

In the report, WTO saw the world economy in 2014 as mixed, with downside risks and significant upside potentials coexisting.

It explained that on one hand leading economies remain fragile, including some of the most dynamic developing countries that until recently were propping up global demand.

Meanwhile, developing economies have slowed greatly due to both internal and external reasons, partially referring to the potential effect of the winding down of U.S. quantitative easing (QE).

On the other hand, the U.S. economy seems to be gaining momentum and the European Union appears to have turned a corner, which would have positive implications, WTO noted.

The report predicted exports of developed economies to grow at 3.6 percent in 2013 while that of developing countries (including the Commonwealth of Independent States, CIS) to be 6.4 percent.

Imports by developed economies were expected to grow at 3.4 percent, while by developing countries (including CIS) at 6.3 percent.

For the very first time, this year's report also detailed the trade outlook for 2014 in regional forecasts.

According to the report, Asia was expected to lead export growth in 2014 at a rate of 6.9 percent, followed by North America (4.6 percent), South and Central America (4.4 percent), Europe (3.3 percent) and other regions that comprise of Africa, the Middle East and the CIS (3.1 percent).

On the import side, Asia would take first place with a growth of 6.4 percent, followed by other regions (5.8 percent), South and Central America (4.1 percent), North America (3.9 percent) and Europe (3.2 percent).

The report said China, with its large economy, would drive strong import growth in Asia.

As for 2013, the WTO said the global economic performance was weak due to several factors including the lingering impact of EU recession, high unemployment in Euro area and uncertainty about the timing of the U.S. easing of its monetary stimulus.

WTO economists noted that the tapering of QE in the U.S. led to financial volatility in developing economies in the second half of 2013. The pinch was particularly felt in certain emerging economies with large current account imbalances, such as in India, which has experienced marked depreciation of its currency, the rupee, between April and September last year.

In 2013, the developed countries witnessed sluggish growth of 1.5 percent in terms of exports, while the figure of developing countries (including CIS) was 3.3 percent. As for imports, developed countries experienced a decline of 0.2 percent and developing countries (including CIS) grew by 4.4 percent.

| | | | |
|---|---|---|---|
| previous | 之前的 | prediction | 预测 |
| watchdog | 监管部门 | coexisting | 共存 |
| stimulus | 刺激；激励 | volatility | 波动性 |
| QE ( Quantitative Easing) | | 量化宽松政策 | |

**Questions**

- How did WTO see the world economy in 2014 in the report?
- How is Asia's performance in the trade outlook for 2014 in regional forecasts?
- List the reasons why the global economic performance was weak in 2013.

# Unit 10

## Counter Offers and Orders

 Learning Objectives

**In this unit, you will learn how to:**

- Make counter offers
- Negotiate prices
- Place orders

## Background Information

It is quite obvious that every business is confronted with a pricing problem. Businessmen are particularly interested in seeing their goods sold in sufficient volume and at profitable prices. Prices occupy a position of first-rank importance and present some of the key problems with which they are forced to contend. The same is true of the foreign trade business. Price is one of the most sensitive factors in the process of negotiation of international business.

To some extent, however, the pricing problem which an exporter tackles is more complicated than that in home trade. In addition to the cost of the goods included in the calculation of the export price, the price quotations in foreign trade are invariably accompanied by an indication as to which party is to pay the expenses of freight, insurance, loading, unloading and other incidental charges, and to bear the risks in case of the goods being damaged. It is essential that a foreign trade merchant knows how an export quotation is constructed.

Sometimes an offeree partly agrees or totally disagrees to the offer and then puts forward his own suggestions. In either case, he is making a counter-offer, which is in fact a new offer from the original offeree.

An order is a request to supply a specified quantity of goods. It may result from an offer or an enquiry with subsequent messages. An order may be given by letter or memorandum, by telex or email message. The importer usually uses printed order forms and the seller uses printed acknowledgements so as to avoid misunderstanding between them.

The buyer's order is an offer to buy. Upon receipt of an order, the seller should acknowledge it as soon as possible.

##  Starting Up

The following chart describes the general trading procedure. Follow the steps in the chart to fill out the missing information.

Offer (a firm offer/non-firm offer)          Counteroffer

Accept and place an order          Confirm the order

| The buyer | | The seller |
|---|---|---|
| Make an inquiry | ➡ | |
| | ➡ | Counter offer |
| Negotiate on other terms such as quality etc. | ➡ | Negotiate on other terms such as quality etc. |
| | ➡ | Accept and confirm |
| Sign the contract | ➡ | Sign the contract |
| Trial order | ➡ | |
| Further order (long-term relationship) | ➡ | Further order (long-term relationship) |

##  Oral Workshop

## A. Negotiating a Better Price

### Dialogue 1 – Discussing an offer

*Mr. Wang is a project manager of an import & export company. He is receiving an regular client Mr. Smith from italy who comes to confirm a purchase of 1,000 metric tons of cotton from China.*

**Mr. Smith：** Good morning, Mr. Wang.

**Mr. Wang：** Good morning. What do you think of our offer?

**Mr. Smith：** Well, I have discussed your offer with my colleagues and I have to be very honest with you. We find the price you quoted rather on the high side.

**Mr. Wang：** Do you really think so? I would like to say my offer was quite reasonable.

**Mr. Smith：** I am saying this because we have received some offers from other resources recently. Most of them are below $1,450.

**Mr. Wang：** Mr. Li gave you a fact sheet to explain our costs of manufacture. You will see from it that our offer is based on reasonable profit.

**Mr. Smith：** But as what I said yesterday, we think supply will continue to exceed demand and prices will continue their downward trend.

**Mr. Wang：** Well, anyway, let's have your counter offer. Are you ready to come up with a figure?

**Mr. Smith：** Considering our good relationship over the past years, we are willing to take the risk of the falling market and make you a counter offer at USD1,450 per metric ton FOB stowed.

**Mr. Wang：** I appreciate your counter offer but find it too low. I'll respond to your counter offer but the best we can do is to make a reduction of 2 dollars. What do you say to that?

**Mr. Smith：** That's not much of an improvement.

**Mr. Wang：** Where do we go from here? How about this? I suggest we take a break and I'll consult with the manufacturers to see what we can do next.

**Mr. Smith：** That's OK.

| | | | |
|---|---|---|---|
| fact sheet | 情况说明 | exceed | 超过 |
| downward | 下跌的 | | |

## Dialogue 2 – Haggling over the price

*Mr. Black, a really smart purchaser of an American company, comes to China for a deal of women's wear. Lucy is receiving him and is cautiously negotiating with this old customer.*

**Mr. Black：** I have to say, your price is unrealistic. It has shot up, almost 15% higher than that of last year.

**Lucy：** I'm a little surprised to hear you say that. The price for this commodity has changed somewhat compared to last year's, but they are still very low compared with the prices of the same kind of products on the international market. Our price is still highly competitive.

**Mr. Black：** I'm afraid I can't agree with you there. The price for this commodity is tending downward on the international market.

**Lucy：** It seems we hold different points of view toward the trend of the international market price. But you need to recognize that the costs for this commodity have gone up since last year. We have to mark up our price to keep our heads above water. Actually, this price leaves us no profit at all. We can't go any lower.

**Mr. Black：** Your price is higher than those we've got elsewhere.

**Lucy：** Taking quality into consideration, I think our price is reasonable. In terms of quality, I don't think that the goods of other brands can compare with ours. To be frank with you, if it were not for the long-standing relationship between us, we would hardly be willing to make you an offer at this price.

**Mr. Black：** Well, we'll have a lot of difficulties in persuading our clients to buy at this price. But I'll have a try, I suppose. How long does your offer remain valid?

**Lucy：** Our offer remains open for three days.

| | | | |
|---|---|---|---|
| unrealistic | 不实际的 | shot up | 暴涨 |
| mark up | 涨价，标高价格 | | |

## Practice

1. You are Mr. Zhang. You are going to import a quantity of chemical fertilizers from Mr. White for your customers. But you find the price quoted on the high side. You try to persuade Mr. White to reduce the price.

2. You find the price Mr. Johnson quoted you on the high side. You want to persuade him to reduce the price by 5%. Mr. Johnson suggests meeting each other half way.

# B. Making Counteroffers

### Dialogue 1 – Making a counteroffer

*After a careful consideration, Hans Schoeman decides to come back and have a further discussion with David Beckham. However, they have very different ideas on price.*

**Hans：** Well, we've studied your offer, and we find your offer too high to be acceptable.

**David:** I'm sorry to hear that. It is our rock-bottom price. The price was closely calculated. We can't make any concession.

**Hans:** I'm afraid I can't agree with you. If you insist on your original offer, I don't think there's any point in further discussion.

**David:** Well, what's your idea of price then?

**Hans:** The best we can do is USD55 per dozen, CIF London.

**David:** Do you really mean that? Our item is quite popular in the world market and your counter offer is not in line with the current market.

**Hans:** But indications show that the price of this item will continue its downward tendency in the future, so I should say the counteroffer is well founded.

**David:** I'm sorry the gap between us is so big. You can't expect us to reduce our price to that extent.

**Hans:** I think it unwise for either of us to insist on his won price. How about meeting each other half way?

**David:** All right, I'll think about it and see whether it is workable.

| | | | |
|---|---|---|---|
| rock-bottom price | 最低价 | concession | 让步 |
| tendency | 趋势 | founded | 有理由的 |
| in line with | 与……相符，与……相一致 | | |

## Dialogue 2 – Meeting each other half way

*Hans Schoeman comes to David Beckham the next day to ask for a final confirmation on price.*

**David:** Mr. Schoeman, we have studied your counter offer and I'm afraid it's difficult for us to comply with your request.

**Hans:** What do you mean?

**David:** We find that the gap between our price and the price you counter-offered is too large. It's impossible for us to bring down our price to your level.

**Hans:** In that case, what about meeting each other half way?

**David:** What is your proposal?

**Hans:** Your unit price is 10 dollars higher than we can accept. When I suggested we meet each other half way, I meant it literally.

**David:** Do you mean to suggest that we have to make a reduction of 5 dollars in our price? That's a big cut, I should say.

**Hans：** Yes. But as your products are still new to our market, I hope you will leave us a margin to cover the advertising expenses.

**David：** I understand your position. OK, with a view to future business, I'll accept your suggestion and reduce the price by 5 dollars. This is really the rock-bottom price.

**Hans：** Thank you for your cooperation. I'm very glad we've come to an agreement on price.

| comply with | 遵从；答应 | literally | 照字面地 |

### Practice

1.  You sell exercise bicycles on behalf of Tianjin Recreation Equipment Imp. & Exp. Co. A businessman from Canada wants to buy 500 sets of your bicycles. Your price is USD 200 per set FOB Xingang, but his counteroffer is USD 180 per set. You start bargaining.

2.  You are a Canadian customer. You have received an offer for mobile phones. You find the price on the high side. You ask the seller to cut the price by 30%. In the end, you and the seller decide to meet each other half way.

## C. Placing Orders

### Dialogue 1 – Placing an order at a Fair

*Mr. Shen works for China Machinery Import & Export Company. He is now at a fair. A foreign customer, David Clerk, comes up to his booth and shows great interest in the wines on display.*

**Mr. Shen：** Hello. Well, what are you interested in?

**Mr. Clerk：** Red wines.

**Mr. Shen：** What's the quality do you have in mind?

**Mr. Clerk：** What is the minimum quantity of an order for your goods?

**Mr. Shen：** Is this your trial order?

**Mr. Clerk：** Yes, since it is the first time.

**Mr. Shen：** 500 scores of bottles.

**Mr. Clerk：** If the first lot is good, we'd like to place a repeat order and then to order regularly.

**Mr. Shen：** Very good, and you can place mail orders in the future. It is convenient.

**Mr. Clerk：** That's good. May I have some samples?

**Mr. Shen：** Sure. We've got several different wines. You can taste them.

**Mr. Clerk：** We are acturally interested in buying different qualities, such as good merchantable quality, fair average quality, sacrifice quality and customary quality, etc., and of-cource the one with the best quality. Oh, by the way, do you have guarantee of quality of all these ones?

**Mr. Shen：** Yes. They all have quality inspection certificates.

**Mr. Clerk：** These are fine. I'm thinking of increasing my order.

**Mr. Shen：** You are quite selective. When can I have your formal order or your firm order then?

**Mr. Clerk：** Okay. Could you arrange a meeting tomorrow and we can talk about them?

**Mr. Shen：** Definitely. Let me check my schedule first. (after checking) Sorry sir, tomorrow morning is all taken. What about tomorrow afternoon between three and four? May I have your name, Sir?

**Mr. Clerk：** Yes. Joe Clerk. This is my name card. And let's make it 3 p.m. then. Thank you.

| | | | |
|---|---|---|---|
| trial order | 试订单 | repeat order | 续订订单 |
| good merchantable quality | G.M.Q 上好可销售品质 | | |
| fair average quality | F.A.Q 良好平均品质 | | |
| sacrifice quality | 降低品质 | | |
| customary quality | 一般品质 | | |
| guarantee of quality | 品质保证 | | |
| quality inspection certificates | 品质检验证书 | | |
| selective | 有眼光的 | | |

## Dialogue 2 – Fulfilling an order

*After a hot discussion at the fair, Mr. Shen and Mr. Clerk are having a meeting on the fulfillment of the order the next day.*

**Mr. Shen：** I'm very glad we've agreed on the terms and conditions of this transaction. We'll make arrangement for the fulfillment of your order when we receive it.

**Mr. Clerk：** Good. And because this is our initial order and your product is new to our market, we just want to place a trial order. I'm afraid it is not a big one.

**Mr. Shen：** No problem. We will carry out the order to your satisfaction, no matter how small it is.

**Mr. Clerk**：That's good. If we find the goods sell well in our market, we will place a repeat order right away. Of course, that relies greatly on the quality of your products.

**Mr. Shen**：We assure you that the delivery will come up to the standard of the sample on which we base our negotiation.

**Mr. Clerk**：Good, in that case, we'll give you our order tomorrow.

**Mr. Shen**：We look forward to that.

| | | | |
|---|---|---|---|
| fulfillment | 履行 | initial order | 首次订单 |
| come up to | 达到；符合 | | |

### Practice

1. You are Mr. Smith. After settling the price, you and Mr. Lee begin to talk about the quantity. Mr. Lee can only supply 500 cartons from stock owing to the increasing domestic demand but you want to place an order for 800 cartons.

2. You have received a shipment of some brand of garments from an overseas company. You find the quality satisfactory and the goods sell well in your market. You want to place a repeat order.

 Language Focus

### Technical Terms

| to make a counteroffer | 还盘 |
|---|---|
| to make a recession | 让步 |
| to cut the price | 削减价格 |
| to meet each other half way | 折中，各让一半 |
| reasonable price | 合理的价格 |
| favorable price | 优惠的价格 |
| bottom price | 最低价格 |
| wholesale price | 批发价格 |
| retail price | 零售价格 |
| fix the price | 定价 |
| price tag | 价格标签 |
| net price | 净价 |

| | |
|---|---|
| price fluctuation | 价格波动 |
| competitive price | 有竞争力的价格 |
| gap in price | 价格差距 |
| commission | 佣金 |
| discount | 折扣 |
| trial order | 试购订单 |
| duplicate order | 重复订单 |
| fresh order | 新订单 |
| initial order | 首批订货 |
| repeat order | 续订订单 |
| to execute an order | 执行订单 |
| to entertain an order | 接受订货 |
| to withdraw an order | 取消订单 |
| ruling price/current price | 现行价格 |
| middleman | 中间商 |
| broker | 经纪人 |

## Functional Expressions

### Making a Counter Offer

- Your quotation of washing machines is too high to be acceptable.
- We regret to say that your price is on the high side; we don't think there is any possibility of business unless you cut your price by 20%.
- We regret to say there is no possibility of business because of your high price.
- We ask for a further reduction of the price by 2%, because your price is not in line with the present market level.
- The price you offered is about 5% higher than the level workable to us, and we cannot but make a counter offer.
- We wish you will reconsider your price and give a new bid.
- Your competitors are offering considering lower prices and unless you reduce your quotations we will have to buy elsewhere.
- I'm afraid we have to call the whole deal off if you still insist on your original quotation.

### Negotiating the Price

- We have cut our price to the limit. So we regret to say we are unable to comply with your request for further reduction.
- Since our prices are closely calculated, we regret being unable to accept your counter offer.
- Our price is reasonable compared with those in the international market.
- Taking the quality into consideration, I think the price is reasonable.
- If you have taken everything into consideration, you may find our quotation lower than those you can get elsewhere.

| Counter Offers under other Terms |
| --- |
| • Unless you make shipment in March, we cannot accept your offer. |
| • We think the price you offered quite reasonable but have to make a counteroffer on the time of delivery. |
| • The price is workable, but the time of shipment is too distant. |
| • We assure you of our prompt and efficient execution of any order from you. |
| • Although the prevailing quotations are slightly higher, we will accept the order on the same terms as before with the view of encouraging business. |

| Placing an Order |
| --- |
| • If the goods you supply turn out to the satisfaction of our users, substantial orders will follow. |
| • If you accept our counter-offer, we will persuade the end-users to place an order with you. |

 Extended Activities

## Role-play

### Task 1

**Group work:** Work in small groups of 2~3. Make sentences with the following phrases.

- place an order
- push the sales
- further reduction
- place a trial order
- make a concession
- as an exception
- meet somebody half way
- make a counteroffer

### Task 2

**Student A:** You are Ms. Bai. You are having a heated discussion on price with Mr. Smith. The price you offered is the rock-bottom price. It may take several rounds of bargaining before you reach an agreement on price with your client. You may need to meet each other half way.

**Student B**: You are Mr. Smith. You find the price offered by Miss Bai unacceptable and ask for a reduction of 5%. However, Ms. Bai insists that the price is the rock-bottom price. It may take several rounds of bargaining before you reach an agreement on price with Ms. Bai. You may need to meet each other half way.

## Task 3

**Student A**: You are Mr. Stevenson. You are prepared to place a large order of 1,500 cases and expect a lower price from Mr. Zhang. But the price offered by Mr. Zhang is USD 185 per case which you find too high to be acceptable.

**Student B**: You are Mr. Zhang, an exporter of canned food. You are having a talk with Mr. Stevenson about the price of luncheon meat. After several rounds of bargaining you reach an agreement at USD 155 per case.

## Task 4

**Student A**: You are Mr. Smith of a shoe company. You wish to introduce the range of "Desert Boots" suede leather men's shoes to California. You are meeting a footwear buyer for California Sales. You insist on USD 35 per pair and would be happy to accept an order of 18,000 pairs on FOB basis.

**Student B**: You are a footwear buyer from California. You are interested in the "Desert Boots" suede leather men's shoes and are prepared to place an order for 3,000 pairs at the price of USD 28 per pair. You strike a hard bargaining with Mr. Smith and finally reach an agreement of an order for 6,000 pairs at USD 30 per pair.

# Discussion

## Topic 1

Prices are very important when it comes to buying and selling. Try to find out some effective ways to make your prices reasonable.

## Topic 2

What are the price terms usually used in international trade?

## Topic 3

What are the differences between discount and commission?

## 📖 Related Information

Business negotiation is an important part of conducting an export transaction. It is the dealing between seller or exporter and buyer or importer in order to reach an agreement on the price, quantity, quality, payment and other terms or conditions of a sale. Evidently, the conclusion of a sales contract results from the business negotiation to the satisfaction of both parties.

No matter in what way the negotiations are held, generally speaking, they consist of the following parts: inquiry, offer, counter-offer, acceptance and conclusion of sales contract. Among them, offer and acceptance are two indispensable links for reaching an agreement and concluding a contract.

Business negotiations are carried out either verbally or in writing. In the latter case, traders talk about the terms or conditions of a sale with each other in person or by telephone. The foreign merchant may call on the domestic trader upon invitation, or the exporter will make a visit to an overseas importer on his own account. Business talks are also held at international fairs where businessmen all over the world can negotiate with one another over export and import trading. Through verbal negotiations, trading transactions between Chinese and foreign merchants are concluded in large amounts at the China Export Commodities Fair in Guangzhou which be held twice a year.

business negotiation 商务谈判，交易磋商

## 📖 Supplements for Reflections

### News Analysis: China's Future Role in Globle Trade

BEIJING, May 6 (Xinhua) – China's import will total 10 trillion U.S. dollars in the next five years, about three times of Germany's gross domestic product (GDP). When Chinese President Xi Jinping announced this figure last month at the Boao Forum, foreign analysts knew its weight.

Against the backdrop of a rapidly changing global trade landscape, will China play a bigger role or be forced to retreat?

In recent years, China's share in global trade has been expanding. In 2012, China registered a total goods trade value of 3.87 trillion dollars, overtaking the United States to claim the top ranking in this regard.

With the unsolved deadlock in the Doha Round and a weak World Trade Organization (WTO), the U.S., as the world's largest economy, is establishing a U.S.-dominated new 21st-century global trade pattern, backed by two pillars – the Trans-Pacific Partnership (TPP) and the Transatlantic Trade and Investment Partnership (TTIP).

TTIP will bind together two large economies – the U.S. and the European Union, with their combined GDP and trade value accounting for half and one-third of the global total respectively.

Using their dominant positions in international trade, the U.S. and EU further push the formulation of new rules for global trade to cope with the rise of new economies, including China, while TPP is aimed at subjecting the stability of Asia-Pacific region to the new order, with security dragging trade against the backdrop of U.S. "Return to Asia" strategy.

The U.S. TPP strategy is clearly targeted at China, said Wang Yong, professor of the School of International Studies of Beijing University.

One and half a year ago, former Secretary of State Hillary Clinton proposed that the U.S. will update the order of priority for its foreign policies and lift economy above anti-terrorism in order to consolidate its leading strategic place.

Some scholars said that the "U.S. Diplomacy Rocket", which carried bombs in the past, will carry U.S. goods in the future.

With more and more countries announcing their decisions to join in TPP talks, China still stays out of it. Under such circumstances, China has to weigh between two options: to stay away from this U.S. initiative and set up its own version or wait to see the progress in TPP negotiations and find an opportune moment to extend its olive branches?

Some observers see that the U.S.-promoted new trade rules set a pretty high bar in regard to intellectual properties, labor protection, transparency and privatization of national enterprises.

Meanwhile, some other observers believe that exterior pressure has never slowed China's pace to move forward. On the contrary, as showed by China's success in three decades of reform and opening-up, the Asian nation is good at using such pressure to fuel progress at home.

The pessimistic voice crying wolf prior to China's WTO entry in 2001 is now remembered only as an interesting episode given the great benefits China has received after becoming a member of the global trade body.

Despite China's gaining of the global laurel in trade of goods, the country has come to a critical point to upgrade the "Made in China" label linked with low tech and high emission.

For China's foreign trade, a smooth transition to quality growth from the past quantity-featured glory holds key to its future boom and even for the sustainability of the overall Chinese economy.

In the months to come, major world economies will have to continue their battle against slow growth amid debt problems and the trend will remain that powers cooperate with and compete against each other at the same time.

| | | | |
|---|---|---|---|
| Boao Forum | 博鳌论坛 | backdrop | 背景 |
| retreat | 撤退 | deadlock | 僵局 |
| TPP（Trans-Pacific Partnership Agreement） | | 跨太平洋伙伴关系 | |
| TTIP（Transatlantic Trade and Investment Partnership） | | 跨大西洋贸易与投资伙伴协定 | |
| dominant | 支配的，统治的 | formulation | 构想，规划 |
| opportune moment | 恰当时机 | olive branch | 橄榄枝 |
| intellectual property | 知识产权 | privatization | 私有化 |
| laurel | 桂冠，殊荣 | | |

## Questions

- What are TTP and TTIP? What are their strategies?
- What options does China have when more and more countries announce their decisions to join in TPP talks?
- According to some observers, what new trade rules has U.S. promoted?

# Unit 11

# Packaging and Shipment

 ## Learning Objectives

**In this unit, you will learn how to:**

- Talk about different types of packaging and functions
- Talk about and understand basic types of shipment
- Set delivery time and select shipment mode

 ## Background Information

In international trade where an exporter and an importer are always far apart, the goods under the contract have to go a long distance and sometimes change several carriers in transit before they reach the importer. So shipment is very important, which is to keep the transported goods in perfect condition with nothing missing on arrival. After settling the terms of prices, quantity and order, shipment is a very important factor to be discussed between the two parties. Shipment covers rather a wide range of work, such as booking shipping space, chartering ships, making customs declaration, etc.

Besides shipment, the exporter has to give considerable attention to the packaging of the goods to be shipped abroad. It is his duty to pack the goods in accordance with the relevant terms in the sales contract and in a manner, which assures their safe arrival and facilitates their handling in transit and at the place of destination. In order to identify the packages easily en route or at the port of destination, the outer packing must be clearly marked with the identifying symbols and numbers in accordance with the instructions of the customer. These symbols and numbers should strictly conform to those correspondingly stated in the commercial invoice, consular invoice, bill of lading and other shipping documents to prevent the goods from going astray. Generally speaking, there are three principal kinds of marking which may have to be done on export package：shipping marks, supplementary marks, indicative and warning marks.

After a contract is made, it is the main task for the exporter to prepare the goods for shipment and check them against the terms stipulated in the contract. The quality, specifications, quantity, marking and the packaging should be in line with the contract, and the date for the preparation should agree with the shipping schedule.

## Starting Up

**1. Match suitable packages from the right column with the commodities on the left. Then try to translate the packages into Chinese.**

| | | |
|---|---|---|
| ☐ | beer | 1. plastic drums |
| ☐ | cement | 2. bale |
| ☐ | tea | 3. crate |
| ☐ | orange | 4. cask |
| ☐ | acetic acid | 5. tin |
| ☐ | cotton | 6. wooden case |
| ☐ | nails | 7. bag |
| ☐ | machine | 8. carton |

**2. Choose the words in the box on the right and fill in the blanks according to the Chinese meaning given.**

| Shipping_____ | 装船通知 |
| Shipping_____ | 装运代理人 |
| Shipping_____ | 轮船公司 |
| Shipping_____ | 船运集装箱 |
| Shipping_____ | 装船单据 |
| Shipping_____ | 装船要求 |
| Shipping_____ | 装船唛头 |
| Shipping_____ | 装货单 |
| Shipping_____ | 装船仓位 |

company
document
advice
space
mark
order
container
instruction
agent

# A. Packaging Goods

## Dialogue 1 — Outer packing

*Mr. Wang and Mr. Smith are talking about the outer packing for the purchase.*

**Mr. Wang**：So, next, shall we talk about packaging of the goods?

**Mr. Smith**：OK. As an experienced exporter, what do you usually do to package electronic products, I wonder?

**Mr. Wang**： As for the electronic products, such as computers, we usually package each set of them in a polythene wrapper.

**Mr. Smith**：What about the outer packing? It's also important.

**Mr. Wang**：We usually use a special corrugated cardboard box with stenciled shipping marks as outer packing.

**Mr. Smith**：I'm afraid the cardboard boxes are not strong enough for such product.

**Mr. Wang**：Such cardboard boxes are very strong and we also reinforce them with nylon straps.

**Mr. Smith**：You are probably right. But if these goods are to be transshipped during transit, don't you think dampness or rain might spoil the goods?

**Mr. Wang**：Oh, don't worry about it. Besides being packaged in polythene wrapper, each box is lined with waterproof material, which serves as the protective outer packing.

**Mr. Smith**：But will the cardboard boxes be strong enough for long-distance ocean transportation?

**Mr. Wang**：Of course, they will. We recommend you the cardboard boxes because we think they are good enough for such lightweight articles as computers. They are comparatively light and easy to handle. We will have reinforcement measures to make the articles inside safe and sound, like what I mentioned just now.

**Mr. Smith**：Anyway, I'm afraid that the insurance company might refuse compensation in case of damage or pilferage, on the grounds of improper packaging.

**Mr. Wang**：There is no need to worry about that. The boxes are strong enough for sea voyage and possible transshipment. What is more, the boxes have been used extensively for such articles in international trade. The insurance company would have no occasion to refuse compensation on such grounds.

**Mr. Smith**： Well, Mr. Li, if you could guarantee that, we'd be quite willing to accept cardboard boxes.

**Mr. Wang**： Then the problem of packaging is settled.

| | | | |
|---|---|---|---|
| polythene | 聚乙烯 | corrugated | 波纹的，有瓦楞的 |
| stencile | 钢印 | shipping marks | 唛头 |
| reinforce | 加固 | waterproof | 防水的 |
| pilferage | 偷盗 | sea voyage | 海运 |
| safe and sound | 安全，平安无事 | | |
| compensation | 补偿；赔偿金 | | |

## Dialogue 2 – Talking about sales packaging

*Mr. Smith comes to Mr. Chen to discuss the sales packaging of his order.*

**Mr.Smith**： Mr. Chen, I wonder if you could tell me a bit about the packaging of your ladies pajamas.

**Mr. Chen**： Certainly. You know, we have definite ways of packaging garments. For ladies pajamas, we use polythene wrappers, ready for window display. Would you like to have a look at the samples?

**Mr.Smith**： Ah yes. Eye-catching packaging will surely help promote sales. With brisk competition from all sources, we must make the merchandise not only superior in quality but also attractive in appearance.

**Mr. Chen**： That's right. One important function of packaging is to stimulate the buyer's desire to buy. We'll try our best to make your end-users fall in love with the products at first sight. We'll make sure that the pajamas will appeal to the eye as well as to the purse.

**Mr.Smith**： That's good. What about the outer packing?

**Mr. Chen**： They will be packaged 10 dozen to one carton, gross weight around 25 kilos a carton.

**Mr.Smith**： Carton? Wouldn't it be safer to use wooden cases? I'm concerned about the possible jolting, squeezing and collision that may take place when these cartons are moved about. And the dampness or rain may get into them, making the goods spotty.

**Mr. Chen**： Well, cartons are comparatively light and easy to handle. They are not stowed away with heavy cargo, and are always handled with care. All our cartons are lined with plastic sheets, so they're waterproof.

**Mr.Smith**: Well, if you can guarantee compensation from the insurance company, and no risk of a claim being dishonored for faulty packaging, we would be willing to accept cartons.

**Mr. Chen**: I'm sorry, but we can't take on any responsibility that is beyond our control. We'll make sure that the packaging is seaworthy, but we can't commit ourselves to being responsible for every kind of mishap. If you want us to use wooden cases, we can arrange that, but the charge will be much higher.

**Mr.Smith**: OK, I see. I think I can accept cartons.

| | | | |
|---|---|---|---|
| garment | 服装 | eye-catching | 引人注目的 |
| jolt | 颠簸；震荡 | squeeze | 挤压 |
| collision | 碰撞 | mishap | 灾难 |

## Practice

1. You are Mr. Anderson. You are talking with Mr. Wang about packaging fragile goods. You're worried that the cartons are not strong enough for such goods.

2. You sell oolong tea on behalf of Fujian Native Produce & Animal By-product Imp. & Exp. Corp. Now a Japanese businessman has ordered a total of USD 18,000 worth of your oolong tea. He wants to make sure the packaging is absolutely moisture-proof and seaworthy. Tell him the way you package and the material you use.

# B. Making Shipment

## Dialogue 1 – Talking about time of shipment

*Mr. Chen is a Chinese importer of China Machinery Import & Export Corporation. He is talking about a contract of 1,000 pieces of home appliances with a German manufacturer Mr. Schneider. After fixing the other items, Mr. Chen asks to talk about the shipment.*

**Mr. Chen**: Can I suggest that we work on the shipment next?

**Mr. Schneider**: Good. What is your specific transport requirement?

**Mr. Chen**: I just want to have an idea of the modes of your practice.

**Mr. Schneider**: For such a big order, we propose to have the goods dispatched by sea. It is usually cheaper to have the goods sent by sea than by other modes of transportation.

**Mr. Chen：** That's OK. But the most important for me is the time.

**Mr. Schneider：** You needn't worry about the time of shipment. We assure you that shipment will be made no later than September.

**Mr. Chen：** Is it possible for you to make shipment a little earlier? I mean early in October?

**Mr. Schneider：** I'm afraid not. There is only one direct liner from here to China every month. The sailings for October have been booked up. The first steamer available now is the steamer due to sail in September.

**Mr. Chen：** But we are in urgent need of the products, because we are going to sell them on the market before National holiday, which is the good season for this commodity.

**Mr. Schneider：** I see.

**Mr. Chen：** You know, good quality, competitive price, all would mean nothing if goods could not be put on the market on time.

**Mr. Schneider：** That's perfectly right. I understand your position.

**Mr. Chen：** So would you try your best to think of a way out?

**Mr. Schneider：** Let me see. OK, I'll consult our freight forwarder to work out a solution, for example, transshipment or something else. Don't worry; I'll give you an answer this afternoon.

**Mr. Chen：** Thank you very much for your help.

| | | | |
|---|---|---|---|
| liner | 班轮 | steamer | 轮船 |
| freight forwarder | 货运代理人 | transshipment | 转船 |

## Dialogue 2 – Wrong Shipment Time

*Mr. Wang, an exporter of Chinese Garment Company, is meeting an regular customer from Germany, Mr. Guete who is coming for a delayed shipment. The situation is quite unfavorable to Mr. Wang. However, he is trying to make an agreement with great effort.*

**Mr. Guete：** What's wrong with your company recently? Last time you made an early shipment and asked us for help, and we did. And this time you delay the shipment again and again. I am thinking of turning to other suppliers, you know.

**Mr. Wang：** I do owe you an explanation.

**Mr. Guete：** Before we get down to specific details, I'd like to review briefly what happened. I hope you don't mind, Mr. Wang?

**Mr. Wang：** No. As a matter of fact, we'd appreciate your doing so. Maybe we'll able to discover what causes the deviation in our position.

**Mr. Guete：** Thank you very much. Now here's a brief account of the deal: in January 2014, the Chinese exporter agreed to sell to the German importer 2,000 kilos of red tea. The deal was set at $30.50 per kilo CIF Hamburg. And the total value of the deal was $70,000. According to the L/C, shipment should be effected in February; and one provision on the L/C also specifically stipulated that the seller had the right to postpone shipment for up to 15-day period. But unfortunately your company was unable to effect shipment until seven days after the 15-day postpone period. This is basically what happened. Am I correct?

**Mr. Wang：** Not exactly. You didn't mention you've rejected our goods at the port of destination and you want to cancel the deal.

**Mr. Guete：** Under the circumstances, I truly can't accept your delayed goods. You have not acted according to the contract, and that's wrong.

**Mr. Wang：** True. It's our fault that we weren't able to deliver the goods on time. However, I feel that your rejection of our goods is mainly market related.

**Mr. Guete：** May I ask the reason why you say so. This sounds like a serious accusation.

**Mr. Wang：** Both of us are clear that in the past few days the market price for this commodity is declining.

**Mr. Guete：** We definitely can't accept your reasoning. Market related or not, you admit it yourself that it's your own fault that shipment was not effected on time.

**Mr. Wang：** Okay. I know you're in a favorable position and I can't argue with you there. But I'd like to remind you that the market is fluctuating all the time. It may boom tomorrow or the day after tomorrow.

**Mr. Guete：** Is this your reasoning? I am afraid I can't agree with you. We've decided to submit this case to arbitration.

**Mr. Wang：** That's fine. It's your right. However I'd like to ask you what is the optimum result you may get out of the compensation? That can't be too much: it might be a few thousands. Now let me make a proposal, and you'd probably make more money.

**Mr. Guete**：Let's hear it.

**Mr. Wang**：You accept our delayed goods. We make some concessions and give you a 20% reduction on price. That means we close the deal at $56,000 instead of $70,000. What do you think?

**Mr. Guete**：It's a good idea, but your price has to be reduced again to 40%; otherwise we have no deal.

**Mr. Wang**：You really want to make money out of this, eh?

**Mr. Guete**：Not my fault. People learn from mistakes, we often say.

| | | | |
|---|---|---|---|
| deviation | 偏差；误差 | account | 描述 |
| provision | 规定，条款 | port of destination | 目的港 |
| accusation | 控告，指控 | arbitration | 仲裁 |
| submit | 提交 | optimum | 最佳的 |

### Practice

1.  You are a merchant from Europe. You intend to purchase from a Light Industrial Products Imp. & Exp. Corporation 3,000 sets of electric ovens and ask for prompt delivery.

2.  You are a Chinese businessman negotiating with a client from Britain the time of delivery. He has ordered 1,000 sets of your products, and asks you to effect an early shipment to catch the season in Europe. You have only 400 sets on hand, and you will not be able to get the entire order completed in a short period of time. Therefore, you suggest a partial shipment and explain to him the arrangements.

## C. Other Modes of Delivery

### Dialogue 1 － Talking about transportation modes

*Mr. Chen comes to Mr. Smith to discuss the modes of transportation for his order.*

**Mr. Smith**：Now that we've settled the most of the terms of this transaction, it's time to talk about shipment.

**Mr. Chen**：Yes, I've heard that you deliver goods by many kinds of transportation. Would you give me a general idea of the different modes of transportation you usually practice?

**Mr. Smith**：With pleasure. In our trade with overseas businessmen, shipping constitutes the principal mode of international transport. Besides that, air transportation is more and more popular with the technology development.

**Mr. Chen：** What else besides that?

**Mr. Smith：** And we also have international rail and road transport, inland waterway transport and multimodal transport.

**Mr. Chen：** Would you be more specific about multimodal transport?

**Mr. Smith：** Currently, different types of multimodal transport operations involving different combinations are used, for example：sea/air, air/road, rail/road/inland waterways, mini-bridge, land bridge, piggyback and sea train, etc.

**Mr. Smith：** That's really interesting. So when we talk about the shipment of this deal, we will choose a most suitable mode.

**Mr. Chen：** Yes, I agree.

| | | | |
|---|---|---|---|
| inland waterway transport | 内陆水路运输 | piggyback | 背负式运输 |
| multimodal transport | 多式联运 | mini-bridge | 小路桥运输 |

## Dialogue 2 – Negotiating Port of Destination

*Mr. Cheng, a Chinese importer of Chongqing Import & Export Co，is talking about a contract of 8 sets of press machines with an American manufacturer Mr. Smith. After fixing the other items, Mr. Smith asks to talk about the delivery. They focus on the port of destination, which is also a key point in shipment.*

**Mr. Smith：** Just now you said you'd like to have our CFR quotation, named port of destination. Do you have a concrete port of destination in mind?

**Mr. Cheng：** Oh, we hope the port of destination to be made in Chongqing.

**Mr. Smith：** Hope you don't mind my asking you where Chongqing exactly is, since I am not good at geography. Actually I mean whether it's a coastal city or not?

**Mr. Cheng：** Chongqing is a landlocked city located on the bank of Yangzi River.

**Mr. Smith：** Is there any other chance? Because Chongqing is not a coastal city, it is not convenient to ship the goods directly there. What about Shanghai? You know what I can do is to ship your goods to a seaport close to Chongqing.

**Mr. Cheng：** OK. Let's make it at Shanghai.

**Mr. Smith：** Yes, I think it a good idea. And from there you'll be able to ship them by means of cargo liner or some other carriers, since the Yangzi River, as you said, leads all the way up to Chongqing.

**Mr. Cheng**：Good. Let's do it that way. By the way, are you going to ship our machine by a liner or a vessel?

**Mr. Smith**：We'll probably charter a vessel since we have got a lot of machines to be delivered this season to Asian area. It seems that you are worrying about something.

**Mr. Cheng**：You know our end users are in urgent need of these machines. I just hope it won't be delayed owing to some details we have overlooked.

**Mr. Smith**：Take it easy, Mr. Cheng. It's probably because I have told you that we had met some difficulties involved in developing your machines based on your design.

**Mr. Cheng**：As an old friend, I have a lot of respect for you. And by all means please make sure the shipment is on time and no partial shipment.

**Mr. Smith**：Please rest assured that we'll do the very best we can to work out the technical problems we're facing. Trust me. It is also in our interests to have the project completed and shipment effected immediately.

**Mr. Cheng**：OK! I really appreciate this.

**Mr. Smith**：Any more questions?

**Mr. Cheng**：No. Thank you very much, Mr. Smith. You've been very helpful.

| | | | |
|---|---|---|---|
| CFR ( Cost and Freight ) | 成本加运费 | | |
| concrete | 具体的 | landlock | 内陆国或地方 |
| charter | 包租 | vessel | 大型货轮 |
| overlook | 忽视，忽略 | | |

## Practice

Suppose you are having a talk with a Japanese merchant about the time of shipment. He asks you to make shipment in April. The reason is that he wants to catch the seasonal demand for swimming suits on the market in time. Since it takes time to find the right manufacturers locally, you could not promise that. The best you can do is mid-May.

## Language Focus

### Technical Terms

| | |
|---|---|
| inner packing | 内包装 |
| outer packing | 外包装 |
| neutral packing | 中性包装 |
| seaworthy packing | 适于海运的包装 |
| shipping documents | 装运单据 |
| manifest | 舱单 |
| shipper | 托运人 |
| consignor | 发货人 |
| consignee | 收货人 |
| carrier | 承运人 |
| sea waybill | 海运单 |
| air waybill | 空运单 |
| rail waybill | 铁路运单 |
| shipping note | 托运单 |
| delivery order | 提货单 |
| mate's receipt | 大副收据 |
| shipping instruction | 装运须知 |
| shipping advice | 装船通知 |
| freight | 运费 |
| freight rate | 运费率 |
| freight space/shipping space | 舱位 |
| accompanying documents | 随附单据 |
| bill of lading | 提单 |
| ocean bill of lading | 海运提单 |
| clean bill of lading | 清洁提单 |
| shipped on board bill of lading | 已装船提单 |
| freight prepaid | 运费预付 |
| freight paid | 运费已付 |
| freight collect | 运费下付 |
| forward shipment | 远期装运 |
| prompt shipment | 即期装运 |
| prompt delivery | 即期交货 |
| time of shipment | 装运期，装运时间 |
| time of delivery | 交货期 |
| loading port | 装货港 |
| unloading port | 卸货港 |
| port of shipment | 装运港 |

| | |
|---|---|
| port of destination | 目的港 |
| ocean transportation | 海洋运输 |
| liner transportation | 班轮运输 |
| chartering | 租船 |
| container transportation | 集装箱运输 |
| international multimodal transport | 国际多式联运 |
| road transportation | 公路运输 |
| inland water transportation | 内河运输 |
| parcel post transport | 邮政运输 |
| pipeline transportation | 管道运输 |
| partial shipment | 分批装运 |
| transshipment | 转运或转船 |
| Incoterms 2000 | 国际贸易术语解释通则 |

## Functional Expressions

### Packaging

- The cartons are comparatively light, and therefore easy to handle.
- Cartons are quite fit for ocean transportation, and they are extensively used in our shipments.
- Cartons are more convenient to handle in the course of loading and unloading.
- We trust that the goods will reach you in perfect condition.
- We trust the consignment will reach you safely and turn up to your satisfaction.

### Shipment

- We have shipped the goods by S.S. "Shanghai" according to your shipping instructions.
- The goods we ordered are seasonal goods. So it will be better to ship them all at once.
- You can rely on us to complete the delivery of the good within the contractual time of shipment.
- If the shipment can not be made within two months as stipulated, the contract will become void.
- As we are in urgent need of the goods under Order No.105, we have to ask you to speed up shipment.
- Could you do something to advance your shipment?
- After shipment, it will be altogether four to five weeks before the goods can reach our retailers.
- We assure you that shipment will be made no later than the first half of April.
- We'd better have a brief talk about the loading port.
- We are always willing to choose big ports as the loading ports.
- Shall we have a talk on the port of discharge this afternoon?
- Sometimes, we have to make transshipment because there is no suitable loading port in the producing country.

## Role-play

### Task 1

**Student A:** You are Mr. Tong from China, the manager of Machinery Import & Export Co., Ltd. in Chongqing. You are negotiating the shipment of 500 sets of ice cream machine with the exporter. You suggest the expected time for shipment is early in May. As this is seasonal product, you insist that the shipment should be made no later than the end of May.

**Student B:** You are an exporter of ice cream machines from Italy. A Chinese importer, Mr. Tong, is negotiating the shipment of 500 sets of ice cream machine with you. The earliest time for shipment will be in late May.

### Task 2

**Student A:** You are Schoeman from Germany, the manager of Dorst Co., Ltd. (Machinery Manufacturer). You are negotiating the shipment of 500 sets of bakery equipment with a Chinese importer. You agree to make the shipment no later than the end of July. Ask your partner for the port of destination preferred. But your usual practice is to ship to Shanghai.

**Student B:** You are negotiating the shipment of 500 sets of bakery equipment with a German exporter. You expect the shipment to be made no later than the end of July.

### Task 3

**Student A:** You are Jane Smith, a business representative of BEC Company, USA. You are negotiating with Mr. Zhao concerning the containers and materials of packaging, because you are afraid that cartons are not quite sea-worthy. The goods have to be transshipped at Hong Kong and if the boxes are moved about on the open wharf, they may be soaked in the rain.

**Student B:** You are Mr. Zhao, a representative of ABC Company. You are negotiating with Jane Smith concerning the containers and materials of packaging. You assure her that the cartons are strong enough to stand rough handling and lined with plastic sheets to be water-proof.

**Task 4**

**Student A：** You are a British importer and you expect to effect the shipment to London in early November. Unfortunately, the shipping space has been booked up till the end of November. Then you ask about the possibility of tramps. With a view to a timely shipment, you agree to transshipment at Hong Kong.

**Student B：** You are a Chinese exporter. You explain to your client the uncertain factors of tramps. Then you suggest transshipment, and at the same time make clear the possible risks involved and the responsibility of extra expenses.

**Task 5**

**Group work：** Work in groups of 3~4 and talk about：

● features of export packaging

● suitable packaging for ocean transportation

● differences between Shipping Advice and Shipping Instructions

## Discussion

**Topic 1**

What are the proper ways of packaging garments?

**Topic 2**

What is the importance of good packaging in transcontinental trade?

**Topic 3**

What should the exporter consider when discussing the time of shipment in the contract?

**Topic 4**

If you cannot meet the date of delivery required by the customer, how would you deal with the problems?

 Related Information

## Shipment in International Trade

The Shipment Clause is an integral and important part of a contract signed between the importer and the exporter. It involves the time of shipment, the port of loading and the destination, means of conveyance, the shipping documents, etc.

Before shipment, the importer generally sends his shipping requirements to the exporter, informing him in writing of the packing and mark, mode of transportation, etc., which are known as the Shipping Instructions. On the other hand, the exporter usually sends by fax a notice to the importer immediately after the goods are loaded on board the ship, advising him of the shipment, especially under FOB or CFR terms so that the importer will effect insurance on the shipment upon receipt of the notice. Such a notice, known as the Shipping Advice, may include the following: Contract and/or L/C number (s), name of the commodity, number of packages, total quantity shipped, name of the vessel and the sailing date and sometimes even the total value of the goods, as the requirements may be.

Partial shipment is necessary to make shipment in several lots by several carriers sailing on different dates, in case of an export covering a large amount of goods. This is done because of the limitation of shipping space available, poor unloading facilities at the port of destination, dull market season, or possible delay in the process of manufacturing the goods. And this is allowable, only if the clause "Partial Shipment to be allowed" is agreed upon in the contract.

Transshipment in marine transport is the movement of goods in transit from one carrier to another at the ports of transshipment before the goods reach the port of destination. Transshipment is necessary when ships going directly to the port of destination are not available, or the port of destination doesn't lie along the sailing route of the liner, or the amount of cargo for a certain port of destination is so small that no ships would like to call at the port. Transshipment is allowed when the contract has a clause like "Transshipment to be allowed".

| integral | 整体的，必需的 | | conveyance | 运输工具 |

 ## Supplements for Reflections

## 2104 Summer Davos Forum in Tianjin Focuses on Innovation

The 2014 Summer Davos Forum and the 8th Annual Meeting of the New Champions of World Economic Forum kicked off at Meijiang Convention Center, Tianjin, China, on September 10, 2014. More than 1,900 leaders in politics, business and media as well as youth leaders, technology pioneers and young scientists from over 90 countries and regions carried out heated discussions on the forum theme, "Creating Value through Innovation". Innovation has become the hot topic in this Summer Dovos forum.

"There generally are several phases in a country's development experience," said Ian Weightman, Vice President of Technology, Research and Operations of global information company IHS, in an exclusive interview with Guangming Daily. In the first phase, it mainly produces basic materials like, in Indonesia. In the second phase, it develops its manufacturing industry with low labor cost, like the clothing and toy manufacturing industries in China. In the third phase, it develops with technology as its engine, meaning that the whole country is integrated with scientific and technological industries, instead of just applying high technologies, and Japanese is the model of this phase.

Weightman says, as the proportion of manufacturing industry is increasingly reducing and capital and technology is flowing into innovation fields, China is moving forwards the third phase. At the moment, there is an obvious trend that China is putting more and more money into research and development, and it enjoys an unprecedented speed of development as well. There have already been some world renowned enterprises in China, including Huawei and Haier, which are representatives of innovation. He said, "I think, China only needs about ten years to achieve fast progress in high-tech fields and compete with U.S. and Japan at the same level."

Klaus Kleinfeld, Chairman and CEO of Alcoa (Aluminum Company of America) and member of the board of directors of World Economic Forum Fund, stressed the significant role the young play in innovation of industry during the discussion at the sub forum themed "China's business environment in changing world". He said, "As a big country of 1.3 billion, China has many smart people as well as its own entrepreneurial spirit. You can see a large number of Chinese people work at Silicon Valley, the hub of innovation in US West Coast, and they have shown really strong entrepreneurial spirit. So that's to say, Chinese people's spirit of innovation is also at work in U.S." Kleinfeld believes that the secret of Silicon Valley is to let the market make choice and give the young opportunities. If young people are provided with capital, they can put their creativities into practice. Therefore, the core of industry innovation is to provide opportunities of equal competition in the market for private enterprises instead of reforms in state-owned enterprises.

Dong Mingzhu, Chairman of the board of directors of Gree Electric Appliances, INC. of Zhuhai, was voted one of the seven forum supervisors which play an important role in discussions in the Summer Davos forum. During the exclusive interview with Guangming Daily, she says, innovation is a process including innovation of culture, system, management and talent, instead of just technological innovation. Only if an enterprise does well in these innovations can it achieve good result and realize true technological innovation. Dong also says, the most obvious characteristic of her company is independent innovation. Its technologies are invented and created all by itself. As to what to create and invent, they are what consumers truly want but haven't thought of, or even what they really want in the depth of their hearts but dare not to think.

| | | | |
|---|---|---|---|
| Summer Davos Forum | | 夏季达沃斯论坛 | |
| kick off | 开始 | convention | 会议 |
| stress | 强调 | Silicon Valley | 硅谷 |
| entrepreneurial | 企业家的 | | |

## Questions

- When and where was 2014 Summer Davos Forum held?
- Who have taken part in 2014 Summer Davos Forum?
- What is the core of industry innovation according to Klaus Kleinfeld, Chairman and CEO of Alcoa?

# $U\,n\,i\,t$ 12

# Payment

## Learning Objectives

**In this unit, you will learn how to:**

- Understand and talk about basic modes of payment in international trade
- Talk about and negotiate L/C and collection
- Persuade the other party to agree to a specific payment mode

## Background Information

In international trade, how and when a seller can get the payment for the goods sold is a key problem that concerns him most, and, particularly in foreign trade, an exporter has to secure payment from an importer who may live on the other side of the globe. This evidently enhances the uncertainty of the payment, as trading with other countries is not the same as trading within one's own country. At home a company or a bank is familiar with people, laws, and business practices of its own, country, where as abroad the picture becomes a complex one. Each country is different and therefore is said to carry different risks. Trading abroad is a risk because the exporter usually does not know the importer.

To guarantee the punctual delivery on the part of the exporter and payment by the importer, different modes of payment have been created. Modes of payment may be on a "cash with order" basis, on open account, by remittance, by irrevocable letter of credit or by bill of exchange. Exporters and importers often prefer the security of payment by confirmed irrevocable letter of credit when dealing with unfamiliar firms in distant countries.

Where and when the payment is to be made depends largely on the political and economic situations of the countries in question and the relationship between sellers and buyers.

## Starting Up

**1. Choose the words in the box on the right and fill in the blanks according to the Chinese meaning given.**

| | |
|---|---|
| _____ L/C 可撤销信用证 | transferable |
| _____ L/C 不可撤销信用证 | revocable |
| _____ L/C 保兑信用证 | sight |
| _____ L/C 不保兑信用证 | divisible |
| _____ L/C 即期信用证 | revolving |
| _____ L/C 远期信用证 | irrevocable |
| _____ L/C 可转让信用证 | time |
| _____ L/C 可分割信用证 | unconfirmed |
| _____ L/C 循环信用证 | confirmed |

**2. Match the English abbreviations with the corresponding Chinese translations. The first one has been done for you.**

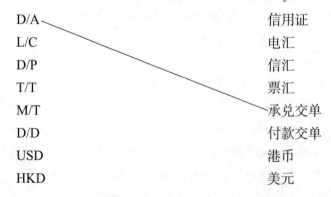

| | |
|---|---|
| D/A | 信用证 |
| L/C | 电汇 |
| D/P | 信汇 |
| T/T | 票汇 |
| M/T | 承兑交单 |
| D/D | 付款交单 |
| USD | 港币 |
| HKD | 美元 |

## A. Making a Payment

### Dialogue 1 – Talking about Terms of Payment

*After fixing the other items of the contract, Mr. Schoeman, an agent of a German manufacturer of hard wares is now talking about the payment with the Chinese importer Mr. Cheng.*

**Mr. Cheng:** Shall we pay by D/A for our imports?

**Mr. Schoeman:** I am afraid you can't. We always require L/C for our exports.

**Mr. Cheng:** You know, this time our order is large in sizes. It's expensive to open an L/C because we need to put a deposit in the bank.

**Mr. Schoeman:** Generally, we only accept payment by confirmed and irrevocable letter of credit payable against shipping document.

**Mr. Cheng:** Could you make an exception and accept D/A or D/P this time?

**Mr. Schoeman:** I am sorry, Mr. Chen. Presently, the situation on the international money market is not stable. To be on safe side, we insist on a letter of credit.

**Mr. Cheng:** Is the credit at sight or after sight?

**Mr. Schoeman:** I agree to use letter of credit after sight. To do so, you won't have your funds tied up.

**Mr. Cheng:** What is your time expectation for this L/C then?

**Mr. Schoeman:** When can you arrange under the new import license?

**Mr. Cheng:** How about an L/C 90 days?

**Mr. Schoeman:** It's OK. Please open the letter of credit in good time, and please make sure that the L/C could reach us a month before the date of delivery.

**Mr. Cheng:** Is the wording of "confirmed" necessary for the letter of credit?

**Mr. Schoeman:** Yes. For payment we require 100% value, confirmed and irrevocable L/C in our favor with partial shipment allowed clause available by draft at sight.

**Mr. Cheng:** Alright, Mr. Scheoman. I understand your situation since this is the first transaction that we have made. I just hope you could offer us a favorable term next time.

**Mr. Schoeman:** Thanks a lot. I'm sure we will cooperate very well in the future.

| confirmed | 保兑的 | irrevocable | 不可撤销的 |
| exception | 例外，破例 | import license | 进口许可证 |
| favorable | 优惠的 | | |

## Dialogue 2 – Insisting on payment by L/C

*Mr. Zhang and Mr. Baker are talking about the terms of payment. As a seller, Mr. Zhang insists on payment by L/C.*

**Mr. Baker：** Well. I'm glad to say that we've settled the price, quality and quantity of the transaction. Now, what about the terms of payment? What terms of payment do you usually accept?

**Mr. Zhang：** We only accept payment by confirmed, irrevocable letter of credit available against presentation of shipping documents. This is the normal terms of payment in international business.

**Mr. Baker：** But I heard you would accept different kinds of payment such as D/A or D/P.

**Mr. Zhang：** Yes, we can accept other modes of payment only when the transaction involves very small amount.

**Mr. Baker：** As this is the first transaction, could you kindly make easier payment terms and accept D/A?

**Mr. Zhang：** Sorry. Since payment by L/C is our usual practice with all customers for such goods, especially with our new customers, I'm afraid I can't grant your request here. As a matter of fact, L/C protects the seller as well as the buyer.

**Mr. Baker：** What about D/P at sight, then?

**Mr. Zhang：** Perhaps we shall consider it at a proper time in the future. But so far, we haven't known much about each other's credit status. So I'm afraid we have to insist on our usual terms. You know, the mode of payment must suit specific circumstances.

**Mr. Baker：** To tell you frankly, when I open a letter of credit, I have to pay a deposit and that will tie up my funds and add to the cost of my imports, especially for such a large order.

**Mr. Zhang：** Consult your bank and see if they can reduce the required deposit to a minimum.

**Mr. Baker：** Still, there will be certain bank charges. It would help me greatly if you would accept D/A or D/P. It makes no great difference to you, but it does to me. Could you be a bit more flexible and bend the rules a little? What do you say to 50% by L/C and the balance by D/P?

**Mr. Zhang**：I'm awfully sorry we cannot promise you even that. As I've said, we do require payment by L/C.

**Mr. Baker**：Well, since there is no other alternative, I think I'll have to arrange for the opening of the L/C as soon as I get home. I hope the goods can be dispatched immediately after you get the L/C.

**Mr. Zhang**：You may be assured of that. We'll book your order and do the preparations right away.

| grant | 允许，同意 | credit status | 信用状况 |
| --- | --- | --- | --- |

### Practice

Suppose you are a Chinese exporter of mini fridges. Considering the size of the order and long-term cooperation, you finally agree to 50% by L/C and the rest by D/P as the British buyer insists. You need to make clear to the buyer the process and procedures of such terms of payment.

## B. Making Payment by Collection

### Dialogue 1 – Payment by D/P

*Miss. Grey and Mr. Shen are having a hot negotiation on payment terms and finally they are about to conclude the business deal.*

**Ms. Grey**：You see, Mr. Shen, the world market has been rather dull recently and we may easily get more favorable terms elsewhere. So we'd like to use D/A this time.

**Mr. Shen**：I'm afraid we cannot accept D/A. That may cause a lot of inconvenience to us. As you know, the international monetary market is unstable; therefore, we find it necessary to handle our business on L/C basis, at least for the time being.

**Ms. Grey**：But you know, opening an L/C is quite costly and will tie up the capital of our company. We do have a cash flow problem this year. What's more, I'm your old customer and we have been cooperating well for years. I hope you can accommodate us in this instance.

**Mr. Shen：** But it is only under very special circumstances that we agree to other payment terms.

**Ms. Grey：** Ours is not a normal case, is it? It is under special circumstances and in the nature of sample order. It doesn't pay to adopt L/C terms for an order as small as ours. The limited profit, if any, is not even enough to cover the bank charges.

**Mr. Shen：** Mmm…well, in order to finalize the business, we exceptionally make a concession and accept your payment by D/P sight, but that's not our normal practice.

**Ms. Grey：** Thank you for your consideration. But still it is not good enough. You know I'm a middleman. I need some time to find a reliable client after I receive your bill. It would help me a lot if D/P after sight is accepted, even 60 days will be enough.

**Mr. Shen：** I'm afraid no further concession can be made. It is just to facilitate your doing business that we make this concession. You can't be better placed elsewhere, can you?

**Ms. Grey：** Well, it seems I have to take things as they are. Let's proceed to contract.

**Mr. Shen：** Ms. Grey, I should mention that we accept such terms only once. It's not our normal practice. When the goods are dispatched, we'll issue a sight draft against you, which will be sent together with the shipping documents through our remitting bank to the collecting bank at your end. The condition of the deal is that you are to honor it on presentation.

**Ms. Grey：** You may rest assured that this documentary draft will be duly honored on presentation.

| | | | |
|---|---|---|---|
| dull | 低迷的 | make a concession | 让步 |
| facilitate | 使便利 | honor draft | 兑付汇票 |
| duly | 如期地 | pay | 值得；回报 |
| accommodate | 照顾；迁就 | | |
| D/P(Documents against payment) | | 付款交单 | |
| D/A(Documents against acceptance) | | 承兑交单 | |

### Dialogue 2 – Payment by D/P after sight

*Mr. Black asks for D/P after sight, a mode of payment that is easier for an importer.*

**Mr. Black**：Hello, Mr. Wang, I've come to continue the topic we've discussed yesterday, about the payment.

**Mr. Wang**：Good morning, Mr. Black. What do you have in mind?

**Mr. Black**：Because of the size of the order that we're placing, we'll need 60 days to pay for it instead of 30 days.

**Mr. Wang**：Can you give me some assurance that your company has sufficient financial resources to draw on?

**Mr. Black**：What kind of assurance do you need?

**Mr. Wang**：Could you provide some credit references and perhaps a letter from your bank?

**Mr. Black**：Sure, if that could help. So, can I count on 60 days if I provide you with all you need on our financial position?

**Mr. Wang**：If your credit rating is acceptable, we can consider you proposal.

| | | | |
|---|---|---|---|
| assurance | 保证；担保 | draw on | 动用 |
| credit rating | 信用等级；信誉评价 | | |

### Practice

A customer asks for payment by D/P as he thinks it is costly to open an L/C. You insist on payment by L/C as it is your usual practice. You try to persuade him/her to accept payment by L/C.

## C. Making Payment through Other Payment Modes

### Dialogue 1 – Making payment in installments

*Mr. Clerk, the buyer, is persuading Ms. Lin to carry on this transaction on the basis of installment.*

**Mr. Clerk**：We would like to make our payment for this complete set of equipment by installments. You know, "payment by installments" is one of the terms of payment that has been widely accepted and often used. It's not out of step with usually practice in international trade. We should adopt payment by installments for some special import items.

**Ms. Lin**：With an eye to future business, we'll accept payment by installments this time. But first of all, may I ask what kind of installment payment you have in mind? Would you explain specifically your proposition about the terms of payment?

**Mr. Clerk**：What we'd like to do is that the payment be divided into four installments in accordance with the progress of the project installation.

**Ms. Lin**：Sorry, I'm afraid I can't agree with you there. You must understand that the progress of manufacture requires a large sum of money and a long time. And we'd like to have our money returned as early as possible. So a down payment is absolutely indispensable. In fact, advance payment is standard practice for international trade.

**Mr. Clerk**：Okay, I agree to make a down payment first. But how much is it?

**Ms. Lin**：20% of the total value.

**Mr. Clerk**：That's too much. We'd have to pay much more interest. I'll only pay 10%, and I'm not prepared to give in.

**Ms. Lin**：All right. To help make this transaction possible, I accept. But your payment will be spread over 4 installments, which is really too long a period for us to finance.

**Mr. Clerk**：What's your proposal then?

**Ms. Lin**：We suggest you divide the payment into two installments. You first make a down payment, which is 10% of the total value, and then pay off 50% of the total sum upon delivery and the remaining 40% after final acceptance.

**Mr. Clerk**：Well, in order to close the deal, I agree to your proposal.

| installment | 分期付款 | with an eye to | 着眼于 |
| installation | 安装 | down payment | 首次付款 |
| advance payment | 预付款 | | |

## Dialogue 2 – Asking for easier payment terms

*Mr. Chang is an owner of a newly established company. He decides to start his business by importing 100 metric tons of canned cod from Russia to China. Now he is meeting a guest from Russia, Mr. Tarasov talking about the terms of payment of the deal. In order not to have his funds tied up, he is making great effort to ask for more favorable payment terms.*

**Mr. Tarasov**：Mr. Chang, I'm glad that we have settled the quality, quantity and price of the transaction. Now, let's come to the terms of payment. What kind of terms of payment do you usually adopt?

**Mr. Chang:** For us it's better to adopt D/A.

**Mr. Tarasov:** Oh, it sounds not so good to us —— You see, you are a new customer, accepting D/A is a risk to us. In most cases we just require payment by L/C.

**Mr. Chang:** A letter of credit would increase the cost of my import. There will be bank charges in connection with the credit. We will have to pay too much for such a letter of credit arrangement.

**Mr. Tarasov:** You know that payment by irrevocable L/C in our favor available by draft at sight is our usual practice. And it is universally adopted in international trade.

**Mr. Chang:** Are there any alternatives? I've heard you would accept different kinds of payment such as D/P or D/A?

**Mr. Tarasov:** Yes, occasionally we do. But it is only under very special circumstances. You must be aware that an irrevocable L/C gives the exporter the additional protection of banker's guarantee.

**Mr. Chang:** I certainly know, but my company is a newly established one, and this transaction is my first deal. Opening a letter of credit will not only increase our cost but also tie up our funds. It would help us greatly if you would accept D/A.

**Mr. Tarasov:** You see, Mr. Chang, just as you have said that you are a new company and D/A offers no protection for the exporter, with this term, whether I can get my money back or not depends entirely on your responsibility. I just can't imagine what situation would be like if you could not sell all these merchandise.

**Mr. Chang:** You should know, Mr. Tarasov, China is a big market. Even if only a small portion of Chinese people like your products, it would be a big amount. I have, moreover, offered some of your samples to some of my friends and relatives, and they like them very much. I have gained confidence in your products. Don't you have confidence in your own products?

**Mr. Tarasov:** I certainly have. I just have no confidence in you and an unknown market (half jokingly).

**Mr. Chang:** OK. Let me make you place confidence in me. You could think this way: This time our order is small and just for a trial sale. Even if I lose money and cannot pay you, it is just a small amount which can be counted as expenditure of promoting products. I actually introduce your product to Chinese market. If, however, the market is good, I will certainly place a large order subsequently because I am a business man. And you may ask for a payment of L/C then.

**Mr. Tarasov**：You are quite persuasive. Let me think about it.

**Mr. Chang**：Could you kindly make easier payment terms or simply accept D/A in our case?

**Mr. Tarasov**：What do you say to 50% by L/C and the balance by D/A?

**Mr. Chang**：Don't you think it is a little troublesome by doing so with only 100 metric tons? Mr. Tarasov, you know quite well that our actual deal price is very competitive and your goods will sell well in our market. I am sure I shall have no difficulty in establishing the market.

**Mr. Tarasov**：OK. I determined to take the risk.

**Mr. Chang**：I really appreciate your way of doing business.

**Mr. Tarasov**：I am looking forward to a big Chinese market.

| | | | |
|---|---|---|---|
| alternative | 选择 | guarantee | 保证；担保 |
| be counted as | 被看作 | expenditure | 支出 |
| subsequently | 随后 | balance | 剩余部分 |

### Practice

You represent Suzhou Arts & Crafts Imp. & Exp. Corp. which sells paper umbrellas. An American businessman has ordered a total of USD 20,000 worth of your products. Since he is an old customer, you agree to grant him easier payment terms.

 Language Focus

### Technical Terms

| | |
|---|---|
| payment by L/C | 凭信用证支付 |
| remittance | 汇款 |
| M/T mail transfer | 信汇 |
| T/T telegraphic transfer | 电汇 |
| D/D demand draft | 票汇 |

| | |
|---|---|
| open account | 赊账交易 |
| payment on delivery | 货到付款 |
| payment in advance | 预付 |
| collection | 托收 |
| D/P = Documents against Payment | 付款交单 |
| D/A = Documents against Acceptance | 承兑交单 |
| D/P at 60 days' sight | 60 天远期付款交单 |
| D/P at sight | 即期付款交单 |
| bill of exchange | 汇票 |
| drawer | 出票人 |
| drawee | 受票人 |
| clean collection | 光票托收 |
| documentary collection | 跟单托收 |
| commercial invoice | 商业发票 |
| L/C at sight, sight LC | 即期信用证 |
| time L/C | 远期信用证 |
| documentary L/C | 跟单信用证 |
| irrevocable L/C | 不可撤销的信用证 |
| transferable L/C | 可转让信用证 |
| divisible L/C | 可分割的信用证 |
| confirmed L/C | 保兑信用证 |
| standby L/C | 备用信用证 |
| payment by installments | 分期付款 |
| deferred payment | 延期付款 |
| to issue/open/establish an L/C | 开立信用证 |
| applicant | 开证申请人 |
| beneficiary | 受益人 |
| opening bank/issuing bank | 开证行 |
| advising bank/notifying bank | 通知行 |
| negotiating bank | 议付行 |
| confirming bank | 保兑行 |
| paying bank | 付款行 |
| payer | 付款人 |
| payee | 受款人 |

## Functional Expressions

| Payment by L/C |
|---|
| • For payment, we require confirmed and irrevocable L/C with partial shipments and transshipment allowed. |

- As agreed, the terms of payment for the above order are letters of credit at 60 days' sight.
- Considering that you're an old client of ours, we can let you make the payment by usance L/C.
- If you do not open the L/C in time, you will be responsible for any loss resulting from the delay.
- Payment by irrevocable letter of credit is convenient for us and we shall draw a 60d/s bill in your bank.
- Please note that this credit is available against Documentary Draft at 60 days' sight.

## Collection

- If you agree to accept D/P, we could compromise on other terms.
- The total amount mush be paid in full upon receipt of the shipping documents.
- The buyer shall duly accept the documentary draft drawn by the sellers at 45 days' sight upon first presentation and make payment on its maturity.
- The shipping documents are to be delivered against acceptance.
- We require full payment within 45 days with a 15% discount for cash payment in advance.
- Kindly send us 2 Bills of Lading by separate posts, together with your draft at 30 days for acceptance.

## Remittance

The buyer shall pay 100% of the sales proceeds in advance by T/T to reach the seller no later than October 10, 2009.

## Payment by Installments

- We would like to make our payment for this complete set of equipment by installment.
- Payment by installments is one of the terms of payment that has been widely accepted and often used.
- We should adopt payment by installments for some special import items.
- You will have to pay $5,000 as a down payment.
- Advance payment of 25% of the contract value shall be paid within 30 days after the date of signing the contract.
- We would like to adopt the terms of payment by installments for our present transaction.

 Extended Activities

# Role-play

## Task 1

**Student A:** You are Mr. Clive, a businessman from England. You are in negotiation with your supplier about a certain business. Everything has been going on quite well except for payment. You insist on D/P terms.

**Student B:** You are a manufacturer. You are now receiving an important client from England. You've agreed on most items, but he insists on D/P terms. After a heated discussion, you finally accept his proposal as his order is quite a big one.

## Task 2

**Student A:** You are having a talk with Mr. King over payment terms. Mr. King wants to pay by D/A, but you insist on L/C at sight because an L/C protects the seller as well as the buyer's interest.

**Student B:** You are Mr. King. You want to make the payment by D/A, but your supplier insists on L/C. In the end, you agree to pay by L/C.

## Task 3

**Student A:** You are Mr. King. You placed an order a long time ago, but you have not made any preparation. Now the supplier is making a call, urging you to open the relative L/C as soon as possible.

**Student B:** You are a supplier. The goods ordered by Mr. King have been ready for shipment for quite a long time, but you have not received any updates from Mr. King. Now, you are calling Mr. King, urging him to open the relative L/C as soon as possible.

## Task 4

**Student A:** You are Mr. White. As the world market has been rather dull recently, you would like to pay by D/A. Finally you agree on payment of 50% of the total value by D/A and the balance by L/C.

**Student B:** You are Mr. Lee. Your client would like to make a payment by D/A because of a weak market. However, you are not willing to accept his proposal and insist on payment by L/C because payment by L/C is your usual practice with all customers.

**Task 5**

**Student A:** You are Mr. Wood. As an old customer, you ask for an easier payment mode, i.e., when the goods purchased are ready for shipment and freight space booked he will remit the full amount by T/T.

**Student B:** You are a supplier. After long years of pleasant business relations, your client thinks he is entitled to easier payment terms. You make clear that you will consider his proposal.

## Discussion

### Topic 1

In your opinion, what is the best payment mode? Why?

### Topic 2

What are the differences between documentary collection and L/C?

### Topic 3

In what way will an irrevocable L/C protect the seller's interest?

### Topic 4

What are the main differences between D/P and D/A?

 Related Information

## Terms of Payment

### Remittance

Remittance refers to a bank (the remitting bank), at the request of its customer (the remitter), transfers a certain sum of money to its overseas branch or correspondent bank (the paying/receiving bank), instructing it to pay to a named person (the payee/beneficiary) domiciled in that country. Remittance has found its applications in payment in advance and open account.

| beneficiary | 受益人 | domicile | 居住 |

## Payment in Advance

In "payment in advance" method, the entire risk is put on the importer. Under this term of purchase, the importer makes full payment to the supplier before the shipment of goods is done. The importer trusts the supplier that the shipment of the product will be on time and the goods will be as same as advertised. This method of payment generally takes place under the following circumstances:

- If the importer has not been long established.
- If the credit status of the importer is doubtful, unsatisfactory and/or the political and economic risks of the country are very high.
- If the product is in high demand and the seller does not have to accommodate the importer's financing request in order to sell the product.

This method of payment does not involve any commercial bank and is therefore inexpensive. But the buyer faces high payment risk as he can do nothing if the seller sends poor quality goods or incorrect or incomplete documentation.

| commercial bank | 商业银行 |
|---|---|

## Open Account Payment

This method allows the importer to make payments to the exporter on some specific date in the future without issuing any negotiable instrument, only evidencing his legal commitment to pay at the committed time. Usually, this method takes place when either the importer has a strong credit history or is well-known to the seller.

This mechanism cannot offer the seller any protection in case of non-payment. However, the exporter can structure this sale to minimize the risk of non-payment. He can reduce the repayment period and can retain title to the goods until the payment is made.

Though all the risks but still open account payment is more prevailing in the international trade, those exporters who offer such terms are increasingly obtaining credit insurance to mitigate the potential open account credit risks.

| mechanism | 机制 | prevailing | 普遍的 |
|---|---|---|---|
| mitigate | 减少 | | |

## Documentary Collections

This term of payment offers an important bank payment mechanism. It serves the need of both, the exporter as well as the importer. In this mode of payment, the sale transaction is settled by the bank through an exchange of documents. Hence, it enables the payment and transfer of title simultaneously.

> simultaneously    同时地

### Documentary Credits/Letter of Credit

It is a credit instrument like letter of credit or back-to-back letter of credit. In this mode of payment, the buyer's bank undertakes to pay the seller when the terms and conditions have been met. The bank issues documentary credits to a customer according to his credit worthiness. Documentary credits are subject to the international rules, *Uniform Customs and Practice* ( *UCP 500* ) .

 Supplements for Reflections

## China endeavors to boost world economy in 2014

Although China's GDP growth for the past year is likely to slow to around 7.5 percent, its contribution to global and Asian economic growth still accounts for 27.8 percent and 50 percent respectively, according to estimates of the International Monetary Fund.

"China's economic growth has become more stable and been driven by more diverse forces," Chinese President Xi Jinping told at Asia-Pacific Economic Cooperation (APEC) CEO summit in November.

Even a growth rate of around 7 percent would place the Chinese economy among the top in the world in both speed and increment, Xi said, adding that all major economic indicators of the country are "within the reasonable range."

In face of potential economic risks, China has been advancing a new type of industrialization, IT application, urbanization and agricultural modernization in a coordinated way.

| | | | |
|---|---|---|---|
| increment | 增量 | indicator | 指标 |
| urbanization | 城镇化 | coordinated | 协调的 |
| bilateral | 双边的 | substantive | 实质性的 |

## Free Trade Area strategy

In November, China signed a declaration of intent on practically concluding bilateral negotiations on a free trade agreement with Australia, shortly after concluding substantive FTA talks with South Korea.

On Nov. 11, APEC members vowed to kick off and advance the process of the Free Trade Area of the Asia-Pacific, an initiative strongly supported by China and will add $2.4 trillion of output to the global economy.

Multilateral trade systems and regional trade arrangements have always been the driving force behind economic globalization, Xi added.

driving force　　驱动力

## Silk Road Fund

China has been vigorously promoting regional and international connectivity with a series of proposals including the "Silk Road Economic Belt" and the "21st Century Maritime Silk Road" initiatives. These multilateral economic cooperation blueprints are aimed at further facilitating trade and investment in the region and contributing to a more open global economy.

On Nov. 8, China announced a contribution of $40 billion to a Silk Road Fund.

Xi said the new Silk Road Fund will be used to provide investment and financing support for infrastructure, resources, industrial cooperation, financial cooperation and other projects related to connectivity for countries along the "Belt and Road."

vigorously　　大力地　　　　　　　　connectivity　　连接

## Asian Infrastructure Investment Bank

On Oct. 24, up to 21 Asian countries signed a Memorandum of Understanding on establishing the Asian Infrastructure Investment Bank (AIIB), an initiative proposed by Xi in a bid to finance infrastructure projects across Asia.

"China will firmly stick to the opening-up strategy for win-win reciprocity," Xi said. "The establishment of the AIIB will help improve global financial governance, which is very meaningful."

The AIIB should focus on boosting infrastructure inter-connectivity and economic cooperation in the region to inject new momentum into economic development in Asia, Xi added.

| | | | |
|---|---|---|---|
| in a bid to | 为了 | reciprocity | 互惠 |

### Financial opening–up

The Shanghai-Hong Kong Stock Connect was launched on Nov. 17 to give overseas investors easier access to Shanghai-listed shares, a substantial step forward for the internationalization of the Chinese currency, RMB, and opening-up of the capital market of the Chinese mainland.

On April 10, Premier Li Keqiang told a forum that China will carry out a new round of opening-up at a high level.

China will continue to raise the level and quality of opening-up through deeper integration with the international market, he said.

### Questions

● According to the estimates of the International Monetary Fund, what role does China play in the global and Asian economic growth?

● What is the purpose of the new Silk Road Fund?

● What aspects will the AIIB focus on?

# Unit 13

# Insurance

 Learning Objectives

**In this unit, you will learn how to:**

- Talk about types of insurance
- Choose insurance coverage against certain risks
- Talk about insurance premium and coverage

## Background Information

Insurance is a key issue in international trade. The transportation of goods from the seller to the buyer generally covers a long distance and it has to go through the procedures of transit, loading and unloading, storage, etc. These goods, both being imported and exported, are subject to damage or loss. So it is customary to insure the goods against risks of collision, leakage, pilferage, fire or storm, etc.

Insurance is therefore an indispensable part to the import and export practice. So the contracting parties should make clear in a contract as to who will cover the insurance and bear the expenses and what risks should be covered according to the nature of the goods.

In our country, the People's Insurance Company of China underwrites all kinds of transportation insurance. As ocean shipping constitutes the majority of the value of goods transported in international trade, the Ocean Marine Cargo Clauses are the most important ones of the China Insurance Clauses of the said company.

Ocean Marine Cargo Insurance is classified into three forms: Free from

Particular Average (F.P.A.), With Particular Average (W.P.A.) and All Risks. In addition to the three forms mentioned above, there are some additional risks, which are also coverable and classified into two forms. They are General Additional Risks and Special Additional Risks. In case of F.P.A. or W.P.A., one or several kinds of additional risks may be covered in addition.

## Starting Up

**1. Choose the words in the box on the right and fill in the blanks according to the Chinese meaning given.**

| | | |
|---|---|---|
| insurance _____ | 保险条款 | order |
| invoice _____ | 发票金额 | coverage |
| insurance _____ | 保险责任范围 | value |
| insurance _____ | 保险单 | premium |
| insurance _____ | 保险费用 | clause/terms |
| insurance _____ | 货物检查单 | undertaker |
| insurance _____ | 保险承保人 | cover |
| insurance _____ | 保险类别 | policy |

**2. Write down the Chinese equivalents of the following words and expressions.**

Ocean Marine Cargo Clause

PICC (People's Insurance Company of China)

T.P.N.D (Theft, Pilferage & Non-Delivery Risks)

Fresh and/or Rain Water Damage Risks

F.P.A (Free from Particular Average)

W.P.A (With Particular Average)

Shortage Risk

Breakage of Packaging Risk

Leakage Risk (Risk of Leakage)

Cargo Insurance

All Risks

Extraneous Risks

Additional Risks

Basic Risks

 Oral Workshop

## A. Getting to Know Insurance

### Dialogue 1 – Learning about insurance

*Mr. Wang is paying a visit to an insurance company to get to know types of insurance. Miss Liu, the receptionist, is receiving him.*

**Miss. Liu:** What can I do for you?

**Mr. Wang:** It is said that your insurance company is trustworthy.

**Miss. Liu:** You are right. Our company can cover all basic risks such as F.P.A., W.P.A., All Risks and other additional risks. And we have agents all over the world.

**Mr. Wang:** I must admit I'm a layman as far as insurance is concerned. Does All Risks really cover all types of risks?

**Miss. Liu:** No. All Risks is actually the most comprehensive basic coverage. Aside from the risks covered under the F.P.A. and W.P.A. conditions, this insurance also covers all risks of loss or of damage to the insured goods whether partial or total, arising from external causes in the course of transit.

**Mr. Wang:** Now I see. And what is the difference between F.P.A. and W.P.A.?

**Miss. Liu:** F.P.A. provides coverage only for total loss of cargo together with ship or aircraft and general average. It means no partial loss or damage is recoverable, which is the minimum coverage and offers limited protection. Aside from the risks covered under F.P.A. conditions as above, W.P.A. also covers partial losses of the insured goods caused by natural calamities, such as heavy weather, lightening, tsunami, earthquake and/or flood.

**Mr. Wang:** That means W.P.A. insurance covers more risks than F.P.A. Then can I present a claim with the insurance company if the goods are damaged in the process of transportation?

**Miss. Liu:** It depends on whether you have taken out the certain sorts of insurance policy.

**Mr. Wang:** Thanks a lot for your help.

**Miss. Liu**：You're welcome. If you need further help, please feel free to contact me.

| | | | |
|---|---|---|---|
| general average | 共同海损 | partial loss | 单独海损 |
| F.P.A. | 平安险 | W.P.A. | 水渍险 |
| natural calamities | 自然灾害 | | |

## B. Talking about Insurance Practice

### Dialogue 1 – Talking about usual practice of insurance

*Mr. Wang is having a meeting with Mr. Smith, discussing the insurance stipulations.*

**Mr. Smith**：Your quotation is on CIF basis. How do you cover insurance?

**Mr. Wang**：We always insure our goods with the People's Insurance Company of China as per their Ocean Marine Cargo Clauses.

**Mr. Smith**：I have to say that I know very little about that. Could you be more specific?

**Mr. Wang**：OK. The Ocean Marine Cargo Clauses provide coverage of three basic risks, some additional risks and some special additional risks. The three basic risks are Free from Particular Average, With Particular Average and All Risks.

**Mr. Smith**：What do they mean respectively?

**Mr. Wang**：Well, roughly speaking, F.P.A. covers total losses resulting from both natural calamities and accidents, and partial losses caused by accidents.

**Mr. Smith**：What about W.P.A.?

**Mr. Wang**：W.P.A. has a broader coverage. It covers everything in F.P.A. plus partial losses caused by natural calamities.

**Mr. Smith**：And All Risks?

**Mr. Wang**：All risks provides wider coverage than FPA and WPA.

**Mr. Smith**：I see. Now, for this particular article, what risks do you usually cover?

**Mr. Wang**：We usually insure the goods against All Risks for 110% of the invoice value.

**Mr. Smith**：Does All Risks include War Risk?

**Mr. Wang**：No. War Risk is special additional risk, and it has to be arranged separately.

**Mr. Smith**：But judging from the recent situation in the Middle East, I think War Risk should be covered.

**Mr. Wang**：We can certainly do this, but it is subject to an additional premium, because our CIF quotation doesn't include this risk.

**Mr. Smith**：Additional premium? That's not a problem. There's no harm in doing things on the safe side.

**Mr. Wang**：Then we will cover War Risk for you.

**Mr. Smith**：Good.

| | | | |
|---|---|---|---|
| People's Insurance Company of China | | 中国人民保险公司 | |
| Ocean Marine Cargo Clauses | | 海洋运输货物保险条款 | |
| invoice value | 发票金额 | War Risk | 战争险 |
| as per | 依据；按照 | | |

## Dialogue 2 – Talking about additional risks

*Mr. Clerk, a buyer, is negotiating additional risks with Mr. Han.*

**Mr. Clerk**：Mr. Han, this time our clients want to buy on a CIF Marseilles basis. This will save us the trouble of going to our underwriters to cover insurance by ourselves.

**Mr. Han**：You said it. The People's Insurance Company of China can offer good services. The PICC at present maintains hundreds of cargo surveying and claim-settling agents in about 100 countries and regions, to conduct on-the-spot surveys. Most of the agents are authorized to effect settlement locally. If any damage occurs, you may file a claim with the local insurance agent within 60 days after the arrival of the goods. Of course, claims should be supported by survey reports. Then the PICC will undertake to compensate you for the loss according to the risks insured.

**Mr. Clerk**：These are attractive provisions. Then how is the rate of premium?

**Mr. Han**：Our insurance rates are much more favorable than those of our competitors.

**Mr. Clerk**：Good. Mr. Han, I presume W.P.A and War Risk are general clauses of marine insurance that PICC underwrites.

**Mr. Han**：Well, Mr. Marceline, the PICC can cover all basic risks as required so long as it is stipulated in the Ocean Marine Cargo Clauses of the PICC.

**Mr. Clerk**：Then do you cover risks other than WPA and War Risk?

**Mr. Han**：Certainly. Risks such as Leakage, Fresh and Rain Water Damage, Hook

Damage, Clashing, TPND and so on are offered.

**Mr. Clerk**： I suppose they are classified under additional risks.

**Mr. Han**： Yes. OK, then let's talk about what risks should be covered in this transaction.

| | |
|---|---|
| underwriter | 保险公司 |
| Clashing Risk 碰损险 | Hook Damage Risk 钩损险 |
| Fresh and/or Rain Water Damage Risk | 淡水雨淋险 |
| TPND (Theft, Pilferage and Non-Delivery) | 偷窃，提货不着险 |

### Practice

1. You are Mr. Martin, an importer from USA. You are going to purchase Chinese dinnerware on CIF basis. Talk with Mr. Li about covering insurance on the goods with PICC.

2. You are a buyer of 1,000 garments and you learn that your Chinese customer only wants to insure W.P.A. for the goods. Talk to your customer and persuade him/her to add Strike Risk. Work out the problem with your partner according to the following situation.

**Situation**： Shipments are often delayed to discharge in France, and your clients have endured a great deal of loss in the past.

**Reason**： There are frequent strikes of workers at the destination port in France.

**Solution**： The seller agrees to insure Strike Risk besides W.P.A., the buyer bears the premium of the additional risk.

## C. Talking about Premium and Coverage

### Dialogue 1 – Covering all risks

*Mr. Wilson, a buyer, asks Mr. Zhang to cover All Risks on his own account.*

**Mr. Zhang**： In terms of CIF, we would cover W.P.A. on your behalf. Do you have any specific requirements?

**Mr. Wilson**： Could you tell me if W.P.A. coverage includes compensation for breakage of the goods?

**Mr. Zhang**： The compensation for breakage is covered in the insurance of additional risks, that is Risk of Breakage. If you need, we can cover that, but the extra premium should be for buyer's account.

**Mr. Wilson**： I see. Then what about insurance for All Risks?

**Mr. Zhang**： Insurance against All Risks can also be covered at the buyer's request.

But the premium will be relatively higher.

**Mr. Wilson：** It doesn't matter. What we want to have most is the safety of goods.

**Mr. Zhang：** OK, we'll arrange to cover the goods against All Risks.

| | |
|---|---|
| on one's account | 由……支付 |

### Dialogue 2 － Talking about insurance value

*Later, Mr. Wilson and Mr. Zhang continue to discuss the insurance value.*

**Mr. Wilson：** I'm sorry to have to mention this again. After a second thought I think we'd better have the insurance of the goods covered at 130% of the invoice value. Do you think that can be done?

**Mr. Zhang：** I think so, but please note that according to our usual practice, our insurance coverage is for 110% of the invoice value only. Therefore, the premium for the difference between 130% and 110% should be for your account.

**Mr. Wilson：** I see. Then, how about your covering All Risks and War Risk for 130% of the invoice value with PICC?

**Mr. Zhang：** I'll do that. You can rest assured that we will have the goods insured as soon as they are shipped.

### Practice

1. You are exporting Black Tea to an American client. Talk with him about the insurance under CIF terms.

2. Your customer only insures W.P.A. for the goods. But you've heard there is a strike in the destination. Persuade your customer to insure Strike Risk and also bear the premium of the additional risk.

 Language Focus

### Technical Terms

| | |
|---|---|
| to cover insurance/to insure the goods | 投保 |
| Free from Particular Average | 平安险 |
| With Particular Average | 水渍险 |

| | |
|---|---|
| All Risks | 一切险 |
| insurance policy | 保险单 |
| insurance certificate | 保险凭证 |
| open policy | 预约保单 |
| Actual Total Loss | 实际全损 |
| Constructive Total Loss | 推定全损 |
| Partial Loss | 部分损失 |
| General Average | 共同海损 |
| Particular Average | 单独海损 |
| insurance premium | 保险费 |
| insurance coverage | 保险范围 |
| insurance company | 保险公司 |
| the insured | 被保险人 |
| insurance agent | 保险代理人 |
| underwriter | 保险商 |
| Theft, Pilferage, & Non-Delivery Risks | 偷窃、提货不着险 |
| Fresh and/or Rain Water Damage Risks | 淡水雨淋险 |
| Risk of Shortage | 短量险 |
| Intermixture & Contamination Risks | 混杂，玷污险 |
| Risk of Leakage | 渗漏险 |
| Clash & Breakage Risk | 碰损，破碎险 |
| Sweating & Heating Risks | 受潮受热险 |
| Rust Risks/Risk of Rust | 锈损险 |
| War Risk | 战争险 |
| SRCC (Strike, Riots and Civil Commotions) | 罢工，暴动，民变险 |
| franchise | 免赔率 |

## Functional Expressions

### Insurance Value

- We usually insure the goods against All Risks for 110% of the invoice value.
- We can insure the shipment for 130% of the invoice value, but the premium for the difference between 130% and 110% should be for your account.
- We have covered insurance on these goods for 10% above the invoice value against all risks.
- We shall effect the insurance of the goods for 110% of their CIF value.
- We'd like to cover our ordered goods against WPA for 120% of the invoice value according to our usual practice.

| Insurance Premium |
|---|
| • We may cover the inland insurance on your behalf, but you will pay the additional premium. |
| • What is the insurance premium for these goods? |
| • We can insure the porcelain vases on your behalf, but at a rather high premium and all the additional premium will be for your account. |
| • Since the premium varies with the extent of insurance, extra premium is for buyer's account, should additional risks be covered. |
| • Buyer's request for insurance to be covered up to the inland city can be accepted on condition that such extra premium is for buyer's account. |

| Insurance Practice |
|---|
| • What kind of insurance do you usually provide? |
| • Underwriters agree to insure this risk at 2% extra premium and with 5% franchise. |
| • We require the current insurance rates for land transportation. |
| • We need to send a shipment to England. We want to find out about your marine insurance. |
| • We have effected marine insurance on your behalf for the gross amount of the invoice plus 10%. |
| • For FOB and CFR sales, insurance is to be covered by the buyers. |
| • Please effect insurance on your side covering All Risks and War Risk. |

 Extended Activities

### Task 1

**Student A:** You are a foreign merchant who shows little interests in effecting insurance with the PICC, which is preferred by your business partner from China.

**Student B:** You are a Chinese businessman. You are requested to try to persuade your foreign client to cover insurance with the PICC.

### Task 2

**Student A:** You are Mr. Johnson. As an old customer, you have done business with the supplier on FOB basis for years. This time you request a quotation on CIF basis for a repeat order of 500 pieces of alarm clock Type 835. As you are not very familiar with insurance clauses of the PICC, you go to your supplier for relevant information.

**Student B**: You are Mr. Baker, a clerk from a trading company. Mr. Johnson, one of your old customers, comes to you to inquire about insurance matters. Try to explain briefly the Ocean Marine Cargo Clauses of the PICC and sort out appropriate coverage for alarm clocks.

## Task 3

**Student A**: You are an importer. About 70 out of 1,000 chests of Chinese green tea were contaminated with the odor of peppermint, and will have to be disposed of at a considerably reduced price. You lodged a claim against China National Native Produce Import and Export Corporation for the loss arising from contamination, but the claim was declined. Then you go to China National Native Produce Import and Export Corporation to find out why.

**Student B**: You are a clerk of China National Native Produce Import and Export Corporation. You need to explain to a client why his claim is declined. The reason is that contamination is not considered a marine risk and must be insured against a special risk, which the importer failed to do.

## Task 4

**Student A**: You are an Italian customer. You want Mr. Zhang to introduce in detail the insurance coverage issued by PICC and then ask him to insure the goods with PICC against All Risks for 110% of the invoice value.

**Student B**: You are Mr. Zhang, a spice exporter. You have just concluded a deal on CIF terms with a businessperson from Italy. Introduce to your customer the insurance coverage issued by PICC.

## Task 5

**Student A**: You are Mr. Zhang, a manufacturer of LCD monitors. You are talking with an importer from Britain and advise him to cover the Risk of Breakage as well and you discuss the premium.

**Student B**: You are an importer from Britain. Talk with your supplier and tell him that you would like to have the goods covered under W.P.A.

## Discussion

### Topic 1

What will the insured do if any damage occurs?

## Topic 2

What are the differences between F.P.A and W.P.A ?

 Related Information

# Understanding Insurance

### Choosing the Right Coverage

The clear distinction among the clauses F.P.A., W.A. or W.P.A. and All Risks is of great practical significance. It may help exporters choose the right coverage.

Most exporters will probably want to have the widest form of coverage they can get "All Risks" coverage. But because of the nature of their goods, underwriters may agree to provide only a more limited form of cover. Moreover, even though an exporter can get "All Risks" coverage, he may well decide that it is uneconomical.

An experienced exporter will come to know the losses he can expect, and may find it cheaper to write them off as trade losses than to pay the relatively high All Risks premium.

### Insurable Value

Insurable value, in marine cargo insurance, is the actual value of the insurable cargo. It is generally calculated as: cost of goods + amount of freight + insurance premium + percentage of the total sum to represent a reasonable profit for the buyer. Insurable value is the maximum amount payable by the insurance company in case of loss and premium is calculated and paid on the basis of this amount.

### Insurance Premium

The insurance premium is payable to the insurer when he issues the insurance policy or certificate. The premium charge for the insurance policy is calculated according to the risks involved. A policy that protects the holder against limited risks charges a low premium, and policy which protects against a large number of risks charges a high premium.

The most frequently used trade terms which affect insurance arrangements are FOB, CFR and CIF. Where the contract between the exporter and the foreign importer is FOB contract, it is the importer's responsibility to insure the goods. If the goods are contracted to be sold on CIF term, then it is the exporter's turn to take out the policy and pay the costs of insurance.

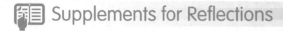 

## Officials Express Optimism as Trans-Pacific Trade Talks Head into 2015

Negotiations for a trade deal among 12 Pacific Rim countries that would cover over 40 percent of global GDP are set to continue into 2015, despite prior hopes that an agreement ——even "in principle" —— might be announced before this year draws to a close.

However, officials involved in the Trans-Pacific Partnership (TPP) talks have indicated in recent weeks that a final deal is close, and analysts suggest that the recent election victory in Japan of incumbent Prime Minister Shinzo Abe could pave the way for Tokyo to make some difficult concessions in areas such as agricultural trade.

Meanwhile, the New Year is also expected to see a potentially more favorable political climate in Washington for passing trade-related legislation, including bills seen as key to advancing TPP.

A brief update on the officials' meeting posted on the Canadian trade ministry website noted that the Washington talks addressed legal and institutional issues, textiles, rules of origin, state-owned enterprises, and the environment, among other subjects.

With 2014 now largely in the rearview mirror, the U.S. President has since indicated that he is increasingly confident in the prospects for the trans-Pacific pact, while not publicly placing any new timeframes on it. Analysts have suggested, however, that officials are likely to push for a final result in 2015, given the upcoming 2016 general election in the U.S.

"I'm much more optimistic about us being able to close out an agreement with our TPP partners than I was last year," Obama said last week at a meeting of the Export Council.

"Doesn't mean that it's a done deal, but I think the odds of us being able to get a strong agreement are significantly higher than 5050, whereas last year I think it was still sort of up for grabs," the U.S. leader said.

Trade Promotion Authority sets the priorities for the U.S. executive branch in negotiating international trade deals, while ensuring that any completed pact submitted to Congress can only face a straight up-or-down vote, without amendments. Without it, analysts say, Washington's trading partners are unlikely to make major concessions in negotiations, out of concern that a final deal could then be unravelled in the U.S. legislature.

| head into | 走向；进入 | incumbent | 现任的 |
| pave the way for | 为……做好准备 | | |

## Questions

- What subjects did the Washington talks address according to the brief update on the officials' meeting posted on the Canadian trade ministry website?
- What is the the U.S. President Obama's attitude towards TPP chances?

# 14 Unit

# **Conclusion of Business**

 Learning Objectives

**In this unit, you will learn to:**

- Confirm acceptance
- Review contract terms and conditions
- Make amendments or supplements to the contract

 Background Information

When the buyer and the seller have finally agreed upon all the terms and conditions of a transaction, they will sign a contract. A contract is an agreement between the seller and the buyer to confirm the sale and stipulate their rights and obligations respectively. A sales contract or sales confirmation contains some general terms and conditions as well as the specific terms that vary with the commodity.

The composition of a formal business contract usually consists of three parts: preamble, body and witness clause. It includes all the main clauses of the contract, reflecting duties and obligations of both parties. The preamble usually includes title, number, date of signing, signing parties, place of signing, each party's authority, recitals, whereas clause, and so on. The body of a business contract usually includes definition clause, general terms and conditions, basic conditions, duration, termination, force majeure, governing law, arbitration, jurisdiction, notice, entire agreement clause, amendment, and so on. The witness clause usually includes language validity, copies, signature, seal, and so on.

A contract can be worked out either by the seller or the buyer, and is called sales contract or a purchase contract respectively. The same is also applicable to sales confirmation or a purchase confirmation.

 Starting Up

**Read the description of a transaction between two companies and complete the sales contract.**

China Oriental Company and P&D Company from the U.S. have concluded a transaction. The business is for 20,000 kilograms of red dates, Grade One, at USD 3 per kilo, CIF New York, Shipment in July, 2010, with 30 days after receipt of L/C allowing transshipment and partial shipment, payment by confirmed, irrevocable, transferable and divisible sight L/C. One kilo of red dates are packed in one poly bag, 25 bags into one carton. The order is covered against W.P.A. and Fresh and/or Rain Water Damage Risks for 110% of CIF invoice value as per the ocean marine cargo clauses of the PICC.

---

**Sales Contract**

NO.:

Signed at:

Date:

Seller: _____ Address: Tel: Fax: E-mail:

Buyer: _____ Address: Tel: Fax: E-mail:

The undersigned Seller and Buyer have agreed to close the following transaction according to the terms and conditions set forth as below:

1. Name, Specifications and Quality of Commodity: _____

2. Quantity: _____

3. Unit Price and Terms of Delivery:

The terms FOB, CFR, or CIF shall be subject to the *International Rules for the Interpretation of Trade Terms* (*INCOTERMS 2000*) provided by International Chamber of Commerce (ICC) unless otherwise stipulated herein.

1. Total Amount: _____

2. Time of Shipment:

Within_____days after receipt of L/C allowing transshipment and partial shipment.

3. Terms of Payment:

By_____L/C. The L/C must specify that transshipment and partial shipments are allowed.

The Buyer shall establish a Letter of Credit before the above–stipulated time, failing which, the seller shall have the right to rescind this Contract upon the arrival of the notice at Buyer or to accept whole or part of this Contract non fulfilled by Buyer, or to lodge a claim for the direct losses sustained, if any.

1. Packaging：

2. Insurance:

Covering_____Risks for 110% of_____Invoice Value to be effected by the_____.

   …

 Oral Workshop

# A. Confirming Acceptance

### Dialogue 1 – Confirming terms and conditions

*Mr. Jones, an American manufacturer of Automatic Forming Machine, and a Chinese importer Mr. Zheng have come to an agreement. They are confirming the terms and conditions of the business.*

**Mr. Zheng**： Well, Mr. Jones. We've talked about the clauses to be covered by the contract, including formation of the contract, terms of delivery, packaging and inspection, questions of payment, as well as the arbitration clause.

**Mr. Jones**： Yes, Mr. Zheng, it seems to me we've come quite a long way, but there's still a few points left over to be cleared up.

**Mr. Zheng**： I've been looking into the question of having the goods sent by air. It's quick; the goods are less liable to damage than by sea or rail.

**Mr. Jones**： There's only one thing left. Freight costs are higher by air, and if we operate on CIF terms as we've already previously agreed, this might mean a substantial increase in our expenses.

**Mr. Zheng**： All the same, really I believe it would be worthwhile, and we would be prepared to meet you half way with the extra costs incurred.

**Mr. Jones：** I'm certainly with you in principle, but I'll have to take the matter up when I get back to my home office. Perhaps I should make a special note of that.

**Mr. Zheng：** The next point is the guarantee. We should like to have a guarantee for at least six months.

**Mr. Jones：** No problem. We offer a standard guarantee of 12 months in all the countries we're selling, and I think your country should be no exception.

**Mr. Zheng：** So a similar guarantee would also be written into our contract?

**Mr. Jones：** Certainly. Then, one of the things we haven't decided properly yet is who's going to be responsible for publicity.

**Mr. Zheng：** We are prepared to look after that entirely. The only thing I would propose is that you should supply us with as much informative material as possible.

**Mr. Jones：** That's fine. Anyway, we've already settled everything in the contract, and I'll have my secretary prepare the draft contract tomorrow.

**Mr. Zheng：** All right.

| incur | 引发，带来 | in principle | 大体上，原则上 |
|---|---|---|---|

### Dialogue 2 – Reviewing the terms before singing the contract

*Mr. Clark and Mr. Zhao are going through the terms before their signing the contract.*

**Mr. Clark：** Now, we've finally reached a basic agreement on the problems that need to be worked out. Shall we sign the contract now?

**Mr. Zhao：** Just a minute. Generally speaking, a contract cannot be changed once both parties have signed it. So we'd better make sure one more time that we've got them right.

**Mr. Clark：** That's a good idea.

**Mr. Zhao：** First of all, as for the format of our contract, there are two of the originals of the contract both in Chinese and English, so they're equally authentic in terms of law. Here's a copy for you to check.

**Mr. Clark：** Thank you. I have no objections. It contains basically all we have agreed upon during our negotiations. To make sure no important items have been overlooked, let's check all the terms listed in the contract and see if there is anything not in conformity with the terms we agreed on.

**Mr. Zhao：** Okay, let's start from the name of the commodity, specifications, quantity, unit price… Well, it looks good enough to me. You've done a good job.

**Mr. Clark**：Thank you. Since your company enjoys a good reputation, we want to make sure we keep your business.

**Mr. Zhao**：We always think our commercial reputation is of primary importance, and promise that the execution of the contract will not be compromised, no matter what happens.

**Mr. Clark**：It's really nice to get to know all of you. Shall we sign the contract now?

**Mr. Zhao**：Yes, I've been looking forward to this moment.

*(after signing the contract)*

**Mr. Clark**：Let me propose a toast to the success of negotiations and to our future cooperation. Cheers!

**Mr. Zhao**：Cheers! Let's congratulate ourselves on having brought this transaction to a successful conclusion.

---

| | | | |
|---|---|---|---|
| authentic | 权威的 | in conformity with | 与……相符 |

---

## Practice

1. You are David Simpson. You have secured a large order from a Canadian importer for your firm's electric grills. You are now negotiating the terms of a contract with Mr. Gaston from this importing firm.

2. You have accepted Mr. Brown's offer for carpets and are going to conclude a transaction. Before signing the contract, you are now checking up all the main points you've agreed upon. The main points are as follows:

- Commodity：Carpets (Art. No. S009)
- Quantity：500 pieces
- Unite Price：USD 50/PC CIF San Francisco
- Terms of Payment：By irrevocable L/C at sight
- Time of Shipment：In mid-November

# B. Reviewing Contract Details

### Dialogue 1 – Signing a contract

*Mr. Zhang and Mr. Clinton have decided to sign the contract and make a deal.*

**Mr. Clinton**：Mr. Zhang, we have reached an agreement on all the terms. Now we should sign a sales contract, I think.

**Mr. Zhang：** I'm very glad we have agreed on the stipulations of the contract. I asked the secretary to draft a contract yesterday. Here it is. Please go over and see if it contains all we have agreed upon during our negotiations.

**Mr. Clinton：** Let me check all the terms listed in the contract and see if there is anything not in conformity with the terms we agreed on.

**Mr. Zhang：** Yes, you are right. We both should make everything clear so that we can perform our promises written down in the contract smoothly.

**Mr. Clinton：** It looks good. Everything is in order. I'm ready to sign the contract.

**Mr. Zhang：** Let's sign the contract now, and congratulate ourselves that this transaction has been brought to a successful conclusion.

**Mr. Clinton：** I hope the contract will lead to our long-term pleasant cooperation between us.

**Mr. Zhang：** I hope so, too.

| | | | |
|---|---|---|---|
| stipulation | 契约；规定 | draft | 起草 |

## Dialogue 2 – Talking about a draft contract

*Mr. Wilson and Mr. Song are talking about a draft contract.*

**Mr. Song：** Well Mr. Wilson, I've brought with me the draft of our contract. Please have a look and let us know anything you are not clear about.

**Mr. Wilson：** Thank you. Well, there is something we should add to this provision："If one side fails to honor this contract, the other side is entitled to cancel this contract." Do you think so?

**Mr. Song：** Certainly. I shouldn't have ignored it. We should include this provision in it. Anything else you've noticed?

**Mr. Wilson：** There is one more thing to make clear. I'd like to know in case of claims, which institution in China will handle arbitration.

**Mr. Song：** Oh, if we have a dispute, we can resolve the case by submitting the dispute to the Chinese International Trade Arbitration Commission.

**Mr. Wilson：** OK, I think we've got everything clear now. I hope we can sign it very soon.

**Mr. Song：** Thank you. We'll contact you as soon as the formal contract is ready.

**Mr. Wilson：** Good, I'll see you then.

**Mr. Song：** See you.

| provision | 条款 | be entitled to | 有权 |

## Practice

1. After going over the draft of the contract, the foreign buyer finds one thing should be clarified: the deadline for both the first and the second shipment of the goods. He/she also wants the goods to be delivered as soon as possible.

2. Mr. Botha, an Italian importer, discusses with you about an offer on 5,000 sets of cooking utensils. Having bargained for some time, he accepts your revised price. After going over the payment and other general terms, the business is concluded. Both you and Mr. Botha take one more look before signing the contract.

# C. Talking about Contract Terms

### Dialogue 1 – Clarifying a contract

*Peter and Jenny are clarifying the contract they've just signed to make sure everything is clear in the contract.*

**Peter:** If I understand the terms correctly, the length of the contract would be one year with a one-year option. Is that correct?

**Jenny:** Do you mean the contract for equipment rental or the one for training?

**Peter:** I was under the impression that both contracts had the same terms.

**Jenny:** You can say that, but not completely true. I'll try to clarify that. The terms are the same except the fact that the contract for training has a clause that allows for the cancellation after the first six months.

**Peter:** Could you elaborate on that?

**Jenny:** OK. What I mean is that either side could cancel the training contract after the six months as long as it's in writing.

**Peter:** This contract is for six months of training, but if it isn't cancelled, continues for another six months. Is that right?

**Jenny:** Yes, that's right.

**Peter:** OK, that's clear enough. Let's move on to other terms.

### Dialogue 2 – Talking about a long–term contract

*After signing the contract, Mr. Zhang and Mr. Clinton decide to talk about a long-term contract.*

**Mr. Clinton**：I'm so glad we've reached an agreement on this particular contract. I hope the contract will lead to years of friendly cooperation.

**Mr. Zhang**：Maybe it's time now to talk a little about the future.

**Mr. Clinton**：All right. What do you have in mind?

**Mr. Zhang**：Well, we'll face more and more challenges as well as opportunities. Now China has joined the WTO, so I think it's necessary for us to make some long-term business arrangements.

**Mr. Clinton**：I totally agree. Maybe this is the right time for us to talk about it. But I don't really see how we can do it. You see, sometimes we hold different points of view about the trend of the international market price.

**Mr. Zhang**：Oh, that is not really important to a long-term agreement. This agreement needs only concern itself with quantity, specifications, terms and conditions, etc.

**Mr. Clinton**：What about the price?

**Mr. Zhang**：We could meet every three months or so to set the price according to the prevailing world market price.

**Mr. Clinton**：All right. Another question, what if, for one reason or another, we weren't able to buy as many as we wrote down in the contract for one year or you couldn't supply us with as many as in the contract, what would be done about the difference?

**Mr. Zhang**：Oh, that can be easily arranged. We may simply cancel the discrepancy.

**Mr. Clinton**：Do you mean that both sides would then be released from their obligations to fulfill the balance of the quantity for that year?

**Mr. Zhang**：That's correct.

**Mr. Clinton**：Well, I see. I accept your suggestion. Perhaps you may prepare the draft agreement.

**Mr. Zhang**：All right. I'll get it ready for your perusal sometime tomorrow afternoon.

| discrepancy | 差异 | for your perusal | 供你方详阅 |

## Practice

1. You are the Sales Manager representing Tianjin Machinery Imp. & Exp. Corp., a businessperson from Thailand has ordered a total of USD 500,000 worth of your Heavy-duty Machinery equipment. The contract was drafted by the Thai company. You find out one more

provision should be added: the insurance premium should be born by the Thai party since the price is quoted on CFR basis.

2. The draft of the contract is ready, Miss Ma asked Mr. Rush to check the particulars to see if there is anything to be amended. Mr. Rush found that time of shipment was not exact and told her the statement "The seller should notify the buyer by fax after the loading is completed or shall be responsible for the losses incurred." They are having a discussion on this issue.

 Language Focus

### Technical Terms

| | |
|---|---|
| Sales Contract | 销售合同 |
| Sales Confirmation | 销售确认书 |
| Purchase Contract | 购货合同 |
| Purchase Confirmation | 购货确认书 |
| countersign | 签署；会签 |
| counter signature | 会签 |
| transaction | 交易 |
| preamble | (合同的) 约首 |
| witness clause | (合同的) 约尾 |
| whereas clause | 缔约缘由；鉴于条款 |
| force majeure | 不可抗力 |
| contractor | 订约人，承包人 |
| contractual | 契约的 |
| to enter into a contract | 订合同 |
| to sign a contract | 签合同 |
| to draw up a contract | 拟订合同 |
| to draft a contract | 起草合同 |
| original of the contract | 合同正本 |
| a written contract | 书面合同 |
| contract terms | 合同条款 |
| contract stipulations | 合同规定 |
| contract life | 合同有效期 |
| to lay down in the contract | 在合同中列明 |
| to come into effect | 生效 |
| to abide by the contract | 遵守合同 |
| contract of carriage | 运输合同 |
| contract of arbitration | 仲裁合同 |
| contract parties | 缔约方 |

| contractual terms & conditions | 合同条款和条件 |
| interpretation of contract | 合同解释 |
| expiration of contract | 合同期满 |
| gross weight | 毛重 |
| net weight | 净重 |
| theoretical weight | 理论重量 |
| more or less clause | 溢短装条款 |

## Functional Expressions

### Concluding a Business Deal

- After long and friendly discussions, we have now concluded business.
- We are glad to have finalized/put through/closed/concluded this transaction with you.

### Confirming the Conclusion of Business

- We'll have to discuss the total contract price.
- Don't you think it necessary to have a close study of the contract to avoid anything missing?
- We cannot agree to the alterations and amendments to the contract.
- We hope that the next negotiation will be the last one before signing the contract.
- We don't have any different opinions about the contractual obligations of both parties.

### Signing the Contract

- Since both of us two parties have affixed our signature to the contract, it is effective and binding on both parties.
- In international trade, sales confirmation is a document regarded as a contract.
- Here are the two originals of the contract we prepared.
- We have agreed on all terms in the contract. Shall we sign it next week?
- Both versions of this contract are equally authentic.

### Contractual Terms and Conditions

- Any amendment to the contract shall come to force only after the written agreement is signed by both of us.
- This agreement will remain valid for one year and shall become effective on the date of signing.
- In case of breach of any of the provisions of this agreement by one party, the other party shall have the right to terminate this agreement by giving notice in writing to its opposite party.

- If you fail to make the delivery ten weeks later than the time of shipment stipulated in the contract, we should have the right to cancel the contract.
- We hope you will take your commercial reputation into account and execute the contract within the specified time.

 Extended Activities

## Role-play

**Task 1**

**Student A**: You are an export manager of a Chinese foodstuff company. You are telephoning the importer abroad to confirm all the terms and conditions you have agreed upon on the recent deal.

**Student B**: You are an overseas importer. You are answering a call from your supplier, talking about all the terms and conditions of your recent deal.

**Task 2**

**Student A**: You are negotiating with a foreign customer. You have agreed upon all the terms and conditions except the date of delivery. Try to settle this matter with your customer.

**Student B**: You are an importer from America. You have agreed upon all the terms and conditions except the date of delivery. Now you are having a hot discussion with your supplier.

**Task 3**

**Student A**: You are Mr. Lee. Having made a very close study of the drafty contract, you find one more provision should be added to the contract, i.e., "Force Majeure" by which the production and delivery may be affected. You are talking about this clause with Mr. Smith, and add that you are not responsible for the loss thus sustained.

**Student B**: You are Mr. Smith. With regard to Mr. Lee's request, you stress that if "Force Majeure" lasts over 60 days you have the right to cancel the contract or the undelivered part of the contract. Therefore, you are having a heated discussion on this issue.

**Task 4**

**Student A**: You are Mr. Lee. After negotiating with Mr. Brown, you find everything satisfactory regarding the terms and conditions. Before Mr. Brown draws up the contract, you want to make sure what should be specified in the contract as it is a sales contract which is to be made out by your side.

**Student B :** You are Mr. Brown. You find everything satisfactory regarding the terms and conditions after the negotiation with Mr. Lee. Then you begin to draw up a formal contract. In order to avoid subsequent non-performance of the contract and disputes or claims, Mr. Lee wants to make sure what are to be specified in the contract. You tell Mr. Lee that the name of commodity, unit price, total value, port of loading, port of destination, time of shipment, payment terms and some other general conditions of sales are to be specified in the contract.

## Task 5

**Student A :** You are Ms. Mo. The draft of the contract is ready, you ask Mr. Rush to check the particulars and see if there is any thing to be amended.

**Student B :** You are Mr. Rush. You find the time of shipment not exact and require Ms. Mo to add the statement "The seller should notify the buyer by fax after the loading is completed or shall be responsible for the losses incurred." So you are having a discussion with Ms. Mo on this issue.

## Discussion

### Topic 1

What is a formal business contract composed of?

### Topic 2

What is included in the body of the contract?

### Topic 3

What terms should be listed in a sales contract?

 Related Information

## Conclusion of a Deal

A deal is concluded when the exporter's firm offer is accepted by the importer or a non-firm offer, after being accepted by the importer, is confirmed by the exporter. In cases where the importer has made a counter offer, or taken initiative by placing a firm order or a firm bid with the exporter, containing all necessary terms and conditions, the exporter's acceptance concludes the deal.

However, in keeping with the regular practice in international trade, a written contract or confirmation is usually signed to bind both the seller and the buyer. A formal contact or confirmation should be prepared in duplicate; each copy should be signed by both parties, and each party should keep a signed copy of it. Some of the contracts or confirmations commonly used in foreign trade are available in printed form, so that only the date, price, name of commodities, name of parties, and similar particulars need to be filled in.

Legally, both sales contract and the sales confirmation are equally binding on the parties. On the whole, the former is more formal, and the latter is less formal. Besides, the former consists of not only such main terms as the name of commodities, specifications, quantity, packaging, marking, price, shipment, port of shipment and port of destination, and payment, but also those clauses concerning insurance, commodity inspection, claims, arbitration and force majeure; while the latter covers several main items only. It goes without saying that both the parties will best benefit from the sales or the purchase contract if disputes occur because the contract has provided in details the relative terms and the ways of how to handle and settle the disputes. It is, then, appropriate to transactions of large amount and huge quantity. If the amount is not large or the business is done by means of agency arrangement or exclusive sales agreement, the sale of the purchase confirmation is often used.

## Supplements for Reflections

### Is China Still Growing Too Fast?

China may be implementing a series of easing measures to keep its economy expanding, but some analysts believe the mainland should let growth slow instead.

"China's potential GDP (gross domestic product) growth rate is no longer 7~8 percent, because of lack of productivity increases and because of their changing demographic profile and aging workforce," Ruchir Sharma, head of emerging markets at Morgan Stanley Investment Management, said last week.

China set its 2014 GDP growth target at 7.5 percent, unchanged from 2013 —— a sharp slowdown from the double-digit rates of previous years.

| implement | 执行 |

## A turning point at last for China's economy?

In the first quarter of 2014, the mainland's economy grew an annual 7.4 percent, slowing from 7.7 percent in the last quarter of 2013, and marking the slowest annual growth rate since the third quarter of 2012.

"To try to hit a growth target of 7~8 percent is taking on more and more debt," a precursor to likely economic trouble ahead, Sharma said.

China's debt-to-GDP ratio has risen from around 160 percent in 2008 to over 240 percent, he noted. At the same time, the country last year needed to borrow $4.00 to create $1.00 of GDP growth, up from around $2.00 of borrowing for $1.00 of GDP growth just five years ago.

| precursor | 前兆 |

## How much is going clean costing China?

But many analysts expect China's leadership will continue to take easing measures rather than let the economy slow further.

"Policy makers seem to have put deleveraging on the backburner," Credit Agricole said in a note Friday.

"The government has announced numerous stimulus measures, and the PBOC (People's Bank of China) has injected liquidity and used moral suasion to pressure money market rates down and facilitate lending," it noted. It expects China to begin cutting its required reserve ratio for banks in the first quarter of next year to support growth.

"We believe they should not do it, but fear that signs are mounting that they may," it said.

| inject | 注入 | liquidity | 流动资产 |

## China's millionaire machine slows

To be sure, it isn't clear that a sharp slowdown on the mainland is necessarily a worry for all analysts.

"Everyone thinks below 7 (percent) is a disaster. The perception is where the problem is," Sharma said. "To consider China growing at 5 percent in the next five years would still be consistent with an economy that's an economic miracle based on any sort of economic history."

## Questions

- What do some analysts believe the mainland should do about its economy?
- According to Sharma, what is the economic condition in China?

# Trademark, Patent, and Intellectual Property Rights

##  Learning Objectives

**In this unit, you will learn how to :**

- Register a trademark
- Apply for a patent
- Protect intellectual property rights

## Background Information

A trademark is a word, symbol or design, or a combination of these, used to distinguish the goods or services of one person or organization from those of others in the marketplace, which has been legally registered as the property of an enterprise. The essential function of a trademark is to exclusively identify the commercial source or origin of products or services, such that a trademark indicates source or serves as a badge of origin.

A patent is not a right to practice or use the invention. Rather, a patent provides the right to exclude others from making, using, selling, offering for sale, or importing the patented invention for the term of the patent, usually 20 years from the filing date. Like any other property right, it may be sold, licensed, mortgaged, assigned or transferred, given away, or simply abandoned.

The intellectual property protection system emerged as a product of the development of human civilization and commodity economy. And in various countries it has increasingly become an effective legal tool for protecting the interests of the owner of intellectual products, promoting the development of science, technology and the social economy, and allowing international competition.

Today, intellectual property protection is an issue of universal concern in the international political, economic, scientific, technological and cultural exchanges. International bilateral and multilateral negotiations on this topic, especially the reaching of the Agreement on Trade-related Aspects of Intellectual Property Rights in the *General Agreement on Tariffs and Trade* (*GATT*), have raised worldwide intellectual property protection to a new level.

## Starting Up

**Read the following expressions and match the English and the Chinese words according to their meanings. The first one had been done for you.**

| | |
|---|---|
| trademark | 专利代理人 |
| patent | 版税 |
| patent agent | 专利 |
| registered trademark | 专利证书 |
| Patent Office | 专利局 |
| patent certificate | 商标 |
| copyright | 无形资产 |
| copyright royalty | 知识产权 |
| intellectual property | 版权 |
| intangible asset | 注册商标 |

## Oral Workshop

## A. Registering a Trademark

### Dialogue 1 - Learning about trademark registration procedure

*Mr. Wilson from Nordic Import and Export Corporation is paying a visit to Mr. Wang of a Consultative Agency to learn about the procedure of trademark registration.*

**Mr. Wilson：** I'm Carl Wilson from Nordic Import and Export Corporation. I've come to register the trade marks.

**Mr. Wang:** It seems to me that you have put much more stress on trade mark registration now than ever before.

**Mr. Wilson:** Yes, It's true. Our products sell well in the market, so we'd like to have them registered.

**Mr. Wang:** Well, you know that trade mark is an inseparable part of the commodity and an intangible asset of an enterprise. What brands are you applying for registration?

**Mr. Wilson:** Light Breeze brand for bed sheets and Flying Man brand for shirts.

**Mr. Wang:** Let me see. Have you brough't the designs here? Well, a British Company already obtained the registration of Flying Man brand six months ago. The brand name is the same, though the design different.

**Mr. Wilson:** What a shame! You mean we can't have our Flying Man brand registered?

**Mr. Wang:** I'm afraid yes. But the Light Breeze brand is fresh and vivid. There will be no problem for registration.

**Mr. Wilson:** Alright. Could you give me a brief account of the registration here?

**Mr. Wang:** With pleasure. When a foreign enterprise makes application for trademark registration in China, he should entrust a representative from the Trademark Office of CCPIT to go through the formalities.

**Mr. Wilson:** Then what documents do I need?

**Mr. Wang:** You will need an application in duplicate, power of attorney in duplicate and a certificate of nationality.

**Mr. Wilson:** How long do we have to wait?

**Mr. Wang:** Not too long. The Trademark Office examines the application, issues preliminary approval and publishes the trademark; all these will take three or four months.

**Mr. Wilson:** Then how long will the registered trade mark remain valid?

**Mr. Wang:** Ten years from the date of registration. And trade mark registration may be renewed continuously. Each renewal is good for ten more years. Even the producer forgets to apply for the registration renewal, the law grants a 6-month grace period.

**Mr. Wilson:** Thank you for your explanation. I hope everything will go smoothly.

**Mr. Wang:** If you have no more questions, would you please fill in the form? The registration certificate will soon be granted to you upon the approval by the Trade Mark Bureau.

*(after a while)*

**Mr. Wilson：** Mr. Wang. Here is the application form. By the way, will our trademark be legally protected outside China?

**Mr. Wang：** No, trademark is limited by region. That is to say, a trademark registered in China will not be legally protected in another country.

**Mr. Wilson：** That means we need to have the same trademark registered in another country before we sell it abroad?

**Mr. Wang：** Exactly.

**Mr. Wilson：** Then how can we do it in another country?

**Mr. Wang：** For trademark registration, different countries follow different rules. For example, China has adopted the priority-of-registration principle. But other countries, such as USA, prefer the priority-of-use principle.

**Mr. Wilson：** Which principle is more reasonable?

**Mr. Wang：** Well, we can't say one is better than the other. The former seems simpler in terms of the registration procedures.

**Mr. Wilson：** Suppose I seek a trademark registration in the USA, what should I do then?

**Mr. Wang：** You'll have to prepare a lot of documents, and many of them must be notarized. Sometimes the registration fee will be very expensive.

**Mr. Wilson：** In this case who is willing to have their trademarks registered abroad?

**Mr. Wang：** It's still worth trying. Otherwise, it will be hard for your products to cross the boundary.

**Mr. Wilson：** I see. You really help me a lot.

**Mr. Wang：** You are welcome.

| | | | |
|---|---|---|---|
| put stress on | 强调，重视 | notarize | 公证 |
| intangible asset | 无形资产 | What a shame | 太遗憾了 |
| account | 记叙，描述 | entrust | 委托 |
| Trademark Office | 商标局 | grace period | 宽限期 |
| power of attorney | 委托书；授权书 | in duplicate | 一式两份 |
| approval | 赞成；批准 | go through | 经历；办理 |
| inseparable | 不可分割的 | | |
| priority-of-registration principle | | 注册优先原则 | |
| priority-of-use principle | | 使用优先原则 | |

## Dialogue 2 – Other FAQs about trademark registration

*Several days later, Mr. Wilson comes again to consult with Mr. Wang on trademark registration.*

**Mr. Wilson：** Mr. Wang. I've got some questions about our trademark registration. Could you give me some advice?

**Mr. Wang：** With pleasure.

**Mr. Wilson：** Can we assign a trademark to another person or company?

**Mr. Wang：** Of course you can.

**Mr. Wilson：** Then what do we do?

**Mr. Wang：** You can assign your trademark to another person or company by filing a joint application with the assignee with the Trademark Office. The assignee should guarantee the quality of the goods when he uses the registered trademark.

**Mr. Wilson：** Naturally. And what shall we do if we find somebody infringing our trademark?

**Mr. Wang：** You could put in a request to the Administrative Authority for Industry and Commerce and ask them to look into the matter.

**Mr. Wilson：** Then what will the Administrative Authority for Industry and Commerce do with the offenders?

**Mr. Wang：** They have the authority to order the offender to stop the infringement at once and to compensate you for the damage. Or you can take your case to the People's Court.

**Mr. Wilson：** In that case, all the loss we have suffered will be compensated?

**Mr. Wang：** Yes. It is written in the *Trade Mark Law of China*.

**Mr. Wilson：** That's great. Thank you very much.

**Mr. Wang：** You are more than welcome.

| assignee | 受让人 | infringe | 侵犯 |
| --- | --- | --- | --- |
| put in | 提交 | | |

## Practice

1. You are from an American company. You are going to have your new product registered in China. Go to a local consultative agency and ask about the procedures.

2. You are a clerk in a local consultative agency. You are receiving a client, who is

inquiring about the registration procedures.

# B. Applying for a Patent

### Dialogue 1 – Preparing for a patent application

*Mr. Gale is preparing for a patent application. Now he is having a conversation with Ms. Lin who is seeking help.*

**Mr. Gale:** This is our new invention. We have applied for the patent in the U.S. Do we also need to apply for a patent in China before it comes to the market?

**Ms. Lin:** Yes. You need to appoint a patent agency, for instance, the Patent Agent Department, to act as your patent agent.

**Mr. Gale:** Do you think our application for the patent can be approved?

**Ms. Lin:** Well, it depends on whether the invention you apply for qualifies for a patent. According to the Patent Law, you need to prepare the specification for submission to the Patent Office.

**Mr. Gale:** Sounds pretty complicated. Then what are the criteria for granting patent right?

**Ms. Lin:** They are similar to those in other countries: novelty, inventiveness, and practicability.

**Mr. Gale:** Well, in that case I'm sure we can proceed because our process fulfills all these requirements. All we need to do is proving that we are the true and the first inventor.

**Ms. Lin:** That's true.

**Mr. Gale:** But you see, as a foreigner, I'm not quite sure how to apply for a patent right.

**Ms. Lin:** Don't worry. I can take you to our Patent Department. The staff there can help you through all the formalities.

**Mr. Gale:** Miss. Lin you've been most helpful. Thank you!

**Ms. Lin:** With pleasure.

| | | | |
|---|---|---|---|
| qualify | 具有……资格 | Patent Office | 专利局 |
| criteria | 标准 | grant | 授予；准予 |
| patent right | 专利权 | novelty | 新颖 |
| inventiveness | 创造性 | practicability | 实用性 |

## Dialogue 2 – Learning about the patent application process

*Later, Mr. Gale came to the Patent Department to ask about the procedure of patent application. Mr. Chen, a clerk working in the Patent Department, is explaining to him the process.*

**Mr. Gale:** I'm going to apply for a patent, but I am not sure how to prepare the application.

**Mr. Chen:** You need to submit a request, a description, and a claim. If necessary, the description should be supported by drawings.

**Mr. Gale:** How long shall I have to wait for?

**Mr. Chen:** Well, examination takes time. The Patent Office will announce the result and notify the application within 18 months. Even then, you don't get the patent certificate.

**Mr. Gale:** Why?

**Mr.Chen:** The Patent Office needs 90 days to wait for possible oppositions. Only when everything is OK, will the patent be registered.

**Mr. Gale:** I see. How long is the duration of patent right for an invention?

**Mr. Chen:** The term of validity is 15 years. During the 15 years, you hold the exclusive right to exploit it. For utility models and designs, the duration of protection is only 5 years.

**Mr. Gale:** Why is there such a big difference?

**Mr. Chen:** Now technology is developing fast. An invention may be new today, but in a few years, it may be outdated. Better inventions may take its place.

**Mr. Gale:** I see. Does every country specify the same duration of protection?

**Mr. Chen:** No, 15 years protection is the minimum protection any country will grant its patentees. In some countries, the patent right duration for invention is 20 years.

**Mr. Gale:** So the patentees registered in these countries can enjoy longer protection.

**Mr. Chen:** Right. But they enjoy it with a cost. In any country, patentees must pay fees annually. The longer the protection, the more they have to pay.

**Mr. Gale:** Will the right be kept for us if we stop using it?

**Mr. Chen:** No. If you do not use the patent within 3 years, your right to the patent may be granted to another company which applies for it.

**Mr. Gale:** OK, I see. Can I myself assign a patent right in China?

**Mr. Chen:** Of course you can do it through a written contract.

**Mr. Gale:** What if someone infringes our patent right?

**Mr. Chen:** Then you may sue. The new *Patent Law* is quite specific on such matters. If the court finds in your favor, then those who infringe your patent must cease production at once and you are properly compensated for the infringement.

**Mr. Gale:** Well, Mr. Chen, Thank you very much.

**Mr. Chen:** You are welcome.

| | | | |
|---|---|---|---|
| sue | 起诉 | cease | 终止 |

## Practice

You are from a French company. You are going to apply for a patent for your new voice lock. Go to the local paten office and learn about patent application.

## C. Protecting Intellectual Property Rights (IPR)

### Dialogue – Talking about IPR protection

*Andy, a reporter with College Journal, is interviewing Professor Zhou about IPR protection.*

**Andy:** Professor Zhou, as an essential component of China's reform and opening up policy, do you think the IPR protection in China is sufficient?

**Zhou:** Yes, China has done a lot in protecting intellectual property rights. However, China has lagged behind the developed countries in the filed of IPR protection.

**Andy:** It really has. And China needs more laws to protect intellectual property rights.

**Zhou:** As a developing country, China is facing some problems in terms of IPR protection.

**Andy:** Then what do you think is the most serious problem in this respect?

**Zhou:** That could be the general public are lacking in the awareness on IPR protection. This problem has become very urgent since China's entry into the WTO.

**Andy:** So we need to do our bit to help people more aware of the importance of IPR protection.

**Zhou:** As we can see, the protection of the right to the exclusive use of registered trademarks has resulted in the rapid growth of the number of trademarks registered by Chinese and foreign businessmen in China.

**Andy:** And I heard in many universities, teaching and research centre for intellectual property rights have been established, enrolling non-law majors to study for a second degree in intellectual property rights.

**Zhou**： Yes, so there will be more and more qualified personnel in intellectual property rights protection. However, as an important part of IPR protection, the protection of copyright in China also falls behind other countries.

**Andy**： But China has passed many laws in recent years to protect the copyrights.

**Zhou**： But there are still some existing problems. To solve them, China is accelerating its amendment to the *Copyright Law.*

**Andy**： What will be included in the amendment?

**Zhou**： Well, the amendment would clarify the payment system by broadcasting organizations which use the recording product, and it would also include the following provisions： rental rights in respect of computer programs and movies, protection of database compilations, increasing the legitimate compensation amount and strengthening the measures against infringing activities.

**Andy**： That would be great. I'm sure these will guarantee an effective protection of IPR.

**Zhou**： Sure. These laws are also actively encouraging invention and other forms of creation and fair competition.

| lag behind | 落后 | in this respect | 在这方面 |
| do one's bit | 尽自己的力量 | | |

## Practice

You are going to make a short speech about the current situation of intellectual property protection in China. Discuss your points with your partner and ask for his opinions.

 Language Focus

### Technical Terms

| intellectual property | 知识产权 |
|---|---|
| industrial property | 工业知识产权 |
| intangible asset | 无形资产 |
| trademark | 商标 |
| trade mark legislation | 商标法 |

| | |
|---|---|
| trade mark infringement | 对商标专用权的侵犯 |
| patent | 专利 |
| patentee | 专利权获得者 |
| patent agent | 专利代理人 |
| patent agreement | 专利协议 |
| patent office | 专利局 |
| patent specification | 专利说明书 |
| patent tax | 专利税 |
| copyright | 版权 |
| copyright royalty | 版税 |
| registered trademark | 注册商标 |
| royalty | 专利使用费 |
| franchising | 特许经营 |
| licensing | 许可经营 |
| logo | 标识 |
| turnkey project | "交钥匙"工程 |
| expertise | 专业知识 |

## Functional Expressions

### Trademarks

- We should have the brand registered to uphold our just rights and interests.
- Each company tries to establish a well-recognized trademark.
- There is a time limit for trademark right.
- Through preliminary examinations, we have not found any brand names same as yours, therefore, we are going to approve your application before long.
- If there's no justifiable opposition to it, then the registration is approved and a trademark registration certificate is issued.

### Patents

- When a patent right yields no more benefits, protection becomes meaningless.
- The patentees registered in some countries can enjoy longer protection.
- Nobody else has the privilege to use the patent without the owner's explicit written authorization.
- It will grant the rights to produce and sell the licensed products within the validity of the patent.
- The aim of the *Patent Law* is to protect and encourage inventions.

| Intellectual Property Rights |
| --- |

- While improving its legal system, enforcing the laws earnestly and striking relentless blows at infringements and other unlawful s, China has spared no efforts in publicizing and providing education about the intellectual property protection legal system and in accelerating the training of professional personnel in this field.
- The fact that there has been an increasing number of cases involving intellectual property rights in recent years and that these cases have been remedied through recourse to law reflects the people's heightened awareness and the wide spread of intellectual property rights knowledge throughout society.
- In order to speed up the training of personnel in this field, the Chinese government has, in close cooperation with relevant international organizations, sent people abroad to study or to attend training classes and seminars.
- Together with the World Intellectual Property Organization, training classes and seminars, programs in intellectual property rights education and research have been initiated at over 70 institutions of higher learning throughout the country.
- With the implementation of intellectual property laws, intellectual property rights are effectively protected in China.

 Extended Activities

## Role-play

### Task 1

**Student A:** You are a deputy manager of a newly founded Australian company in China. You are going to launch a new product —— a digital clock into the Chinese market. You need some advice from your consultant about trademark registration and patent application.

**Student B:** You are a clerk working in a consultative agency. Now you are receiving a client from Australia, who wants to launch a new product into Chinese market. Explain to him/her how trademark registration and patent application is processed in China.

### Task 2

**Student A:** As a representative from Mario High Tech Company, you are in charge of the China market. You are going to apply for a patent for the company's latest automatic washing machine. Go to the patent office and discuss the procedures with the staff.

**Student B:** You are a staff of the patent office. Now you are serving a representative from Mario High Tech Company who wants to apply for a patent.

### Task 3

**Student A:** You are a government official in charge of intellectual property rights protection. At a press conference, you are required to deliver a speech on intellectual property protection in China.

**Student B:** You act as a journalist attending a press conference. Listen to the speech delivered by a government official on intellectual property protection and raise some questions.

### Task 4

**Student A:** You are Jack Walker, the Customer Service manager of M&C Accessories Company. Your company makes a variety of bags with the trademark of Mark and Claire, which was registered two years ago. But you find the latest model of women's bag was infringed by another company. You received quite a lot of complaints from customers about the fake products. Go to the general manager and report the issue.

**Student B:** You are Andy Linton, the general manager of M&C Accessories Company. Listen to the Customer Service manager's report about the infringement. As you have never met such a problem, you would like to consult the company's attorney about the issue.

**Student C:** You are the attorney of M&C Accessories Company. Listen to the infringement issue and give your suggestions to the manager.

## Discussion

### Topic 1

What can be done to protect intellectual property rights in China?

### Topic 2

What is the best way to prohibit infringement of trademarks and patent rights?

## What's the Difference between Patents and Trademarks?

Patents allow the creator of certain kinds of inventions that contain new ideas to keep others from making commercial use of those ideas without the creator's permission. For example, Tom invents a new type of hammer that makes it very difficult to miss the nail. Not only can Tom keep others from making, selling or using the precise type of hammer he invented, but he may also be able to apply his patent monopoly rights to prevent people from making commercial use of any similar type of hammer during the time the patent is in effect (20 years from the date the patent application is filed).

Generally, patent and trademark laws do not overlap. When it comes to a product design, however —— say, jewelry or a distinctively shaped musical instrument —— it may be possible to obtain a patent on a design aspect of the device while invoking trademark law to protect the design as a product identifier. For instance, an auto manufacturer might receive a design patent for the stylistic fins that are part of a car's rear fenders. Then, if the fins were intended to be — and actually are — used to distinguish the particular model car in the marketplace, trademark law may kick in to protect the appearance of the fins.

## Supplements for Reflections

## Intellectual Property Rights in China

As China implements its reform and opening to the outside world, it is changing with each passing day. Today more than a few international observers have come to the conclusion that in terms of intellectual property protection China has reached international advanced levels. China's backwardness in its intellectual property system is now a thing of the past.

However, there remain some naysayers in the world seemingly willfully blind to China's development and transformation whose incognizant of present realities pass improper judgments on the nation's current situation regarding intellectual property protection. They allege that China has not yet established a "full and effective intellectual property system," and that China "lacks the ability to undertake international obligations." Such unfounded opinions do not bear argument; the truth speaks for itself.

Nonetheless, China cannot remain satisfied with the achievements it has already made. China is a developing country and still has much work towards optimizing its intellectual property system. This system in its modern form was established only a short time ago, and as a result, awareness of intellectual property rights remains underdeveloped in society at large. In some regions and in some governmental departments there is insufficient appreciation of the importance of intellectual property protection. Some serious acts of infringement have violated not only the legitimate rights and interests of the holder of the intellectual property right, but also the dignity of the law. Accordingly, even as the nation continues to otherwise improve the intellectual property legal system, the State Council has drawn up *Decisions on Further Strengthening the Protection of Intellectual Property*. China is confident that the implementation of all the important measures contained in the Decisions will mark a great new step forward in the nation's efforts to ensure the protection of intellectual property rights.

China will continue actively to promote international cooperation in the field of intellectual property. China itself has received active assistance from the World Intellectual Property Organization and from others working in the field in establishing and fine-tuning its intellectual property rights protection system. The nation will, as in the past, actively join in the activities of relevant international organizations and fulfill the obligations described in the international intellectual property treaties and agreements. Operating on the basis of the Five Principles of Peaceful Coexistence and in accordance with the principle of equality and mutual benefit, China will continue to cooperate with the rest of the world's nations, working and making positive contributions towards the development and optimization of the international intellectual property system.

| naysayer | 否定者；反对者 | allege | 断言；宣称 |
| optimize | 优化 | violate | 违反；侵犯 |
| legitimate rights and interests | | 合法权益 | |

## Questions

● How can people's awareness be enhanced to protect the intellectual property rights in China?

● What is the naysayers' view on China's current situation regarding intellectual property protection?

● What will China continue to do on intellectual property protection?

# Unit 16

# Complaints, Claims and Settlement

## Learning Objectives

**In this unit, you will learn how to:**

- Make complaints
- Present proofs
- Settle claims

## Background Information

In international business, complaints and claims from customers, and disputes between buyers and sellers, may sometimes arise although the two parties work very carefully in the performance of a contract. Sometimes they even submit their disputes to arbitration.

Dealing with complaints is the extension of service after a deal. How well a company can deal the complaints often brings impact on the popularity of the company and its products. To receive the person who comes to complain, one should be cooperative in order to work out a solution to the problem as soon as possible. At the same time, one has to refuse some unreasonable complaints politely.

In international trade, claim normally refers to the claim for losses. In the course of executing a contract, if one party fails to perform the contract and thus brings economic loss to another party, the latter may ask the former of compensation according to the contract stipulations. Claims are usually raised by buyers for great loss, for example, loss caused by non-delivery or delay of delivery, short weight or shortage of quantity, inferior quality and improper packaging, breach of contract, etc. However, sellers may also raise claims against buyers for non-establishment of L/C or breach of contract, etc.

Settlement normally refers to the settlement of the party, who is responsible for the claim lodged by the party that suffered loss.

 Starting Up

**Make a list of common causes for complaints or claims in international trade.**

| Common Causes for Complaints/Claims |
|:---:|
|  |

 Oral Workshop

## A. Making Complaints

### Dialogue 1 – Complaining about unconformity

*Mr. Cook bought some spices from Mr. Wong. When the goods arrived, he found that the goods were not in conformity with the contract stipulations. He is now making complaints to Mr. Wong.*

**Mr. Cook**：Mr. Wong, we regret to tell you that the goods you sent us are not in conformity with the contract stipulations.

**Mr. Wong**：What's the problem?

**Mr. Cook**：According to the contract, the expiration date of the spices is November 30th next year. But unfortunately, upon examination of the goods, we found that the expiration date is April 30th next year.

**Mr. Wong**：How can this be? We've never got such a complaint before.

**Mr. Cook**：But the expiration date is clearly printed on the cartons and on the wrappings as well.

**Mr. Wong**：That's incredible. We did have someone go to the factory to supervise the processing of the spices for your order.

**Mr. Cook**：But what I've said is a fact. This is the survey report by China Commodity Inspection Bureau. You need to be responsible for it.

**Mr. Wong**：How about this, you sell them in your market and we reduce the price by 30%?

**Mr. Cook**：I'm sorry, but I can't accept this proposal.

**Mr. Wong**：Then what do you suggest, Mr. Cook?

**Mr. Cook**：You reduce the price by 70% and pay the inspection fee.

**Mr. Wong**：It seems that I have to take your suggestion.

---

spice　　香料

---

### Dialogue 2 – Complaining about inferior quality

*Mr. Jones is complaining about the poor quality of the blenders he bought from Mr. Stevens.*

**Mr. Jones**：I'm sorry, Mr. Stevens, but I have a complaint to address with you.

**Mr. Stevens**：What is it about?

**Mr. Jones**：It's about the quality of the Blender Model CC-323 shipped by you sometime in March. There are rust spots on some of the blades. The quality is by no means satisfactory.

**Mr. Stevens**：Do you have any of the blades with you, Mr. Jones?

**Mr. Jones**：No. But here's a copy of the Inspection Certificate issued by the Shanghai

Commodity Inspection Bureau. The certificate indicates that some of the blades are rusted.

**Mr. Stevens**: When did you receive the consignment?

**Mr. Jones**: About two weeks ago.

**Mr. Stevens**: Did you unpack the cases immediately?

**Mr. Jones**: No, not until about a week ago. Here are the records made and the photos taken on the spot when the cases were unpacked for inspection by the surveyors.

**Mr. Stevens**: What do you think?

**Mr. Jones**: It's quite evident that the rust resulted from poor workmanship.

**Mr. Stevens**: How many blades are in this condition?

**Mr. Jones**: Six out of fifty.

**Mr. Stevens**: I'll ask our manufacturers to look into the matter and let you know once we've got the result.

| | | | |
|---|---|---|---|
| rust spot | 锈斑 | blade | 刀片 |

## Practice

1.　You complain to the seller that there are two pieces of artificial cotton among the shipment of cotton cloth you ordered. You tell him/her that if he/she can offset the price difference and then reduce the price by certain amount, you are willing to sell these two pieces of artificial cotton in your local market.

2.　You ordered 1,000 toasters in black. Upon receiving them, you find 25 of them are in silver. Make a complaint to the seller and ask for immediate replacements.

3.　You bought a desktop computer yesterday, but found it didn't work, as nothing showed on the screen when the computer was on. Call the company and make a complaint.

4.　You are with CPC Company, located in Dalian; lodge a claim concerning the inferior quality of 1,000-metric-tons of Australian wheat supplied by COM, an Australian Import and Export Company. Mr. Howard, the sales manager of COM, negotiates the matter with you.

# B. Raising Claims

## Dialogue 1 – Raising a claim for short weight

*Mr. Blake raises a claim against Mr. Smith for short weight.*

**Mr. Blake**: Mr. Smith, I have to say that on examination, we found a shortage in the shipment.

**Mr. Smith：** If the shortage occurred after shipment, we won't entertain your claim. You may raise a claim against the ship owners as the liability rest with them.

**Mr. Blake：** I don't think we can make a claim against the ship owners because the short weight was due to excessive moisture.

**Mr. Smith：** Then we'd like to have your present proof.

**Mr. Blake：** Here is our onboard bill of lading to claim a settlement.

**Mr. Smith：** Sorry, the evidence you have is inadequate; therefore, we can't consider your claim as requested.

**Mr. Blake：** Inadequate? Do you mean we need more documents?

**Mr. Smith：** Yes, you have to obtain a statement from the vessel's agents certifying that the goods were actually loaded on the vessels at the time the vessel sailed out. You also need to present the full original set of ocean bills of lading, original policy and the original commercial invoice.

| liability | 责任 | moisture | 水分；湿气 |
|-----------|------|----------|-----------|

## Dialogue 2 – Raising a claim for damage

*Mr. Pearson intends to raise a claim against Mr. Kidman for damage.*

**Mr. Pearson：** Mr. Kidman, your shipment of silk shirts arrived at the port yesterday. But upon inspection, we found that two cartons were badly damaged and many of the shirts inside were heavily water-stained and discolored by sea water. They're in such bad state that they are unsuitable for the requirements of the market. Therefore, we decided lodge a claim for the damage.

**Mr. Kidman：** The goods were in proper condition when they left. The damage must have occurred en route.

**Mr. Pearson：** I'm sorry to say that the damage was caused by improper packaging.

**Mr. Kidman：** That's impossible. The packaging was done according to the requirements stipulated in the contract. Ten in a big plastic bag and then ten bags to a carton. Do you have any evidence?

**Mr. Pearson：** Sure. This is the survey report issued by China Commodity Inspection Bureau. The report shows that owing to the inferior quality of the plastic bags and to the application of non-waterproof cartons, the goods were water-stained and discolored by sea water.

**Mr. Kidman：** This is not our fault. We have been using this type of plastic bags to ship shirts all the time and no client has lodged any claims against us for the damage of goods caused by broken bags. I think the broken bags this time was caused by rough handling. Please turn your claim to the shipping company.

**Mr. Pearson:** We went there this morning. They thought that the damage had been caused by the non-waterproof cartons.

**Mr. Kidman:** But there isn't such a stipulation in the contract that we were required to use waterproof cartons. I'm sorry but I can't help. I suggest you go to the shipping company again.

**Mr. Pearson:** Shall I put forward a suggestion? Since the shipping company has admitted to rough handling and the quality of your plastic bag was certified as inferior, can the three of us discuss the matter together and share the loss?

**Mr. Kidman:** Well, it seems to be quite fair.

| | | | |
|---|---|---|---|
| stain | 弄脏；污染 | discolored | 脱色的 |

### Dialogue 3 – Raising a claim for wrong delivery

*Mr. Bond raises a claim against Mr. Sun for wrong delivery.*

**Mr. Bond:** Your shipment of our order No. 597 arrived Monday. Everything appeared to be correct and in good condition except in Container No. 13. When we opened each carton in Container No. 13, we found completely different articles. We had to take them into our warehouse.

**Mr. Sun:** What articles were shipped in Container No. 13?

**Mr. Bond:** Canon BJ1000 Ink Jet Printers. We guess it should be for another order.

**Mr. Sun:** What was your order?

**Mr. Bond:** Canon laser printer. Therefore, we have to file a claim for the wrong delivery.

**Mr. Sun:** What is the amount of compensation you will claim?

**Mr. Bond:** After careful calculation, we decided to make a claim of $80,000.

**Mr. Sun:** I'm very sorry about the wrong delivery. But I'm not convinced that the loss would be that much.

**Mr. Bond:** Because of your shipping the wrong goods, we can't duly satisfy our customers' requirements. Many of them want to cancel their orders, and some of them even ask for compensation.

**Mr. Sun:** Well, this seems to be rather complicated and urgent. I need to report back and discuss with you later. But I can assure you that I will arrange for the right goods to be dispatched to you at once, and relevant documents will be mailed as soon as they are ready.

**Mr. Bond:** What do I do with Container No. 13?

**Mr. Sun:** Please kindly keep the contents for the time being, and we will send our forwarding agent to collect them.

## Practice

1. One buyer lodges a claim against you for short weight on the shipment of your soybeans. After your investigation, you find that the shipping company should hold the responsibility and therefore reject the claim against you.

2. You find that the frozen vegetables of 100 bags you ordered short-weight by 15 kilos. You make a claim with the seller, who believes that the shortage is due to the leak of the packaging and the damage of the packaging has been caused in the course of transit. You are told that you should make a claim with the insurance company.

3. You have purchased some peanuts from a buyer. You tell the seller that the peanuts have been received but some of the bags are broken. The broken bags are caused by the inferior quality, which is not in agreement with the packaging terms in the contract.

4. You raise a claim for the bad quality of bed lamps. When the goods arrived, you found they were not in conformity with the contract stipulations.

# C. Making Settlement

### Dialogue 1 – Inquiring about cargo claims

*Natalie works for a shipping company. Mr. Lee is now speaking with her to inquire about cargo claims.*

**Mr. Lee:** Good morning. I'm here to inquire about cargo claims.

**Natalie:** I hope I can be of help to you.

**Mr. Lee:** I'd like to know what your company's liability is if we damage or lose a customer's freight.

**Natalie:** We are liable for up to $25.00/lb per package, with a maximum of 1 million dollars per shipment. If the actual loss is less than or equal to this amount, we'll pay for the actual loss, but not more than the actual value.

**Mr. Lee:** Does this always apply to all situations?

**Natalie:** No. In fact, there are several exceptions to the rule. The most common are listed within this summary guide. Would you like to take a look?

**Mr. Lee:** Where are the general cargo liabilities listed?

**Natalie:** The Bill of Lading contract for the shipment will determine the extent of our liability.

**Mr. Lee:** What should I do when a customer requests that we transport a Prohibited Article?

**Natalie:** It's in the customer's and our company's best interest that you refuse to transport this freight.

**Mr. Lee:** Who may file a loss and damage claim?

**Natalie:** The shipper, the consignee, or a third party who has title to the goods may file a claim.

**Mr. Lee:** What documentation is needed to file a claim?

**Natalie:** A claim must be presented in writing describing the goods lost or damaged and how the amount of the claim was determined. This statement must identify the shipment and should be supported with a copy of the Bill of Lading or Roadway freight bill, a copy of an inspection report if one was performed, and a copy of the vendor's original invoice or other document to establish the value of the goods.

**Mr. Lee:** What is the time limit for filing a cargo loss and damage claim?

**Natalie:** A cargo claim must be received by the carrier within nine months of the date of delivery, or in the case of non-delivery, within nine months after a reasonable time for delivery has elapsed.

**Mr. Lee:** Then how long does it usually take for a claim to be settled?

**Natalie:** Once a claim has been received with the proper documentation, we will acknowledge receipt of the claim and attempt to settle it within 30 days. Investigation of some claims may take longer. Our company processes over 90% of claims within 30 days or less. If a claim cannot be settled within 120 days, we notify the customer and continue to keep them informed at 60-day intervals until the claim is settled.

**Mr. Lee:** Thank you very much for the information. It's been very helpful.

**Natalie:** You are welcome.

## Dialogue 2 – Discussing the settlement

*Mr. Wong lodged a claim against Mr. Lee for wrong delivery. Now they are talking with each other to discuss the settlement.*

**Mr. Wong：** Good morning Mr. Lee.

**Mr. Lee：** Good morning, Mr. Wong. I'm assigned to come here to settle the claim you lodged against us for our shipping the wrong goods.

**Mr. Wong：** Thank you for coming at such a short notice.

**Mr. Lee：** We're very sorry about the wrong delivery. That was indeed a mistake in the shipping process due to a confusion of numbers. We've already arranged for the right goods which will arrive very soon, I think.

**Mr. Wong：** I appreciate that. Now since everything is clear, let's discuss the settlement.

**Mr. Lee：** We are ready to compensate you for the loss caused by the error in our work, but one container of goods wouldn't make you suffer so much loss. I'm afraid your claim of $80,000 is unacceptable.

**Mr. Wong：** In fact, according to the orders canceled by the customers, we have a loss of nearly $100,000. But for the sake of our long-term cooperation, we only lodged a claim of $80,000 from you. This is reasonable, isn't it?

**Mr. Lee：** This is not right. Mr. Wong, what you have lost is not your net profit, but the value of the customer's orders. The money you paid for the orders still belongs to you. So the loss of nearly $100,000 isn't all you have lost.

**Mr. Wong：** But your wrong delivery not only makes us lose the orders and good opportunity to market, but also delay the time for us to gain.

**Mr. Lee：** That is why we agree to compensate for your loss of $20,000.

**Mr. Wong：** Mr. Lee, you know, we are the leading company in our city and also do business of wholesale and retail. If is not for your wrong shipment, we should have earned net profit of nearly $40,000 from the 400 laser printers. Meanwhile, we have invested much capital in them, but couldn't get our money back. It ties up our capital, and brings us a great deal of difficulty. Compensation of $20,000 for the loss is too little.

**Mr. Lee：** We understand your position, and apologize again for the troubles. So Mr. Wong, what do you suggest?

**Mr. Wong：** We claim at least $50,000. This is the best we can do.

**Mr. Lee：** Well, if you can help to sell out the wrong goods, we'll compensate you $50,000.

**Mr. Wong：** OK, then. Let's discuss how to sell out this lot of goods firstly.

## Practice

1. One of your clients raised a claim against you and required you to replace the

damaged goods and grant him a special discount of 20% to compensate for the loss. After making a thorough investigation, you find you are at fault and decide to accept the claim.

2. A buyer lodged a claim for all the losses incurred due to your delayed delivery. You state that the shipping company should be held responsible for the delayed delivery.

 Language Focus

### Technical Terms

| | |
|---|---|
| inferior quality | 质量较差 |
| improper packaging | 不当包装 |
| breach of contract | 违反合同 |
| delay in delivery | 交货延迟 |
| recourse | 追索权 |
| faulty goods | 有缺陷的货物 |
| faulty packaging | 有缺陷的包装 |
| short delivery | 短交 |
| short shipment | 短装，装载不足 |
| short-landed | 短卸 |
| short-paid | 少付 |
| short weight | 短重 |
| short-calculated | 少算 |
| short-invoiced | 发票少开 |
| short-shipped | 短装 |
| dispute | 争议 |
| file/register/lodge/raise a claim | 索赔 |
| settle a claim | 理赔 |
| defendant | 被诉人，被告 |
| consultation | 协商，磋商 |
| conciliation | 调解 |
| litigation | 诉讼 |
| certificate | 证明书 |
| inspection/survey report | 检验报告 |
| notice of claim | 索赔通知 |
| claim statement | 索赔清单 |
| insurance claim | 保险索赔 |
| Inspection Certificate of Quality | 质量检验证书 |
| Inspection Certificate of Quantity | 数量检验证书 |
| Inspection Certificate of Weight | 重量检验证书 |
| Certificate of Origin | 原产地证明书 |

| China Import and Export Commodity Inspection Bureau | 中国进出口商品检验局 |
|---|---|

## Functional Expressions

### Raising Claims

- I've got a complaint to make.
- On the basis of clauses of the contract, we place our claims before you as follows.
- We have to file a claim against you for all the losses sustained.
- We have to hold you responsible for the loss caused by the shortage.
- Please give our claim your favorable consideration.
- We shall lodge a claim for all the losses incurred as a consequence of your failure to ship our order in time.
- We have to ask for a compensation of … to cover the loss incurred as a result of the inferior quality of the goods concerned.
- We require you to replace the damaged goods and grant us a special discount of … to compensate for the loss.
- According to the contract, you are responsible to compensate us for the loss we have suffered.
- The quality of you shipment for our order is not in conformity with the specifications, we must therefore lodge a claim against you.
- After re-inspection, we found that the quality of the goods was not in conformity with the contract stipulations. There is a difference of … between the actual landed weight and the invoiced weight.
- The landed goods were quite different from what expected.
- This consignment is not up to the standard stipulated in the contract.
- Due to your delayed delivery, we have sustained heavy loss amounting to …
- We hope you will settle this claim as soon as possible.
- Claims for shortage must be made within 30 days after arrival of the goods.
- I'm afraid that we can't withdraw our claim.

### Presenting Evidence

- Here is the survey report issued by China Commodity Inspection Bureau. It shows evidence of …
- The survey report can certify that the weight shortage was caused by improper packaging.
- The survey has revealed that the damage to the goods is attributable to rough handling.

| Settling Claims |
| --- |

- We will get this matter resolved as soon as possible and hope to compensate you for your loss.
- We'd like to express our sincere apologies for the poor quality of the products.
- If we were at fault, we would be very glad to compensate for your losses.
- We regret for the loss you have suffered and agree to compensate you.
- We agree to replace the defective products for you.
- Considering our long-standing business relations, we agree to accept all your claims. We'll send you a replacement right away.
- After making a thorough investigation, we have decided to accept your claim and to compensate you for the sum involved.
- We are not in a position to entertain your claim.
- You should claim compensation from the insurance company.
- The claim should be referred to the ship owners.
- Your claim should be supported by sufficient evidence, otherwise we cannot entertain it.
- The shipping company must be held responsible for the delayed delivery.
- We suggest that you approach the insurance company for settlement as the shortage occurred in transit.

 Extended Activities

## Role-play

### Task 1

**Student A:** You ordered 180 Printed Circuit Boards (PCB) on June 16, for delivery on July 22, at $9.60 each. However, by July 22, you received only 150 pcbs, 25 of which were found faulty. You call the manufacturer to complain.

**Student B:** You are a manufacturer of PCB. A customer ordered 180 pcbs on June 16, for delivery on July 22, at $9.60 each. Unfortunately, you had a fire in the factory on June 18. Production has been limited and quality control is made difficult. You receive a call from the customer. Explain to him/her and express that you will try your best to supply and replace any faulty boards.

### Task 2

**Student A:** You are an American businessman. You ordered 5,000 digital cameras on CIF terms from a Chinese company at a trade fair. Upon arrival, approximately 1,000 cameras were found broken due to rough handling and improper shipment. You raise a claim against the shipping company.

**Student B:** You represent a shipping company that shipped 5,000 digital cameras for an American businessman. The businessman raised a claim against your company. Talk with the client to figure out what the problem is. Also express that you need to make some investigation before deciding whether to refuse or entertain the claim.

## Task 3

**Situation:** Mr. Cooper, a German trader, lodges a claim with Mr. Wang for short weight on the soybeans he sold. Mr. Cooper says that the 10,000 metric tons of soybeans arrived at Rotterdam with a short weight of 12.55 metric tons. Mr. Wang's Sales Confirmation stipulates that he sells the goods on shipping weight against the Certificate of Weight issued by the Shanghai Commodity Inspection Bureau, which is to be accepted as final and binding upon both parties. Mr. Wang needs to talk with Mr. Cooper out of his claim in a satisfactory manner.

## Task 4

**Situation:** Mr. Jackson, an American buyer, has signed a contract with a Chinese seller of frozen vegetables on the terms of CIF. When the goods are unloaded at the port of destination and are moved to the warehouse, he finds the goods inferior to the sample. Mr. Jackson then makes a claim, and refuses to accept the whole lot.

## Task 5

**Situation:** The buyer, Mr. Smith, has ordered 800 electric razors and finds they do not agree with the original sample supplied by the seller. He lodges a claim and asks for a compensation of $5,000 for inferior quality. The disputes then arise. Finally, Mr. Smith presents the Inspection Certificate. The seller then promises to compensate him the full amount requested if there is sufficient evidence.

# Discussion

## Topic 1

What are the common reasons for lodging a claim?

**Topic 2**

Suppose one of your clients, an American buyer, has ordered 1,000 cases of woolen sweaters. When the products arrive at port New York, 30 cases were found wet. The buyer then lodges a claim against this. How are you going to talk him/her out of the claim and settle it in a satisfactory way?

 Related Information

## Claims

Claims offer the opportunity to discover and correct defects existing in the goods and services. In making a claim, one of the major jobs is to keep negatives from worsening the situation when making a direct claim. In international business, claims do not happen in every transaction but often occur. Sometimes when the loss is not serious, the party who suffered the loss may not lodge a claim for compensation. Instead she/he writes a complaint to call the other party's attention to avoid of this matter happening again.

Because different causes of loss are with different ranges of responsibility, different parties will be liable for the claim lodged. If the seller breaches the contract, which incurs loss, the seller will should take the responsibility and the buyer should raise a claim against him according to the contract stipulations. If the buyer breaches the contract, the buyer will be responsible for the loss sustained and the seller should claim with him on actual case. If the loss takes place during transit, it is within the responsibility of the insurance company or the shipping company. It should be noted that a claim must be lodged within the term of validity stipulated in the contract.

 Supplements for Reflections

## How to Resolve a Client Complaint?

In order to keep your client happy, it is vital to handle his complaints in no time and properly or else they simply will not shop or approach you any longer. You definitely need to take each criticism right away and seriously even though it seems to be quite amusing and not to the point. That can happen too.

- Taking care of the client that facing you and answer every question that he has. Moreover, you need to show him that you are really on his side so he can trust you as his ally and not his enemy. You are highly appreciating his concern of the matter not less than him as well as wanting to improve the situation as quickly as possible. To smile and be kind.

- When he talk to you, as possible, note down the complaint. It shows that you are taking the issue seriously and in friendly manner, while at the same time, you ensure therein, that you have records on file of the complaint for a future use.

- Needless to mention, you should not never, never show impatience, roll your eyes etc. These are all noted by the client and can simply take his complaint to a whole new level that you are there to prevent.

- In order to get your client from effect up to a cause level, you can get him to participate by feeling free to consult with him on how he would propose to handle the issue. It will show your kindness and might restore the communication faster than you would think. As the golden law is, when you find yourself in communication disagreement or dispute the solution is always to get in more communication and not less.

- Do not have a bad approach towards the client, as a client does not care if you are annoyed, have a bad day or whatever. It is actually makes things worse. As much as it sounds as mission impossible sometime, keep your profile low, and acknowledge him as much as necessary to a positive result.

## Questions

- As a consumer, how do you make a complaint to the business about the product or service you have paid for?

- What can be done to increase your chances for a satisfactory settlement of your complaint?

- Make a list of do's and don'ts for people who are responsible for resolving complaints.